Globalization is often described as the spread of western culture to other parts of the world. How accurate is the conventional depiction of 'cultural flow'? In *Counterworks*, ten leading anthropologists examine the ways in which global processes have affected particular localities where they have carried out research. They challenge the validity of anthropological concepts of culture in the light of the pervasive connections which exist between local and global factors everywhere.

These essays contend that culture is itself a representation of the similarities and differences recognized between forms of social life. Focusing on specific local situations, including Bali, Cuba, Bolivia, Greece, Kenya and New Zealand, the contributors argue that the apparent opposition between strong westernizing, global forces and weak local resistances is ideologically loaded. Through detailed case studies, the contributors demonstrate that the anthropological concept of culture needs rethinking in a world where a marked sense of culture has become a widespread property of people's social knowledge.

Counterworks is an important contribution to current debates on cultural globalization in the social sciences, and will therefore be of great interest to students of sociology, cultural studies and social geography as well as to anthropologists.

Richard Fardon is Reader in West African Anthropology, School of Oriental and African Studies, London and Chairman of the Centre of African Studies, University of London.

ASA Decennial Conference Series
The Uses of Knowledge: Global and Local Relations
Series editor: Marilyn Strathern

Other titles in this series include:

Worlds Apart
Edited by Daniel Miller

The Pursuit of Certainty
Edited by Wendy James

What is Social Knowledge For?
Edited by Henrietta Moore

Shifting Contexts
Edited by Marilyn Strathern

Counterworks

Managing the Diversity of Knowledge

Edited by Richard Fardon

London and New York·

First published 1995
by Routledge
11 New Fetter Lane, London EC4P 4EE

Simultaneously published in the USA and Canada
by Routledge
29 West 35th Street, New York, NY10001

© 1995 Association of Social Anthropologists, selection and editorial matter; the
individual chapters, the contributors

Typeset in Times by
Ponting–Green Publishing Services, Chesham, Bucks
Printed and bound in Great Britain by
Mackays of Chatham plc, Chatham, Kent

British Library Cataloguing in Publication Data
A catalogue record for this book is available from the British Library.

Library of Congress Cataloguing in Publication Data
A catalogue record for this book has been requested.

ISBN   0–415–10792–X (hbk)
ISBN   0–415–10793–8 (pbk)

Contents

vi *Contents*

Contributors

Arjun Appadurai Professor in the Department of Anthropology, and Director of the Chicago Institute of Humanities, University of Chicago, USA.

Richard Fardon Reader in West African Anthropology in the University of London, School of Oriental and African Studies, UK.

Olivia Harris Senior Lecturer in Anthropology, Goldsmiths' College, University of London, UK; Visiting Professor, Department and Museum of Anthropology, University of Oslo, Norway.

Michael Herzfeld Professor of Anthropology, Harvard University, and Curator of European Ethnology, Peabody Museum, USA.

Mark Hobart Senior Lecturer in Anthropology with reference to South East Asia, School of Oriental and African Studies, University of London, UK.

Signe Howell Professor of Anthropology, Department and Museum of Anthropology, University of Oslo, Norway.

Stephan Palmié Assistant Professor of American Cultural History at the Amerika Institut of the University of Munich, Germany.

David Parkin Professor of African Anthropology in the University of London, School of Oriental and African Studies, UK.

Anne Salmond Professor in Maori Studies and Social Anthropology, Department of Maori Studies, University of Auckland, New Zealand.

Piers Vitebsky Director, Scott Polar Research Institute, University of Cambridge, UK.

Series editor's preface

This book is one of five to have been produced from the Fourth Decennial Conference of the Association of Social Anthropologists of the Commonwealth held at St Catherine's College, Oxford, in July 1993. Sections were organized by Richard Fardon, Wendy James, Daniel Miller and Henrietta Moore, each of whom has edited their proceedings. In addition Wendy James acted as Oxford Co-ordinator, and it is principally due to her untiring efforts that the conference took place at all. As Convenor, I take the opportunity of acknowledging our debt to her, and of registering gratitude to Priscilla Frost for her organizational assistance and to Jonathan Webber for acting as conference Treasurer.

The Institute of Social and Cultural Anthropology at Oxford gave material as well as moral support. The following bodies are to be thanked for their generous financial assistance: the Wenner–Gren Foundation for Anthropological Research, the British Council, the Oxford University Hulme Trust Fund, the Royal Anthropological Institute and the Association of Social Anthropologists itself.

To suppose anthropological analysis can shift between global and local perspectives may well imply that the two coexist as broader and narrower horizons or contexts of knowledge. Indeed, the relationship seems familiar from the ethnographic record: in cosmologies that set a transcendent or encompassing realm against the details of everyday life; or in systems of value that aggrandize this feature while trivializing that; or in shifts between what pertains to the general or the particular, the collective or the individual. And if knowledge consists in the awareness of context shift, then such scaling may well seem routine. However, this book does not take scale for granted. It examines certain contexts in which people (including anthropologists) make different orders of knowledge for themselves as a prelude to questioning assumptions about the 'size' of knowledge implied in the contrast between global and local perspectives.

Marilyn Strathern
University of Cambridge

Preface

These papers derive from the first, full-day session of the Fourth Decennial Conference of the Association of Social Anthropologists of the Commonwealth, held at St Catherine's College, Oxford, in late July 1993 under the overall rubric of 'The uses of knowledge: global and local relations'. Planning such an occasional, large-scale event occupied three preceding years, and the intellectual agenda – of which this volume and its argument represents only one part in five – was agreed under the direction of Marilyn Strathern with three other section convenors: Wendy James, Daniel Miller and Henrietta Moore. Wendy James also undertook the onerous responsibilities of local convenorship with the practical assistance of Priscilla Frost as organizer and Jonathan Webber as treasurer.

The volume is also a collective enterprise by virtue of the intellectual contributions of those represented here only by their influence on the final form of the revised papers: Ruth Finnegan and Ladislav Holy who chaired proceedings, and Talal Asad, Keith Hart and Judith Okely who acted as discussants. Because Maurice Bloch's paper, 'Time, narratives and the diversity of ways of knowing the past', is to appear in a further volume of his essays, he graciously withdrew it from this collection to allow other contributors his word allowance. Particular thanks are due to Arjun Appadurai who was prevented by family circumstances from attending the conference but consented to the editor presenting his paper and continued to be an encouraging virtual presence from afar – lending weight by example to his theoretical arguments about the moral dimensions of an electronically mediated community. The contributors have tolerated being harried and queried by the editor with a cheerfulness that puts him in their debt. Judy Sterner is gratefully acknowledged for her help in formatting some of the papers on disk.

The Decennial Conference was made possible by the practical support of the Institute of Social and Cultural Anthropology of the University of Oxford and the financial assistance of: the Wenner–Gren Foundation for Anthropological Research, the British Council, the Oxford Hulme Trust Fund, the Royal Anthropological Institute and the Association of Social Anthropologists itself.

Richard Fardon

1 Introduction

Counterworks

Richard Fardon

The papers collected here address the status of 'global' and 'local' as organizing terms of social knowledge with imagination and subtlety, but I shall begin literally and simple-mindedly[1] with an invitation that seems to involve. . .

'TAKING SIDES' IN A TROPE

The sides in question are the global and the local polarity and, on one reading, the invitation is to act as 'western' sociology's significant other in a debate over the globalization of (largely western) culture. Given how 'local' in sociological agendas is often conflated with non-western, and that anthropology's historical concern has been largely with non-western peoples, it is irresistible to note that – according to the latest report from the UN Population Fund (*The State of the World Population 1993*) – forty years ago 'developing countries' accounted for 77 per cent of world population growth but now they account for 95 per cent of it; global population is set to reach 6.25 billion by the end of this century. If sociology wishes to concede 95 per cent of the increment to anthropology, being local may be the only global option. But this is a gross argument from gross figures: perhaps, strategically useful on occasions when anthropologists need to dispute their own marginality on university committees, it begs questions about the categories of 'developing' and 'non-western' countries and, if these hurdles were negotiated, leaves intact the common impression that anthropology remains specifically about such places. The massiveness of the numbers does, however, underline both the massive and changing context we might mean by global – not to mention the size of some localities – and the sense of the world as a finite space that motivate an emergent style of social knowledge concerned with spatial relations and expressed in a language itself saturated with spatial images.

More troubling about the global/local contrast is the knowledge that it *is* going to work and, thus, the suspicion that what it appears to illuminate is already present in the terms it offers us. If knowledge, as Marilyn Strathern suggests (Strathern 1995), can be treated as the capacity to transform perceptions, we know at the outset that we *shall* manage to show (among other things) that global is also local and vice versa. The terms work off one another through mutual provocation (literal calling forth of one another) – neither makes sense alone. This is an initial referent of my title, 'counter-works'. The same distinction between global and local could have been applied, though not to identical effect, almost any time in the last two, even five, hundred years (Said 1993). So, of what is the contemporary prominence of the pair symptomatic? I think it is a matter of the varied conjunctures of unequally empowered processes and imaginings that are localized conceptually as figures against the ground of a global space that is both traversed and simultaneously classified, possessed and defended exhaustively. In consequence, it is a matter – even shorter – of the complexity of agency recognized in particular places. The counterworks ineluctably provoked by the terms 'global' and 'local' demand contests over the scale of units of analysis and the definition of their boundaries symptomatic of our turn-of-the-millennium times; and these concerns with spatial relations are themselves articulated through concepts and metaphors so imbricated with spatiality that the difficulty of distinguishing between real spaces and the allegorical spaces of theory has become a distinguishing feature of a post-colonial, political agenda cross-cutting the disciplinary boundaries of the humanities and social sciences. It is unnecessary, therefore, to reach agreement about the exact referents of 'global' and 'local' to argue that things look different in these terms than they did in terms of – just-as-contested – ideas of society and culture. If we give ourselves some elbow room with respect to the present, these preoccupations with space and locality, both as real and theoretical, and with how things occur in spaces and how they seem, appear symptomatic of the same condition.

To search only for definitional stability in such key terms as 'global' and 'local', or 'society' and 'culture', risks missing their significance as lexical markers of the fuzzier currents of ideas that are a backdrop to the intellectual contests occurring in particular disciplines (for instance, as Herbert 1992 argues for culture). The early promise of key terms may accrue through definitional slippage that allows them to resonate with widely felt intellectual and moral concerns. But as the range of potential definitions, and the consequences of defining a term this way or that, are worked through, slippage comes to seem more like sleight of hand. Each use of the terms involves all the problems that previous usage has made familiar. Culture and society reached this pass after a century of intensive use but, remarkably, the terms local and global – which have been called upon to qualify or even replace them in some usages – were problematic from the instant of their popularization.

Perhaps not so remarkable, though: anthropologists are all too sensitive to the traces of binary thinking (courtesy of structuralism), the pitfalls of essentialization (courtesy of deconstruction), and thinking through spatial metaphors (courtesy of tropic analyses). Scant wonder if the global/local pair in action promises few surprises, since it has characteristics of all three of these old friends. In common with other spatial analogies for social conditions (right/left; east/west; north/south; up/down; centre/periphery ...), global/local crystallizes matters not just by the attraction of its poles but by their unequal strength. This metaphorical strategy invites the constrained, somewhat mechanical but nonetheless effective, subversions: of inversion, akin to switching the charges on the poles,[2] or else of demonstrating 'resistance', a kind of friction model. However, the wider frame (which makes both inversion and resistance discernible as tactics or strategies) derives from overall positional images that orient by placing interacting parties within a theoretical landscape (Salmond 1982) the envisaged topography of which influences what is able to be said about relations between them. This is of more than intellectual curiosity, because the notion of orientation (getting one's bearing from the east, or – literal-mindedly – 'occidentation' for movements which take their bearings from the 'West', Carrier 1992) is the prelude to organizing directed movement. Defining entities and placing their interaction in a non-neutral space prejudges the meaning and likely outcome of whatever occurs. Particular metaphors of emplacement and movement are readily spotted once the trick is learnt (Hobart, Chapter 3); and they may as easily be essentializations of those whom anthropologists study as of anthropological theory (Herzfeld, Chapter 6). Metaphor is already party to this, since it is predicated etymologically on movement and containment. This much is familiar, but are there peculiarities of a world in globalization as the thinkable space in which real interactions occur?

As a concept, the globe blurs distinction between space, as suppositional to trope making, and place, as a trope of the particular. The globe is all the space that most of the members of a methodologically agnostic discipline are likely to be concerned with professionally. In this sense, the global context encompasses and produces all differences, rather as if it were thought itself. This 'globe' is shorthand for conceptual totality. But the globe is also a place that can be envisaged from a variety of perspectives – and sometimes seen from as close to 'nowhere' as our contemporary imagination permits, as here by the geographer Doreen Massey,

> Imagine for a moment that you are on a satellite, further out and beyond all satellites; you can see 'planet earth' from a distance and, rare for someone with only peaceful intentions, you are equipped with the kind of technology that allows you to see the colours of people's eyes and the number on their number-plates. You can see all the movement and tune-in to all the communication that is going on. Furthest out are the satellites, then aeroplanes, the long haul between London and Tokyo and the hop from San Salvador to Guatemala City. Some of this is people moving, some of it is physical trade, some is media broadcasting. There are faxes, e-mail, film distribution networks, financial flows and transactions. Look in closer and there are ships and trains, steam trains slogging laboriously up hills

somewhere in Asia. Look in closer still and there are lorries and cars and buses and on down further and somewhere in sub-Saharan Africa there's a woman on foot who still spends hours a day collecting water.

(1993: 61)

Within a unitary place, the populations of the globe are unequally globalized technologically (what Massey calls the 'power-geometry of time–space compression'), and this can be represented in terms of the trails they leave on the face of the globe, as well as in terms of the resources they extract unequally from within it. The moral is well taken and neatly pointed, but the trope is interesting in itself. Whoever is crewing the satellite has a quite different view of proceedings from the African water-carrier – or anyone between. And we have to be asked to suspend disbelief that anyone with that kind of totalizing vision, even after the Cold War, harbours only peaceful or disinterested intentions.

Human co-occupation of the world materially transgresses any pre-supposition of equality. In their ability to operate at a distance, some people(s) effect more, finite, global space than do others. And there is no imaginable, vacant 'somewhere else' – as there once was – where these others could rectify the fact. Conceptually, globalization is transgressive in related senses. Writers have described the globe as a shrinking space – undergoing time/space compression (Giddens 1981) or the annihilation of space through time (Harvey 1993 following Marx).[3] Concurrently, the scope of the local is described as expanding (for instance through electronic mediation (Appadurai, Chapter 10)). Spatial polarities – having, as it were, reached maximal logical extension in the contrast between global and local – finally collapse. What's more, the collapse is precipitated from both poles: since locals are shown to harbour projects of global scope, while global schemes are revealed in their provinciality. Simultaneously, locality itself (Appadurai) as well as the globe, comes to seem increasingly fragile. Social interaction within this fragile world of unreliable contexts is sometimes attributed characteristics reminiscent of Durkheim's notion of dynamic density – a concentration of energy channelled into exchanges that are becoming homogenized with the effect of producing a global culture within a world system (Robertson 1991). But this is only half a picture, and its plausibility rests on a contrary imagining it only seems to contest.

BOUNDARIES: ONCE – SOCIETY AND CULTURE; NOW – NATION, ETHNICITY, IDENTITY

One effect of a conceptual shift in favour of the relational parameters of global and local has been to make fixity seem intrinsic to anthropology's middle-range concepts of society and culture (Strathern 1995). To continue to write as if societies and cultures were stable spatializations risks irrelevance in the form of perverse attachment to conventions that fly in the face of the way the world now seems to be pictured credibly. The disappearance of anthropology's subject in this manner would involve not the demise of the exotic, which Malinowski foresaw, but rather the demise of societies and cultures describable distinctly. Another way of becoming irrelevant, however, would involve letting go of the assumption of the exotic – what resists comprehension by being outside one's previous experience. If to nothing else, the epithet 'exotic' seems appropriate to the opaque imaginings – good or bad – of a common global future. But if the exotic, both present and future, is no longer exogenous then existing concepts of society and culture do not seem appropriate spatializations in which to figure it. Bounded ideas of society and culture tended to produce an image of the inhabited world as a patchwork quilt, but the dialectic of global and local portends either final synthesis, as distinctions collapse and dissolve into a homogenized global culture, or unresolvable contradiction, as cultures shadow one another in mutually defined antipathy.

A sense of pervasive transgression results from retaining an attachment to the older tropes of society and culture while at the same time conceding the normality of the global/local pair. For some writers things appear increasingly to be out of place, or else chaotic such that there is no place where things might any longer belong. Evocative talk of jumbling, mixture and juxtaposition, or of hybridity and mongrelism, is symptomatic of this sense, but the effect occurs not as a raw reflection of the state of the world but as a consequence of the simultaneous appeal of two different ways of spatializing facts about it.

There are alternative ways of dealing with this. The simplest is to suggest that a world once made up of distinct cultures and societies is moving through a phase of transition towards becoming something different. Argument then revolves around the time-depth required to account for this change historically, as well as identification of the factors responsible for it. More radical is the suggestion that the world was never accurately described as an array of cultures and societies, but that people were once predisposed to see it that way. Argument then might concern why it was so imagined and – given the inaccuracy of that imaginary – in what respects the present really is different. A third, or at least the last, possibility I wish to consider here is that both spatializations make partial sense of different aspects of connection and distinction between populations, but the propensity to privilege one or the other, and the criteria made prominent by any particular way of doing this, require senses to be discovered for the two pairs of key terms (society and culture; global and local) such that their combination (global society; local culture etc.) does not simply compound the problems each term might beg singly. In all three cases, making sense of the world seems to involve addressing the relation between these two ways of spatializing facts about it; but only the third concedes that how the world is, and how it seems, are aspects of the same condition, and that recognition of partial global connections does not imply the existence of a privileged account to which all, however positioned, might be expected to subscribe.

Theoretical limitations of some notions of society have been widely debated of late (GDAT 1989; Kuper 1992). In some hands, 'society' has been employed as an essentialist, totalizing term, with the effect of precipitating a dichotomy between society and the individual prejudicial to understanding people who do not recognize any such antinomy (and, as tellingly, prejudicial to arguing sensibly with those who do essentialize in that fashion). On this issue, I am in sympathy with those who find concepts of sociality irreplaceable in anthropology (and politics) but seek to avoid totalizing ideas of society (Fardon 1992: 35–36). My own preference is for attempts to define analytic notions of sociality which throw 'native' categories of 'individual' and 'society' into sharp relief (partly because natives who classify like this, and with whom I disagree, live in my neighbourhood). Apart from remarking in passing that when the 'natives' (here or elsewhere) disagree one cannot agree with all of them (even describing the extent of contention among their opinions usually betrays a preference for one party or for an account that envelops them all), I rehearse this issue only to note that if formally similar arguments are applied to culture as have been applied to society, the concepts are not affected identically. This makes culture the more pressingly problematic of the pair, and it points to senses in which – despite the conventionality of the phrase 'society and culture' or the vacuity of the hybrid 'socio-cultural' – society and culture are not easily interchangeable. At least for my part, and perhaps also for others who still concede some heuristic use to distinguishing the social as an object of analysis, I suspect it is easier to begin to give some substantive sense to global and local society, and to social complexity, than to global and local culture, and to cultural complexity.

In high cultural circles, fragmentation, juxtaposition and the unhinging of signifiers from signifieds (itself a telling deterritorialization) may be signs of cultural postmodernism experienced as irony. Elsewhere, formally rather similar phenomena may be described as: pidginization, creolization, hybridization, McDonaldization, superficial cosmopolitanism and so forth (Twitchell 1992). Frequently the latter typifications are tragic rather than ironic. 'High' and 'low' society are hardly persuasive ideas these days as they were once. The lexicon to describe states of social mixing in the abstract has attenuated rather than multiplied – for instance, what are the equivalents of transculturation and acculturation, or of syncretism (Palmié, Chapter 4)? Who you are speaks volumes of how your capacity to cope with cultural diversity is liable to be moralized (Howell, Chapter 8). The ability to appropriate the exotic instrumentally – that is to de-originate the externality of what crosses to the inside, rather than to be culpable oneself of de-origination by it – is to be found in a cluster of attributes of power. The sum of this reconfiguration of mutual appropriations may then be termed cultural complexity (presumably the obverse of cultural simplicity) – but it is neither clear what is to be gained by doing so nor is it demonstrated that this apprehension would be shared by the human agents of the change. Indeed, it is more likely that appropriation is experienced as an, albeit possibly short-term, resolution to or simplification of complexity. It seems unsatisfactory to argue that people act in ways that make their lives more complicated, and simply leave it at that.

The evaluation of complexity draws credibility from its internal coherence with assumptions concerning differential local, worldmaking capacities, and by virtue of drawing selectively – as any way of worldmaking must – upon some perceptions that are difficult to deny. Predominantly, these perceptions draw upon the more manifest effects of the refashioning of the production of material space during, at the least, the last five hundred years. The expansion of the circuits of profitability across the globe have been accompanied by the deterritorialization of the idea of the market (Dilley 1992). People, ideas and things move faster, further than before[4] with the result that the viability of projects in different places (once iron smelting in India and Britain, now car production in India and Japan) become interrelated. It would be as foolish to deny this as to imagine that its consequences are uniform or predictable. Indeed, Appadurai (1990) has argued that disjuncture rather than conjuncture is characteristic of the different aspects of transnational movements. Larger numbers of people may move faster than before, but the effect of their doing so is mediated by internationalized norms of citizenship and the nation-state. Cosmopolitans and tourists move in the expectation of returning whence they came, not of remaining to refashion the places they go to by intention.[5] Refashionings, which are not the objective of movement (of tourists, cosmo-politans, *gastarbeiter*, refugees) have come to seem transgressive of the autonomy of the nation-state as custodian of culture – and perversely contrary to the interests of those who desire to be cultural tourists or markedly cosmopolitan. More than other elements of its definition, the exclusionary logic of culture has suggested it to be compromised both practically and ethically as a conceptual tool. Nation, ethnicity and identity – which are complex, provocative and explicitly interested terms – have been used to challenge the autonomy of culture and society, and the latter pair have come to seem (to put it most starkly) innocent dupes of the political triad. Innocent because they were naively employed, and dupes because of their complicity in the historical plots of the more definitively 'possessed' (in two senses I am coming to) characteristics of nation, ethnicity and identity. Recent debates over the global genealogies of nationalism, ethnicity and identity add to the growing opinion that previous tendencies to spatial representation of the globe as an array of societies and cultures be seen as a derivative fact.

Etymology cannot determine how terms are used in argument, but often it does indicate why a term appeared so helpful before its insights were exhausted or the term started, as it were, misbehaving. Culture – defined at its boldest in the productive, semantic overlap of generation, gender and genre – suggested the mutual cultivation of people and place according to conventions that intensified over generations. Culture does not only lend itself to being seen as possession, but as hereditary possession representing the investment of the lives of a people's predecessors. Over time, left alone, the anticipation of the image in its nineteenth-century evolutionary form is that cultures should differentiate. Suitably reified this image can satisfy cultural relativist and cultural supremacist alike. The recent appeal to cultural flows seems multiply transgressive to both – since it threatens incomparability (in senses dear to both). Not being made of rooted stuff, culture seems to be in free flow – in food, music, language, commodities, etc. The culture trope worked better as evaluative, localized and internally responsive to its own dynamic totality. In the light of the reconfiguration of relations in the aftermath of overt imperialism and colonialism, sticking with culture cannot but suggest inauthenticity as a globalized condition, precisely because of the terms in which authenticity became established. Globalization appears as a pervasive condition of transgression not only because it suggests culture to be fluid (a landscape become waterland), but because culture was conceptualized proprietorially. People possessed culture, but were also possessed by it so that nothing else could possess them without displacing, diluting or hybridizing inherited genius. Perception of cultural globalization relies, necessarily and without paradox, upon recognition being accorded more local cultural boundaries; globalization would not be discernible were there no such boundaries to be transgressed (or transcended) and affirmed as 'real' in consequence (see Harris (Chapter 5) on how Latin American *mestizaje* underwrites the reality of Indian and Spanish, and Palmié (Chapter 4) on *syncretismo* as explicit Cuban ideology).[6] Thus, the equivocation over whether globalization encounters boundaries or whether:

> The twentieth century has been a unique period in world cultural history. Humankind has finally bid farewell to that world which could with some credibility be seen as a cultural mosaic, of separate pieces with hard, well-defined edges. Because of the great increase in the traffic in culture, the large-scale transfer of meaning systems and symbolic forms, the world is increasingly *becoming one* not only in political and economic terms, as in the climactic period of colonialism, but in terms of its cultural construction as well; a global ecumene of persistent cultural interaction and exchange.
>
> (Hannerz 1991: 107, my emphasis)

The quotation hesitates before a distinction I drew earlier – was the world really the sort of place to be described as a cultural mosaic, or could it only 'with some credibility' be seen as such? A global perspective suggests that the idea of the world as cultural mosaic arose, not because it was such a glittering fabrication, but because projects to create such a world proliferated. Reification of boundaries and discovery of their transgression, even negation, are dialectically related (and common to political projects that might otherwise be deemed distinct as radical and reactionary). The increasing performativity of 'culture' – which I mean in several senses – only makes the point impossible to ignore. Commentators on globalization frequently privilege two instances of the globalizing process: the pervasion of production and consumption in the pursuit of profit (see Miller 1995), and the proliferation of international media and the creation of a transnational public sphere of information, arts, opinion formation and life-style (see Moore 1995). These two instances share more than the obvious nexus that the media industry is commonly a capitalist industry. The related point is that production as well as consumption can be portrayed as performances of informational simulacra. Capital operates in an increasingly 'footloose' fashion (Harvey 1989, 1993), contributing to the shortening of its own remunerative cycle, and giving rise to a late (Jameson 1991) or disorganized capitalism (Offe 1985; Lash and Urry 1987). Profit threatens to follow consumption in loosening its material foundations and transforming into information to be massaged. Computerized informational technologies have created a pervasive market in the digitalized traces of products and money in which the performative utterance involved in purchase or sale has a materiality no more immediately substantial than a pulse. In analogue language, the same effect ensues when representatives of the world's largest net debtor state through the International Monetary Fund and World Bank can, under the rubrics of structural adjustment, international competitiveness, accountability and democratization, effect such wide-ranging changes in the lives of peoples in sub-Saharan Africa. However much they seem to be losing their immediate materiality, the performative effects of empowered utterance, digital or analogue, have increased capacity to bring about effects of much greater materiality – and the upshot is experienced as extraversion in national terms. Even if money makes our (globalized) world go around, much of that 'money' is virtual (Rotman 1987) – or purely performative – a functionally powerful version, in the immediate term, of the many performances in which we are mutually engaged. So many of the means that establish and maintain unequal relations between us nowadays are susceptible to accretion to the historical senses of the term 'culture', that there is little cause for wonder that the term itself becomes problematically overloaded.

COMPLEXITY: FROM CULTURE TO 'KNOWLEDGE ABOUT "CULTURE"'

To argue that culture is becoming more complex (*pace* Hannerz) seems mistakenly concrete. Is the problem not that the range of phenomena subsumed under the rubric of 'culture' is becoming unruly? After all, how would we calibrate the instrument designed to measure cultural complexity? Given that culture is often analogized to language, does it make as little sense to talk about simple cultures as it does to talk about simple languages (a score on which anthropologists – who no longer, one hopes, claim to have 'mastered' simple languages in months – should feel proper humility)? The reasonable response to the claim that someone's language is simple is to question whether our witness fully understood what was being said. Furthermore, how do we reconcile 'cultural complexity' with claims about emergent 'cultural homogeneity' (Robertson 1991)? At first sight we might feel that these are antithetical: to the extent that we all become similar, complexity – say as a term indicative of the effort that goes into understanding something – ought to diminish. However it might be objected that a featureless (homogeneous) scene is peculiarly difficult to read. In short, it is not that we cannot debate issues of cultural complexity and simplicity, homogeneity and heterogeneity, and so forth; rather, it is a question of what, other than perplexity, we achieve by entanglement in this particular web of words.

Global, applied to culture, often functions adjectivally as a late-coming analogue of the universal in two senses. As certain products are universally diffused into daily lives so culture appears to become globalized, but this globalization highlights different modes of appropriation thus producing an equally concrete sense of cultural pluralization (Friedman 1988: 458, 1990). The 'universal' of some earlier writings implied 'intrinsically human'; latterly, the distinction of local cultures has suggested their incommensurability and put the intrinsically human in question; globalization, by destabilizing the space of locality, restores universality historically. But this new universality differs from its original by virtue of succeeding locality: whatever is now globalized has the historical potentiality to have once belonged locally – or to have been the outcome of a localizable process. Because globalization is historic rather than intrinsically human, it seems that everything can be marked either as deriving locally or extraneously. Thus, although concern with authenticity seems peculiarly globalized, usually it is claimed only in relation to some things and not others and even then with different degrees of knowingness.[7] These things then stand, metonymically, for 'culture'. The same is true of 'mixture'; as Olivia Harris (Chapter 5) remarks of Bolivia, everything may be mixed but not everything is *mestizo*. Because authenticity is unevenly claimed, there is an open invitation to anthropologists to contest the selectivity and logic of local claims to exceptionalism (compare Tonkin *et al.* 1989 for ethnicity and history). Cultural claims thus become bracketed by claims about knowledge generally and knowingness in relation to particulars; the effect is that relative to our knowledge of what it purports to describe, the culture trope appears to imply closure and coherence that can be challenged either by demonstrating the diversity of the bits from which every culture is fashioned or the knowingness with which people articulate them. From this perspective, it seems that representations of 'culture' are, as J.D.Y. Peel suggests of ethnohistory, the more 'serious aspect of social self-reproduction' (1993: 178). The attempt to recoup the culturalist position from this dilemma, by arguing that representations of culture are themselves 'cultural', threatens endless regression, or unhelpful confusion of distinct senses of the same term, or controversy over proprietorship of the culture concept itself (and probably all three).

Although a modest conceptual and semantic move might promise to dissolve the boundedness of culture – by analogy with the way that sociality transforms society – the outcome is not the same. Margaret Thatcher[8] might consign British society to oblivion but she did not attempt, and one cannot imagine her even trying, to see off British culture (Winston Churchill and all) in the same fashion – the great and dead are more intrinsic to the concept of culture than to society (though why is a peculiarity of language). Languages other than English seem to manage the unbounding of culture more easily – for instance Spanish-speakers might use the ungendered, *lo cultural*, derived from the adjectival form of *la cultura*; and this form resists other adjectival accretions, as might 'the cultural' in English. Resistance to possession only highlights the fact that culture is usually someone's. As such, culture is a particularistic claim – one that requires other cultures with other identities. The statement that global culture is as meaningful as other cultures is, thus, not sustainable innocently (Robertson 1991) because possession is now part of the meaning of culture: global culture could be meaningful to the same extent as other cultures only by being someone's (and correlatively not someone else's).

Rather than being an innocent term of anthropological analysis – what key term ever is? – 'culture' has become established as a crucially productive token in a discourse that is rapidly becoming the taken-for-granted account not just of the world in which we live, but of its history and its future. Like terms that promised similar unification to human self-knowledge, much that appears to be its explanatory power derives from its role in constituting the object it purports to explain. Worse, because culture is widely seen as human essence, the constitutive function of the term threatens to become total. The argument that there are different cultures then becomes tantamount to the claim that there are different types of humans – which might be deemed a dangerous turn on the part of so apparently amiable a concept.[9] Claims to knowledge about 'culture' are, therefore, of great and increasing moment.

KNOWLEDGE AS COUNTERWORK

Anthropological theory and writing achieves some of whatever relevance and cogency it has through positioning a reader in interrelated spatial and temporal terms. This is not the whole story so far as textual conviction is concerned (a more comprehensive checklist would – according to taste – include an appreciation of clarity, coherence, bias, language proficiency, research methodology and so forth), but spatio-temporal textualization has become impossible to ignore since ethnography has been read in the literary *cum* deconstructive mode. Like the tropic construction of knowledge mentioned earlier (Hobart, Chapter 3), tendencies to the temporalization of spatiality in evolutionary writing, or conversely detemporalization by spatialization in structural functionalism and cultural functionalism, become difficult not to notice once remarked. If, as has been argued, the anthropologist's view was once construed as the capacity either to step outside spatio-temporal coordinates to which others were consigned, or to occupy some privileged position within them, then under conditions of globalization of culture, when externality has become impossible, the position of privilege is accorded instead to hybridity – the capacity for multiple positioning. That this stance is 'there' to be adopted results both from tropic spatialization of the capacity to know, and from the possessive qualities of the relation between culture and the individual. Possessive in the double sense I flagged earlier: that culture has proprietors and that the individual is possessed by the culture – as if under the sway of an external agency.[10] Once construed thus, the capacity for multiple possession, in both senses, cannot but offer grounds for contention between different writers claiming this capacity for themselves on the basis of life-history, learning, experience, method or some combination of these.[11]

The idea of 'multiple positioning' as a 'stance' occurs in the broader context of a, widely remarked, move in western social theory to valorize space over time. I have difficulty understanding how one can change without the other, but there is no denying increasing, explicit concern with space in the take-up of Foucault's work on disciplinarity and surveillance or, for instance, in the influence of Henri Lefebvre's attempted unification of the levels of production of space upon social geographers (e.g. Harvey 1989; Smith 1993; Watts 1992).

> Much social and cultural theory in the last two decades has depended heavily on spatial metaphors. The myriad 'decentrings' of modernism and of reputedly modern agents (e.g. the working class), the displacement of political economy by cultural discourse, and a host of other 'moves' have been facilitated by a very fertile lexicon of spatial metaphors: subject positionality, locality, grounding, travel, (de/re) centring, theoretical space, ideological space, symbolic space, conceptual space, space of signification and so forth.
>
> (Smith 1993: 97–98)

As Neil Smith goes on to note, 'Absolute space can no longer be equated with "real space" even for the purpose of grounding alternative metaphors' (1993: 99). Similar observations can be attested in anthropologists' writings (e.g. Parkin 1990, 1992: 81; Gupta and Ferguson 1992). How writers place those they write about, and whether this placement is obvious or requires close reading, have become grounds on which to 'place' the writers themselves in some 'theoretical space'. Given the pervasive spatialization of theoretical language, writers and 'written about' are constrained to be located somewhere – often several somewheres – and are open to being impugned for not being elsewhere. So here I rejoin the original observation that the local/global polarity is symptomatic rather than diagnostic. 'Taking sides' in the trope involves the recognition that those who speak globally are no less locals of a kind. Perhaps the more empowered of them are locals of the kind whose culture is so performative that a few computer key strokes in one global financial centre affects the livelihoods of people remote from such technologized culture, and may even threaten their lives and security by destabilizing their political arrangements. But in making this perceptual transformation – seeing the local and global in one another – it would be rash to believe that we are doing more than carrying through the counterwork this trope asks of us, or that this trope carries less metaphorical baggage than others. Nonetheless, the local/global pair brings a series of tensions to bear upon the bounded tropes of societies and cultures; not least because it makes the 'design features' of the latter pair so prominent by contrast. Such tensions import intellectual discomforts and falterings into the production of anthropological knowledge which – for all the tribulation they cause – are, as David Parkin argues below, also the strengths of a method that tacks between global theory and ethnographic particularity.

Anthropological notions of the boundedness of cultures and societies enabled a productive comparability between the units they defined; yet this success in creating comparable entities now seems part of the problem. In relation to culture, complexity is produced on two principal fronts: self-conscious, local 'cultures', that are recognizably reified and selective (and also recognizably cognate with the essentialized culture concepts used by anthropologists in the 1953 report on acculturation, see note 6), and powerful localizable knowledges that do not represent themselves as cultural. To the extent that knowledges with global effect (i.e. effect that is pervasive or at least broad) lay claim to self-evident truth, then it may be worth arguing that they are cultural, in that sense susceptible to being localized. But there is an equal challenge to see beyond the tropes of essence or possession of self-proclaimed 'cultures'. No-one, in the papers that follow, suggests that attention to the global/local pair is a panacea; but a way of looking at our crowded end-of-the-millennium world that self-consciously spatializes tropes of knowledge, and makes the possession of culture problematic, may be a means to question the human boundaries otherwise immanent in a world of 'cultures' awkwardly related (almost as after-thought) in: acculturation, transculturation, cultural pluralism, creolization, cultural syncretism and so forth.

Somewhat artificially, given how much they share, the following chapters have been arranged in pairs. Anne Salmond (Chapter 2) and Mark Hobart (Chapter 3) are concerned to question the agency that makes connections between different knowledges. In Salmond's rescension of the history of a relationship, Maori (that is 'people') produced themselves as a collectivity by wresting reciprocity from pale-skinned, *pakeha* and, in so doing, refused simply to be an 'other' to Europeans. Through numerous personal exchanges she traces how Maori and European ways of thinking entered into reciprocal entanglements across 'borderlands' (a metaphor she chooses from Maori perceptions). Borderlands were at once the physical places of early encounters and the metaphorical horizons of expectation each entertained of the other, which shifted over three and a half centuries as anticipations were adjusted on both sides. Like Hobart, Salmond finds anthropology largely to have been a vehicle of Euro-American hubris – unwilling to enter properly dialogic relations with others that would extend to debating their questions rather than attributing them voices to answer our own. She demonstrates how it was Maori activism that forced Europeans into the relationships that now prevail in New Zealand. Hobart's vignettes from Bali, prefaced by a vigorous analysis of the ways in which images of knowledge are constructed in the English language, are designed to contrast ideas of knowing that Balinese bring to episodic appreciation of mediumship and theatrical performance with those that westerners entertain of systematic knowledge. Anticipating discussion of the 'uses of knowledge' (see, Moore 1995), Hobart examines the metaphors of knowledge which allow us to imagine that knowledge grows, is managed or expended. In common with Parkin, who also compares differing presuppositions of knowledge, he suggests that knowledge might with equal plausibility be construed as fragmented, or confused. To systematize knowledge beyond episodic actions of knowing itself prejudices the likelihood of grasping how others apprehend complexity by subordinating their agency to our own controlling metaphors.

The authors of these two papers find distinctions between European and Balinese/Maori knowledges useful exegetical devices to make epistemological points. Stephan Palmié (Chapter 4) and Olivia Harris (Chapter 5), studying Hispanic America, show that relations and influences between Europe and Africa, for one, and Europe and Amerindia, for the other, have become internal to local ethnographic arguments over identity into which outside ethnographers cannot help but be drawn. Palmié tracks the mutually reactive syncretic moves and resistances between the histories of Cuban *oricha* worship and Yoruba Reversionism in the USA set against the different contexts of the semi-official syncretism of Cuban nationalism and North American cultural pluralism. Black American, Yoruba-derived religion is reliant on its 'syncretic' Cuban counterpart for 'source' material while defining itself as the purer, more Yoruba, eventually more African version. In common with Harris, Palmié found the complexity of attributions of knowledge highlighted in personal experience – when Yoruba Reversionists submitted to Cuban tutelage in ritual, tacitly ignoring the manifold ideological contradictions into which both parties might stray. A similar learning experience for Harris concerned the way her own writings on Laymi Bolivians evoked contradictory responses – from Katarismo ethnic nationalists, nostalgic for a lost past, and *mestizo* appreciative of 'civilization'. *Mestizaje*, as part of the ideology of Latin American nationhood, is a historically selective rendition that implicitly retains the distinction between Indian and Spanish, just as the psychic *mestizaje* attributed to Cuba retains the division between African and Spanish. Harris reminds us that issues of mixing (its politicization and moralization) are foundational in Latin America, rather as Benedict Anderson has argued the non-derivative nature of nationalism in the same sub-continent (Anderson 1991; see also Segal and Handler 1992). Tracing the routes of Cuban African would lead us back to the nexus between a Yoruba ethnicity coming into being, a Creole identity in formation around Freetown in Sierra Leone, and the proselytizing by Victorian, Yoruba, recaptive, Sierra Leonean, Christian missionaries of the Yoruba on whom they simultaneously bestowed Yoruba ethnicity while defining their own roots (Peel 1989, 1990; Wyse 1989). Writing history without recourse to stabilizing devices of unitary cultures and societies makes anthropologists sensitive to the fact, as Palmié puts it, that in some respects we are 'all in the same boat' – all trying to make sense from differently interested positions of the creation and backwash of boundaries from transcontinental political, economic and ideational processes. Rhetorics of ethnicity, nationhood, authenticity, originality and so forth are the serially invented, discarded, devalued and revalued coinage of these dealings.

Essentialization is also the subject of papers by Michael Herzfeld (Chapter 6) and David Parkin (Chapter 7). The productivity of a reified mind/body dichotomy in Greek national culture, which overlaps similar distinctions in most European cultures, is the source of a sense of 'Greekness' that is naturalized to the degree that it 'goes without saying'. Mutual recognition of these shared features of embodiment allows the achievement of 'cultural intimacy', as Herzfeld dubs it, by virtue of establishing convertible boundaries subject to delicate manoeuvres of subversion, analogy, resistance, blaming and complicity (Herzfeld 1992). Greeks know one another – and thus themselves – by their capacities to play with virtuosity on these embodied states, and thus reproduce themselves as distinct from their European others. Such 'latticing' of effects is similar to the more general strategies of applied knowledge explored in Parkin's discussion of medical and religious discourse among coastal Kenyan Swahili (and social theory among island-dwelling social anthropologists). Containment, elimination and dispersal, as formal solutions to problems demanding immediate address, are as discernible in Swahili medical and religious discourse as they are in contemporary anthropological theorizing. As Keith Hart remarked at the time, these papers suggest that anthropology is practically the study of who essentializes what, where and when. While ethnographic fieldwork typically supplies a specific 'who' and 'what', the conjunctural logic of the 'where' and 'when' requires contextualization in broader spatial and temporal terms than was typical of the early generations of professional ethnographic reporting, and such contextualization cannot but revise assessment of identity and activity (the 'who' and 'what').

A concluding trio of papers by Signe Howell (Chapter 8), Piers Vitebsky (Chapter 9) and Arjun Appadurai (Chapter 10) are avowedly comparative in ways that complement one another. While Howell concentrates on relations between existing localities, Appadurai highlights the production of locality. Howell introduces the notion of 'cultural lacunae' to express the way in which people's consciousness of 'cultural difference' suggests 'gaps' in their own cultural lives. Such conjunctures – compounded of how people reify their own lives as 'culture', how they are able to conceptualize what they know of other lives as 'cultures', and how they deal with the juxtaposition of the two images – determine whether 'appropriation' will occur and the manner in which any such appropriation will be construed. She points out a tendency to overestimate the degree to which cultural diffusion is from the 'West' to the 'Rest' – in part as a consequence of judgements of scale and importance (the Rest appropriate more, and what they appropriate is considered somehow more important), and in part a matter of the way appropriation is moralized (Westerners remain themselves through appropriation – indeed become even more themselves – while the Rest are diluted by borrowing).

Enlarging on one of the subjects Howell introduces, Vitebsky compares the global contexts of 'shamanism' among the Sora of tribal India, the Sakha of Siberia, and in its appropriation by 'New Age' movements. Sora soul-force, which is transmitted from the dead to their crops, leaches from its local cycle in the reproduction of life as grain, is commodified and sold outside the community. Unaware of their own beliefs as something that might be called shaman*ism*, Sora have rapidly become Baptists. Sakha have few shamans but a thriving ideology of shamanism which local intellectuals promote, in part as an ethnic argument for exclusive claims to their mineral-rich lands in the context of the break-up of the USSR. Sakha knowledge of shamanism as a fact of their older life-style shares something with New Age appreciation of shamanism as an exogenous system of belief. But whereas Sakha self-consciously revive a knowledge that was locally their ancestors', New Age thinkers try to import a knowledge marked as 'local' into a global outlook. New Age shamanism serves as a system of verbalized beliefs that are psychotherapeutic for the individual, to whom they offer an intensely personalized surrogate for theistic religion, and powerfully convey a 'post-Edenic' desire to save planet earth from looming environmental disaster.

In Arjun Appadurai's phrase, Sora, Sakha and New Ageists are all engaged in the 'production of locality' under different conjunctures of circumstance. Appadurai's concluding essay begins from the supposition that the production of locality has always been a fragile and multi-faceted social achievement. Starting from the least complex case for his argument, he notes how the maintenance of 'neighbourhoods', as actual social forms, requires not just the production of reliably local subjects, but also the material production of locality, as well as the practices of performance, representation and action that produce local time–space. Even in the ideal-typical case of relatively small, autonomous neighbourhoods, locality production is subject to the corrosion of context that occurs, if in no other way, through the attempt to realize locality against the resistance of a material world.

In developing this processual, or social reproductive, argument from its simplified starting point, Appadurai eschews the assumption that the existence of societies is unproblematic, presuming instead that the production of sociality necessitates unremitting and accident-prone work. Few social forms are, or ever were, isolates. Instead, differentially empowered institutions compete to produce locality. In the contemporary world, the most powerful of these institutional complexes is the nation-state, which seeks to control the production of locality within its national territory by making itself the focus of commitment. The success of this endeavour is challenged not just by the difficulties intrinsic to all locality production but also by the potentially competitive contexts produced by sub-national and transnational productions of locality. Sub-nationally, locality may be produced by encapsulated neighbourhoods of different scope (communities or regions) or in terms of identities defined by national or transnational ethnoscapes. Transnational challenge to nation-states' monopoly of the production of locality has been facilitated by electronically mediated technologies capable of creating virtual neighbourhoods (whether ethnic or not). Pursuing his argument, Appadurai envisages that all actual and virtual forms of association come into existence and are maintained within cross-cutting currents of locality production: only some of which are produced by these associations or serve to reproduce them. Conjunctural relations between the agencies producing locality has proved particularly difficult to theorize, in part, he suggests, because the value to be attributed to locality is part of what they contest. This is particularly clear in the case of, what here and elsewhere he has called, 'ethnoscapes' – ethnic classifications of populations in space (Appadurai 1990, 1991) – which constitute easily visible challenges to the historical ambition of nation-states to achieve identity with both an 'interpretive neighbourhood' and a distinguishable population. A nation-state's success in achieving these goals has been an index of its power to produce 'subject-citizens', a material locality (homogeneous in terms of its possession, but studded with national sites) and representations and actions consistent with these. Globalization of the means for producing locality challenges national orders in unprecedented ways through the creation of transnational virtual neighbourhoods made possible by technologies that permit international contacts of both a public and private nature to become routine.

The preceding papers can be read as responding to different aspects of the comparative approaches in the final three papers. Herzfeld's insistence on the embodiment of a reified aspect of national character in Greece adds a populist dimension to the idea of the nation as an intimate, interpretative community and translocality beyond its national space. Palmié and Harris add detail to the complexities of the relations between nation, interpretative community and ethnoscape in circumstances when criteria of identity are established not just transnationally but inter-continentally. Salmond's account of Maori/ *pakeha* relations illustrates a historical contest for the definition of national identity. These papers show that anthropologists have moved beyond questionable claims to have reinstated the 'voices' of the marginalized to examine the diverse ways in which localities, and the concerns of those who live in them, are created in contests over the shape and coherence of social knowledge (Hobart, Chapter 3; Parkin, Chapter 7).

Devoid of much specialist vocabulary to call its own, anthropology has always been involved in the give and take of terms with its historical contemporaries (these days such terms would include society, culture, ethnicity, identity, nation and so forth, as they once included primitive, totemism, animism, etc.). If it has any special competence, this may concern an accumulating disciplinary familiarity with how such terms of engagement tend to come out as counterworks: to every hegemony – a resistance (Salmond), to every knowledge – an ignorance (Hobart), for every mixture – – terms that must be imagined as separable (Harris), for every syncretism – a play of parts (Palmié), for each essence claimed – a deconstruction (Herzfeld), and to every containment or elimination – a potential dispersal (Parkin). General recognition of human diversity in a post-colonial order has bestowed celebrity, and notoriety, upon anthropology as the discipline to which responsibility for making sense of this variety was once shunted off. If the number of scholars hovering over the corpus of every dead anthropologist now rivals the number of anthropologists once proverbially attached to each Eskimo family, one can only applaud the change. But Ulf Hannerz has wondered why anthropologists are not as happy as they might be that their 'culture concept' has lately been on a 'winning streak' and become everyone's favourite idea (1993: 95). The answer I have been suggesting is that the 'culture concept' has been borrowed both as the presupposition and the butt of globalization theory. Culture makes globalization theory go around. But David Parkin suggests that subversion of grand narratives has been a necessary consequence of anthropologists' engagements with the particular rather than the 'local'. If the anthropological concept of culture is anchoring a grand narrative with which anthropologists feel ill at ease, then its subversion may be timely.

NOTES

1 Although this version of the paper delivered to the Decennial Conference is heavily revised, I have generally not included references to literature published since mid-1993. Gratitude for not being more simple-minded is owed especially to Talal Asad and Judith Okely who were section discussants, to Robert Paine who thoughtfully commented on a draft and, of course, to the authors of the papers. Keith Hart, to whom responsibility for summarizing the day's proceedings fell, will recognize his specific influence in this version. Undated author references are to essays in this collection.

2 See for instance, Dumont's (1992) discussion of right and left, and nationalist ideology in France; and Stuart Hall's account of the strategic acceptance of black/ white polarity: 'The Black I'm talking about is a historical category, a political category, a cultural category. In our language, at certain historical moments, we have to use the signifier' (1991: 53).

3 'The *nineteenth* century had seen time collapsed and space contracted as never before' (Richards 1993: 5, my emphasis). The periodization and specification of temporal/spatial shifts remain moot and crucial to a broad context, not least because scholars seem to concur in attributing an exceptional standing to the different periods they study.

4 But it is important not to overstress the exceptionalism of the contemporary situation: the rapid diffusion of early expansionary Islam or of more secular

revolutionary ideas (for instance as dramatized in the transnational movements of the protagonists of Alejo Carpentier's *Explosion in a Cathedral*), caution against underestimating this capacity previously.

5 This is especially so of migration as a proportion of population:

> Compared with migration rates in the nineteenth and early twentieth century, present day rates are small and account for a very small proportion of total population increase. Between 1840 and 1930 for example, approximately 52 million people left Europe for North America, Australia and New Zealand and, at the peak of emigration between 1881 and 1910, the number of emigrants was equivalent to something like 20 per cent of the population increase in Europe. It has been calculated that present-day migration is less than 3 per cent of population increase in Latin America and 0.5 per cent or less in Africa and Asia.

> (Hall 1991: 48)

The relation between population growth and the rate of forced emigration from Africa during the period of the slave trade remains contentious; clearly the proportion was substantial and some commentators have claimed sufficiently so to cause population to decrease.

6 Exactly forty years ago, at the time of speaking, a Social Science Research Council 'Seminar on acculturation' in the USA met to discuss 'acculturation [which] may be defined as culture change that is initiated by the conjunction of two or more autonomous cultural systems'. The main report (authored by Broom, Siegel, Vogt and Watson) achieved an apotheosis of the organismic metaphor for culture in the distinction between 'hard-shelled vertebrate' and 'soft-shelled invertebrate' cultures, going on to discuss a variety of relations which might hold between them. The dissenting voice of Barnett appeared in an appended statement arguing an essentialist and nominalist (though highly reductionist) concept of culture. Initially, he stated, the culture concept seems to 'put order into confusion and explain much that is otherwise nonsensical. At the same time, a working familiarity with the idea tends to produce more perplexity than clarification' (1953: 1000–1001). This effect (often worse than perplexity) is not confined to anthropologists' essentializations (compare Herzfeld); indeed, would it were.

7 As Hall (1991) observes, marks of cultural authenticity – for pasta-eating Italians as well as tea-drinking English – are often appropriated and their origins forgotten. The centrality to national culture of cricket in the West Indies and in South Asia, which C.L.R. James described with dignity, has become the object of a more self-consciously ironic, or knowing, post-colonial play with authenticity: witness wits in the press (both in England and in India and the West Indies) celebrating successive 'brownwashing' and 'blackwashing' (i.e. the kind of complete drubbing once called 'whitewashing') of England's hopelessly outclassed, touring cricket teams. The situation allowing this to be funny and acceptable has at least three characteristics: that the joke is instigated outside England and appropriated within, that England continues to oblige by losing handsomely, and perhaps also that the England team is not wholly 'white'. Signe Howell's reference to cricket brings this to mind.

8 A theoretician whose dicta on the ontological primacy of individuals and families have now appeared on the examination papers of a majority of British departments of anthropology.

9 Noting that the notion of culture took over some of the burden of explaining difference once carried by race is not meant to suggest that this change was not for the good, but that – in the longer term – there is a tendency to discover how much the definition of key concepts carries over from those they displace (Appiah 1992; Abu Lughod 1991, see note 11).

10 My general inspiration here derives from Fritz Kramer's argument that Africans managed the externality of foreignness through spirit possession and masquerade, thus localizing external forces (by tested methods) while not dispelling their strangeness (Kramer 1993). Without endorsing every ethnographic particular of this imaginative reading, it seems intriguing to treat 'culturing' analogously. As a technique, 'culturing' (explaining behaviour by redescribing difference as 'culture') requires possession in two senses. Others 'possess' their culture (like the proprietors of a masquerade), and this makes them 'locals' of a particular type, but they are also 'possessed' by it, and thus their 'possession' by another culture raises problems of proprietorship (whose culture it is) and self-consistency (how can one be doubly possessed?). I am not seriously suggesting another definition of what culture *is*, but implying that the logic of 'culturing' can be made to seem every bit as exotic as the logic that Kramer imputes to spirit possession and masquerade.

11 For instance, I find myself in agreement with much of the argument of Lila Abu-Lughod's paper 'Writing against culture' (1991). However the 'halfies', as she describes those whose cultural or national antecedents are 'mixed', are 'halfies' only in terms of the idea of 'culture' she is 'writing against'. Given the tenor of her discussion, I presume her choice of an ironic term signals the provisionality of the identity. As she cogently argues, despite its differences from race, the culture idea possesses some of the same tendency to 'freeze difference' (1991: 144).

REFERENCES

Abu-Lughod, L. (1991) 'Writing against culture', in R.G. Fox (ed.) *Recapturing Anthropology: Working in the Present*, Santa Fe, New Mexico: School of American Research Press.

Anderson, B. (1991) *Imagined Communities*, Revised Edition, London: Verso.

Appadurai, A. (1990) 'Disjuncture and difference in the global cultural economy', *Public Culture* 2(2): 1–24.

—— (1991) 'Global ethnoscapes: notes and queries for a transnational anthropology', in R.G. Fox (ed.) *Recapturing Anthropology: Working in the Present*, Santa Fe, New Mexico: School of American Research Press.

Appiah, K.A. (1992) *In My Father's House: Africa in the Philosophy of Culture*, London: Methuen.

Barnett, H.G., Broom, L., Siegel, B.J, Vogt, E.Z, and Watson, J.B. (1954) 'Acculturation: an exploratory formulation' (Social Science Research Council Summer Seminar on Acculturation, 1953), *American Anthropologist* 56: 973–1002.

Carrier, J. (1992) 'Occidentalism: the world turned upside down', *American Ethnologist* 19: 195–212.

Dilley, R.(ed.) (1992) *Contesting Markets. Analyses of Ideology, Discourse and Practice*, Edinburgh: Edinburgh University Press.

Dumont, L. (1992) 'Left versus right in French political ideology', in J.A. Hall and I.C. Jarvie (eds) *Transition to Modernity. Essays on Power, Wealth and Belief*, Cambridge: Cambridge University Press.

Fardon, R.O. (1992) 'Postmodern anthropology? Or, an anthropology of postmodernity?', in J. Doherty, E. Graham and M. Malek (eds) *Postmodernism and the Social Sciences*, Basingstoke: Macmillan.

Friedman, J. (1988) 'Cultural logics of the global system: a sketch', *Theory, Culture & Society* 5(2–3): 447–460.

—— (1990) 'Being in the world: globalization and localization', *Theory, Culture & Society* 7(2–3): 311–328.

Giddens, A. (1981) *A Contemporary Critique of Historical Materialism*, Vol.1 *Power, Property and the State*, Basingstoke: Macmillan.

Group for Debates in Anthropological Theory (1989) *The Concept of Society is Theoretically Obsolete* (M. Strathern, J.D.Y. Peel, C. Toren and J. Spencer), T. Ingold (ed.), Manchester: GDAT.

Gupta, A. and Ferguson, J. (1992) 'Beyond "culture": space, identity, and the politics of difference', *Cultural Anthropology* 7(1): 6–23.

Hall, R. (1989) *Update: World Population Trends*, Cambridge: Cambridge University Press.

Hall, S. (1991) 'The local and the global: globalization and ethnicity', 'Old and new identities, old and new ethnicities', in A.D. King (ed.) *Culture, Globalization and the World-System. Contemporary Conditions for the Representation of Identity*, Basingstoke: Macmillan.

Hannerz, U. (1991) 'Scenarios for peripheral cultures', in A.D. King (ed.) *Culture, Globalization and the World-System. Contemporary Conditions for the Representation of Identity*, Basingstoke: Macmillan.

—— (1992) *Cultural Complexity: Studies in the Social Organization of Meaning*, New York: Columbia University Press.

—— (1993) 'When culture is everywhere: reflections on a favourite concept', *Ethnos* 58(1–2): 95–111.

Harvey, D. (1989) *The Condition of Postmodernity: An Enquiry into the Origins of Cultural Change*, Oxford: Blackwell.

—— (1993) 'From space to place and back again: reflections on the condition of postmodernity', in J. Bird, B. Curtis, T. Putnam, G. Robertson and L. Tickner (eds) *Mapping the Future. Local Cultures, Global Change*, London: Routledge.

Herbert, C. (1992) *Culture and Anomie: Ethnographic Imagination in the Nineteenth Century*, Chicago: University of Chicago Press.

Herzfeld, M. (1992) *The Social Production of Indifference. Exploring the Symbolic Roots of Western Bureaucracy*, Oxford: Berg.

Jameson, F. (1991) *Postmodernism, or the Cultural Logic of Late Capitalism*, London: Verso.

Kramer, F. (1993 [1987]) *The Red Fez: Art and Spirit Possession in Africa*, London: Verso.

Kuper, A. (ed.) (1992) *Conceptualizing Society*, London: Routledge, European Association of Social Anthropologists.

Lash, S. and Urry, J. (1987) *The End of Organized Capitalism*, Cambridge: Polity.

Lefebvre, H. (1991) [1974] *The Production of Space*, trans. D. Nicholson-Smith, Oxford: Blackwell.

Massey, D. (1993) 'Power-geometry and a progressive sense of place', in J. Bird, B. Curtis, T. Putnam, G. Robertson and L. Tickner (eds) *Mapping the Future. Local Cultures, Global Change*, London: Routledge.

Miller, D. (ed.) (1995) *Worlds Apart*, London: Routledge.

Moore, H. (ed.) (1995) *What is Social Knowledge For?*, London: Routledge.

Offe, C. (1985) *Disorganized Capitalism*, trans. J. Keane, Cambridge: Polity.

Parkin, D. (1990) 'Eastern Africa: the view from the office and the voice from the field', in R. Fardon (ed.) *Localizing Strategies. Regional Traditions of Ethnographic Writing*, Edinburgh: Scottish Academic Press.

—— (1992) 'Nemi in the modern world: return of the exotic?', *Man* (NS) 28(1): 79–100.

Peel, J.D.Y (1989) 'The cultural work of Yoruba ethnogenesis', in E. Tonkin, M. McDonald, and M. Chapman (eds) *History and Ethnicity*, London: Routledge, A.S.A. Monograph 27.

—— (1990) 'The pastor and the *babalawo*: the interaction of religions in nineteenth century Yorubaland', *Africa* 60(3): 338–369.

—— (1993) 'Review essay', *History and Theory* 32(2): 162–178.

Richards, T. (1993) *The Imperial Archive: Knowledge and Fantasy of the Empire*, London: Verso.

Robertson, R. (1991) 'Social theory, cultural relativity and the problem of globality', in A.D. King (ed.) *Culture, Globalization and the World-System. Contemporary Conditions for the Representation of Identity*, Basingstoke: Macmillan.

Rotman, B. (1987) *Signifying Nothing. The Semiotics of Zero*, New York: St Martin's Press.

Said, E. (1993) *Culture and Imperialism*, London: Chatto & Windus.

Salmond, A. (1982) 'Theoretical landscapes. On a cross-cultural conception of knowledge', in D. Parkin (ed.) *Semantic Anthropology*, London: Academic Press, A.S.A. Monograph 22.

Segal, D.A. and Handler, R. (1992) 'How European is nationalism?', *Social Analysis* 32: 1–15.

Smith, N. (1993) 'Homeless/global: scaling places', in J. Bird, B. Curtis, T. Putnam, G. Robertson and L. Tickner (eds) *Mapping the Future. Local Cultures, Global Change*, London: Routledge.

Strathern, M. (ed.) (1995) *Shifting Contexts*, London: Routledge.

Tonkin, E., McDonald, M. and Chapman, M. (eds) (1989) *History and Ethnicity*, London: Routledge, A.S.A. Monograph 27.

Twitchell, J.B. (1992) *Carnival Culture: The Trashing of Taste in America*, New York: Columbia University Press.

United Nations Population Fund (1993) *The State of the World Population, 1993*, New York: United Nations.

Watts, M.J. (1992) 'Space for everything (a commentary)', *Cultural Anthropology* 7(1): 115–129.

Wyse, A. (1989) *The Krio of Sierra Leone: An Interpretive History*, London: C. Hurst.

2 Self and other in contemporary anthropology

Anne Salmond

We know the other by the self, but also the self by the other.[1]

(Tzvetan Todorov 1982: 241)

Since Descartes, the 'self' in European intellectual discourse has been literally 'self-evident'. The thinking self, by virtue of its thinking, constitutes its own existence. Self looks at reality, measuring and describing, and so has being. Other becomes object, resource for self's own projects. Measured and described, other constitutes self's self-consciousness (Heidegger 1978: 247–282). And so in anthropology, the anthropologist describes the other, and thus 'is' anthropologist. Other is means for anthropology's being, resource for anthropology's projects. Asad (1975), Said (1978) and others have shown how far imperialism and colonialism have held 'the other' in thrall for such uses. As European powers took indigo, spices, flax and timber for European production and consumption, so too people were taken – as labour, but also as 'curiosities', exhibited as savages, noble or ignoble, produced as exotic oddities for European consumption.

In anthropology, the ethnographic 'I' (eye) has been a trope for Euro-American hubris. From its (Euro-American) location the cosmos is carved up – into centre and periphery, First, Second, Third (Pletsch 1981) and Fourth Worlds, simple and complex, developed and undeveloped societies – all images echoing ancient European metaphors of hierarchy and control. The thinking 'I' remains the final point of reference, the centre of control in an intellectual panopticon. Metropolitan languages of description, by self-definition, are always 'strong' and those of others 'weak'. How, in such a cosmology, could it be otherwise?

It is no wonder that 'others' have resisted such processes of definition. Yet as others have spoken, not in answer to anthropology's questions but from their own interests; as others have shouted or argued back, snubbed or excluded anthropologists, what has anthropology done? By and large, carried on regardless or shifted its gaze, from 'other' to ethnographic texts or historical documents (which can't talk back); its dialogics have been curiously one-way.

Foucault has talked of 'insurrections of knowledges', uprisings of ways of knowing defined by science as local, disqualified and illegitimate (1980: 81–87). In anthropology this is happening everywhere, as peoples defined as 'local', 'tribal' or 'villagers' assert ancestral ways of knowing, and resist the imposition of global scientific framings. Shared projects between knowledges have always been possible in anthropology, yet exchanges of questions as well as answers, reciprocities of insights have hardly ever happened. The very possibility has been obscured by the calm, one-way imperialism of anthropology's gaze.

This paper will investigate a 'genealogy', both in Maori and in Foucault's sense.[2] In particular I wish to explore the possibility of a collaboration between local knowledges (both Maori and European), to see whether this might illuminate past (and contemporary) relations between Maori and Europeans in New Zealand. In the process, ideas of self and other will be considered from the vantage point of Maori, as well as European formulations about relations between people, and between people and the wider world.

SOME MAORI VERSIONS OF 'SELF' AND 'OTHER'

> *He iwi kee, he iwi kee*
> *Titiro atu, titiro mai.*
> One strange people, and another
> Looking at each other!

In this recent *haka* (chant of challenge), Merimeri Penfold speaks of Maori–Pakeha relations in New Zealand. Each 'side' is defined as an '*iwi*' (ancestral grouping), gazing at the other. The metaphor evokes memories of encounters on *marae*, or ceremonial meeting grounds. Here ancestral groups meet in ritual order, as *tangata whenua* ('land people', the local owners) to welcome *manuhiri* (visitors) to their *marae*. Ranged in front of their meeting house, local people challenge the visitors in high, floating calls (*karanga*), which summon up ancestors. *Tangata whenua* and *manuhiri* sit apart, facing each other across an open space in which the exchanges of speeches and songs proceed. The groups then come together to *hongi* (press noses), exchanging the breath of life, and the visitors are taken to the dining hall and fed.

The syntax of this *haka*, like *marae* rituals, is riddled with reciprocities. Ideas of 'self' and 'other' are framed, not in unilateral and individual, but in relational and collective terms. Groups meet, each of which is '*kee*' (different) to the other. 'Otherness' resides in the relationship; it is mutually, not self-produced. As groups face each other across an open ground, each gazes away from itself (*titiro atu*, look away) and in turn is gazed upon (*titiro mai*, look towards). The *haka* speaks of a tangling exchange of gazes, quite unlike the characteristic one-way visualist metaphors of western science (Salmond 1982). There is a consonance, though, with Foucault's ideas of strategies of power, for *marae* encounters negotiate *mana* (ancestral power to act in the world), and with his metaphor of genealogy, the language in which Maori thinkers speak the world.

As I understand it, ancestral Maori modes of understanding were inherently relational. The world was/is grasped not as Sahlins would have it, in a mytho-praxis, [3] but genealogically (1985: 54–72). From the beginnings of the world until now, the patterns of reality were genealogically described. The very capacities of the knowing self – thought, memory, the mind-heart, knowledge and desire – emerged in genealogical stages before the rest of reality was formed. This cosmological chant recorded by Te Kohuora of Rongoroa in 1854 tells the story:

Naa te kune te pupuke	*From the source the rising*
Naa te pupuke te hihiri	*From the rising the thought*
Naa te hihiri te mahara	*From rising thought the memory*
Naa te mahara te hinengaro	*From memory the mind-heart*
Naa te hinengaro te manako	*From the mind-heart, desire*
Ka hua te waananga	*Knowledge became conscious*
Ka noho i a rikoriko	*It dwelt in dim light*
Ka puta ki waho ko te poo	*And darkness emerged*
Ko te poo i tuturi, te poo i pepeke	*The dark for kneeling, the dark for leaping*
Te poo uriuri, te poo tangotango	*The intense dark, to be felt*
Te poo wawa, te poo te kitea	*The dark to be touched, unseen*
Te poo i oti atu ki te mate	*The dark that ends in death*
Naa te kore i ai	*From nothingness came the first cause*
Te kore tee whiwhia	*Unpossessed nothingness*
Te kore tee rawea	*Unbound nothingness*
Ko hau tupu, ko hau ora	*The wind of growth, the wind of life*
Ko noho i te aatea	*Stayed in empty space*
Ka puta ki waho te rangi e tuu nei	*And the atmosphere emerged*
Te rangi e teretere nei	*The atmosphere which floats*
I runga o te whenua	*Above the earth*
Ka noho te rangi nui e tuu nei	*The great atmosphere above us*
Ka noho i a ata tuhi	*Stayed in red light*
Ka puta ki waho te maarama	*And the moon emerged*
Ka noho te rangi e tuu nei	*The atmosphere above us*
Ka noho i a te werowero	*Stayed in shooting light*
Ka puta ki waho ko te raa	*And the sun emerged*
Kokiritia ana ki runga	*Flashing up*
Hei pukanohi mo te rangi	*To light the atmosphere*
Te ata rapa, te ata ka mahina	*The early dawn, the early day, the midday*
Ka mahina te ata i hikurangi!	*The blaze of day from the sky!*

. . . and then the land was produced, then the gods, and man.

The ancestors who emerged in this genealogical succession could collapse space–time to become co-present with their descendants, moving from an invisible dimension of experience variously described (as *Poo, Hawaiki, Tawhiti,* etc.) into the being of their descendants. A contemporary 'self' as the 'living face' of his/her ancestor could share their experiences, or act for them in *Te Ao Marama* (the world of light). It is this interlock of being between ancestors and their descendants, rather than some heroic identification, that defines the so-called 'Maori kinship I' (Johansen 1954; Sahlins 1985: 35, 47). As Hohepa has put it, 'time is a moving continuum if seen through Maori language, with ego being a particle whose own volition and direction is not bound to time. Time swirls like *koru* patterns, three-dimensional spirals' (MS, Hohepa n.d.). The self turns now towards one set of ancestors and kinsfolk, now towards another, engaging different *taha* (sides) in different contexts – this is the relational 'I' (rather than say, the 'partible I' (Strathern 1992: 155)).

Whakapapa (genealogy) was and is not static, frozen at the moment of creation and ceaselessly recapitulated. It grows (*tupu* – issue, bud, grow, unfold essential nature – whether of rock, plant, animal or person) through time, shooting out tendrils which may thrive or wither in successive generations (*whakatupuranga*) (Salmond 1984: 246–247; 1982). Ancestors (*tupuna*) and descendants, *Te Poo* and *Te Ao Maarama* (at once 'worlds' of darkness and light, and evolutionary epochs) and ancestral groups meet on *marae*, and in the past on battlefields or at *tuuaahu* (shrines). These places were the *pae* or borderlands; powerful places where history was negotiated out of the edges of existence in magic, feasting and war (Salmond 1978: 15–28).[4]

Maori cosmology is intrinsically dynamic, and developmental through genealogical time. It is thus puzzling to encounter metropolitan analyses which identify Maori logic with mythological re-enactment, or authenticity with the period before European contact. European myths (the 'Savage Mind', the 'Golden Age', the 'Fatal Impact') seem to have been more persuasive here than Maori experience, past or present – a case, maybe, where strong languages have got it wrong. The result has been implausible, ahistorical versions of Maori reasoning, [5] false problems about the 'invention of tradition' (Hansen 1989), and mechanistic accounts of historical change. A serious recourse to Maori, as well as European ways of thinking may well serve better to illuminate the nature of early (and more recent) exchanges between Maori and Europeans.

'MAORI' AND 'PAKEHA' AS SELF AND OTHER

At the end of 1910, Te Waaka Te Ranui of Ruatoki wrote a letter to the editor of *Te Pipiwharauroa,* a Maori-language newspaper, asking '*He aha tatou i kiia ai he Maori?*' (why are we called 'Maori'?). He offered some answers, both to this question and to another on the origin of the term '*Pakeha*' (European). First, Te Waaka claimed that when Captain Cook arrived at Tuuranga (Poverty Bay), he was almost out of potatoes, so he asked the local people if they had any. They answered that they had a similar root, and when he asked for its name, they said that it was '*Maori*' (ordinary). Cook turned to his companions and said, 'These people are *Maori*!'. Secondly, according to Te Waaka, when the local people first saw Europeans' faces, they thought they were as pale as some of their garments, and so they called them '*Pakeha*' after a particular type of white cloak.

In the next issue of *Te Pipiwharauroa*, there was a scathing response to Te Waaka's letter from Nikora Tautau of Uaua. Nikora began by rehearsing both Te Waaka's questions and his answers, dismissing these as '*koorero puuraakau*', '*paki waitara*' (incredible stories, fiction). He lampooned Te Waaka's account of the conversation with Captain Cook, asking whether he thought Cook was mad, for it was as though a person, having asked a horse its name and having been told 'horse', turned to his companion and said 'This is a cow!'. He then proceeded to give his own answers to Te Waaka's questions.

According to Nikora, the term '*Maori*' was a description for ancient things, ordinary things, things from inland and for local people. '*Wai Maori*', for instance, was fresh water, in contrast to '*wai tai*', the salty waters of the sea. As for '*Pakeha*', this was an ancient term for pale-skinned folk who were also called '*tuurehu, patupaiarehe, urukehu, pakepakeha*'. When local people first saw Europeans with their pale skins, they called them '*pakepakeha*' after an ancient people who had arrived from the sea, from outside Maori territories.

In the next issue of *Te Pipiwharauroa*, a letter was published from the East Coast tribal expert Mohi Turei, 'graduate' of the Taapere-nui *Whare Waananga* ('School of Learning') and a deacon of the Church of England, in response to this exchange. He supported Nikora's account and further corrected Te Waaka's claims, but with a display of erudite authority that outmatched them both. He explained that the term '*Maori*' was indeed ancient, for in the old days there had been two peoples in the land, the tribe of '*atua*'(supernatural beings) and the tribe of '*taangata Maori*' (ordinary people). Everything in the everyday world was '*Maori*' – descent groups, chiefs, *paa* (fortified villages), treasures and food. When people died they were farewelled – '*Hei konei raa i te ao Maori, i te ao tuuroa*' – 'farewell from the "Maori" world, the "established" world'. '*Maori*' people were ordinary and everyday, unlike the new arrivals with their white skins and strange ways of speaking. He then told of the arrival of a boat-load of pale-skinned people to the East Coast, called '*pakepakeha*' after part of a *haka* (chant) they performed, long before the arrival of Captain Cook in the *Endeavour* in 1769. This chant, according to Turei, was the origin of the term '*pakeha*'.[6]

EUROPEAN OTHERS AS *ATUA* 'GOD' OR *TUPUA* 'GOBLIN'

In a recent work *Two Worlds: First Meetings Between Maori and Europeans 1642–1772* (1991), I studied all surviving textual Maori versions of those early meetings. On the basis of that evidence, as well as Mohi Turei's explanations, it became clear that at first 'Maori' people thought that Europeans were part of the supernatural, extraordinary world rather than the everyday world of light. In Tuuranga (Poverty Bay) in 1769, for instance, the local people (according to William Williams in 1888 and Mohi Turei in 1911) thought that the *Endeavour* was a floating island or (according to Polack's East Coast informants in 1838) a great bird, or a houseful of 'divinities' (Salmond 1991: 123–124). In Te Matau-a-Maui (Hawkes Bay), Ngarangi-kamau told Colenso in 1851 that although Tupaia warned the local people not to approach the *Endeavour* in a hostile manner, the chiefs contemptuously over-ruled him, saying *'kahore he raakau o te hunga o Hawaiki; he puu kaakaho, he korari!'* (the people of Hawaiki have no weapons, only reeds and flax-stalks!) (Salmond 1991: 150–151). They evidently understood the *Endeavour* to be a vessel from the mythical homeland, Hawaiki, crewed by ancestors, yet were far from awe-struck by the new arrivals. In Whitianga, according to Te Horeta Taniwha in 1852, Cook's crew were thought to be 'goblins' (translated by John White as *'tupua'*), a kind of supernatural being. Horeta was given a nail which he treasured as an *'atua'* until he lost it one day when his canoe capsized (Salmond 1991: 87–88). In all of these encounters, the local people challenged the Europeans vigorously with *haka* (chants), the ritual throwing of spears and with *karakia* (incantations). It was thus unpleasant to find Gananath Obeyesekere, in his recent debate with Sahlins over whether Polynesians had 'deified' Captain Cook, castigating Horeta Te Taniwha as an 'Uncle Tom' for having described Cook's party as supernatural in quality (1992: 135). Maori understandings were barely investigated in Obeyesekere's polemic; he simply assumed that to describe Europeans as *'tupua'* or *'atua'* was a form of colonial flattery, rather than a common-sense interpretation within a *'Maori'* version of the world.

Interestingly, *'Maori'* people (as they came to define themselves in contradistinction to *'pakeha'* or Europeans) seem to have treated human-like *'atua'* much the same as other unidentified visitors. Given the notion that visiting parties might include ancestors (for instance on *marae*), this is perhaps not surprising. Indeed, the first Maori visitors on board European vessels acted with great aplomb, examining the crews, guns and physical layout of the ships, and often staying on board all night. Horeta's account of the *Endeavour's* arrival at Whitianga in 1769 gives some idea of the rapidity with which local people relaxed when they realized the Europeans were not intent on fighting them.

We lived at Whitianga, and a vessel came there, and when our old men saw the ship they said it was an *atua*, a god, and the people on board were *tupua*, strange beings or 'goblins'. The ship came to anchor, and the boats pulled on shore. As our old men looked at the manner in which they came on shore, the rowers pulling with their backs to the bows of the boat, the old people said, 'Yes, it is so: these people are goblins, their eyes are at the back of their heads; they pull on shore with their backs to the land to which they are going'. When these goblins came on shore we (the children and women) took notice of them, but we ran away from them into the forest, and the warriors alone stayed in the presence of those goblins; but, as the goblins stayed some time, and did not do any evil to our braves, we came back one by one, and gazed at them, and we stroked their garments with our hands, and we were pleased with the whiteness of their skins and the blue of the eyes of some of them.

These goblins began to gather oysters, and we gave some *kumara*, fish and fern root to them. These they accepted, and we (the women and children) began to roast cockles for them; and as we saw that these goblins were eating *kumara*, fish and cockles, we were startled, and said, 'Perhaps they are not goblins like the Maori goblins'. These goblins went into the forest, and also climbed up the hill to our *pa* (fort) at Whitianga. They collected grasses from the cliffs, and kept knocking at the stones on the beach [no doubt Banks and Solander, 'botanizing' and 'geologizing' on behalf of the Royal Society]. We said, 'Why are these acts done by these goblins?'

We and the women gathered stones and grass of all sorts, and gave to these goblins. Some of the stones they liked, and put them into their bags, the rest they threw away; and when we gave them the grass and branches of trees they stood and talked to us, or they uttered the words of their language. Perhaps they were asking questions, and, as we did not know their language, we laughed, and these goblins also laughed, so we were pleased.

(Salmond 1991: 87–88)

As Horeta's account suggests, Maori people were from the outset formulating guesses about the nature of their extraordinary visitors; as the debate in the pages of *Te Pipiwharauroa* indicates, it is unlikely that unanimity was quickly achieved. All the various surviving Maori accounts of first meetings with Europeans share the supposition, however, that these new arrivals were not '*Maori*', or ordinary. The newly constituted groups were defined in relation to each other; what are now commonplace ethnic labels in New Zealand ('*Maori*' and '*pakeha*') at first meant simply 'familiar, everyday', and 'extraordinary' in some way.

EUROPEAN OTHERS AS '*TANGATA*' (PEOPLE): '*MARIAO*' – MARION DU FRESNE

It seems it was not long before Maori decided that Europeans were human beings. In the north of New Zealand, that moment probably came some time during the sojourn of Marion du Fresne and his expedition in the Bay of Islands in 1772. Marion and his men stayed in the Bay for about a month, in largely peaceful intimacy with local groups. As Crozet later commented

The friendship which they showed us was carried to the extremest familiarity; the chiefs on boarding our vessels entered our rooms without ceremony, and slept on our beds, examining all our furniture piece by piece; they asked about the meaning of our pictures, and of our mirrors, of which they of course understood nothing. Indeed, they spent whole days with us with the greatest demonstrations of friendship and confidence.

(Salmond 1991: 427)

For thirty-three days Marion lived among Maori in blissful ignorance of their mores and politics, assuring his officers that 'since I do them nothing but good, surely they will not do me any harm?'(Salmond 1991: 388). Towards the end of his time in the Bay, in a poignant precursor to Cook's 'apotheosis', Marion was taken to a high hill and installed as a chief (or prepared for ritual sacrifice?).

He received many caresses from them, then they put a sort of crown of feathers on his head, showing him the whole expanse of land and making him understand that they recognised him as their king. They carried out several ceremonies and treated him with much respect; they made him a present of fish and of a stone on which an image of their deity was carved [probably an ancestral *tiki* ornament]. For his part he also gave them presents and many caresses and they escorted him back on board ship.

(Salmond 1991: 387)

Two days later he was dead, killed by one of the principal chiefs of the Bay. According to several tribal manuscript accounts from the 1850s, the cause that finally provoked Marion's killing (after a series of lesser offences) was a fishing expedition when, ignoring the advice of his Maori companions, he insisted on hauling his net in a *tapu* bay where two drowned men had recently been washed up. A number of northern tribes formed an alliance to attack his expedition, and the tribal accounts are matter-of-fact about his fate.

Marion was cooked and eaten by the chiefs Te Kauri and Tohitapu, as they were priests, and it was for them to eat these foreigners, so that evil might not come on their tribes for the evil of these people for ignoring the *tapu* of the beach where corpses had lain . . . . The bones of the foreigners who had been killed were made into forks for picking up food, and the thigh bones were made into flutes.

(Salmond 1991: 401)

None of the Maori accounts asserts that Marion and his men, despite their peculiarity, were regarded as other than human. They had arrived in the Bay during a period of inter-tribal hostilities, and after various attempts by particular groups to acquire the French as allies, it was decided that they were too unpredictable and disrespectful of the gods, and must be got rid of. Marion himself was sacrificed, not as a god, but like any enemy chief who had desecrated a *tapu* place. Despite its fine beginnings this proved to be one of the most destructive of all early Maori–European encounters; it led to the slaughter of hundreds of local Maori as well as many of Marion's companions, and consequential inter-tribal battles and expulsions of whole descent groups from the Bay.

'*KAAWANA KINGI*' (GOVERNOR KING) AND TUKI AND HURU

The episode of Marion du Fresne's killing and the subsequent shootings by the French became notorious in the north; Maori as well as Europeans came to regard their newly encountered 'others' as dangerous in the extreme. This opinion was confirmed in Europe by news of the killing and eating of a party of Cook's men in Grass Cove in 1773; but this by no means deterred Europeans from making further forays to New Zealand. The imperial powers maintained an officially rosy view of 'discovery' and 'exploration', which held that the process was beneficial both to the powers themselves and to the 'savages' encountered. Thus in 1798, George Vancouver could begin his *A Voyage of Discovery to the North Pacific Ocean and Round the World*:

> In contemplating the rapid progress of improvement in the sciences, and the general diffusion of knowledge since the commencement of the eighteenth century, we are unavoidably led to observe, with admiration, that active spirit of discovery by means of which the remotest regions of the earth have been explored; a friendly communication opened with their inhabitants; and various commodities, of a most valuable nature, contributing either to relieve their necessities, or augment their comforts, introduced among the less-enlightened part of our species. A mutual intercourse has also been established, in many instances, on the solid basis of a reciprocity of benefits; and the productive labour of the civilized world has found new markets for the disposal of its manufactures. . . . It should seem, that the reign of George the Third had been reserved by the Great Disposer of all things, for the glorious task of establishing the grand key-stone to that expansive arch, over which the arts and sciences should pass to the furthermost corners of the earth, for the instruction and happiness of the most lowly children of nature.
>
> (Lamb 1984: 272–273)

Vancouver conceded that these 'lowly children' had food and refreshments, or the skins of hunted animals and similar foods to offer Europeans, but the epistemological benefits, as he conceived it, were all one way. Ironically, however, his supply ship the *Daedalus* inverted these ideas about exploration when it went south in 1793 to capture some 'natives of New Zealand', to teach the convicts at the newly established 'thief colony' of Norfolk Island how to weave their clothes from local flax.

The two young men kidnapped by Lieutenant Hanson in the Bay of Islands, Tuki-tahua and Huru-kokoti (or Toha-mahue), knew little enough about weaving, but their paradoxical experiences as tutors for 'civilized men', captured yet living free in a convict society, were to have profound effects on subsequent Maori–European relations in New Zealand. Tuki and Huru later recounted the story of their capture to Lieutenant-Governor King, their host on Norfolk Island.

> They were some time about the Ship, before the Canoe in which Tooke and Woodoo were, ventured alongside; when a number of Iron Tools and other Articles were given into the canoe, the Agent Lieutenant Hanson (of whose kindness to them they speak in the highest terms) invited and pressed them to go on board, which Tooke and Woodoo were anxious to do immediately, but were prevented by the persuasion of their Countrymen [this being the very place where Marion's killing had occurred]. At length [they] went on Board, and according to their Expression, they were blinded by the Curious things they saw; Lieutenant Hanson prevailed on them to go below, where they Eat some meat; At this time the Ship made sail, One of them saw the Canoes astern, and perceiving the Ship was leaving them they both became frantic with Grief and broke the Cabbin Windows, with an intention of leaping Over Board, but were prevented; whilst the Canoes were in hearing they advised [their chief] to make the best of his way home for fear of his being taken also.
>
> (King 1791–1794, ML, A1687: 179–181)

After a brief detour to Port Jackson, Tuki and Huru were taken on board the *Shah Hormuzear* to Norfolk Island. It has often been forgotten in New Zealand history that during the late eighteenth century, the European settlements nearest to New Zealand were penal colonies, bleak outposts in which the 'criminal classes' (an 'excrementitious mass' according to Jeremy Bentham) of the home society were unceremoniously dumped. In fact, one early plan for New Zealand dreamed up by Arthur Philip, the first Governor of New South Wales, suggested that these islands might become a place of ultimate punishment. He thought that convicts who committed murder or sodomy in Botany Bay could be shipped to New Zealand and left there 'and let them [the Maori warriors] eat them. The dread of this will operate much stronger than the fear of death' (Historical Records of New South Wales 1892 (1787): 53). This plan failed, however, so remote and tiny Norfolk Island was set up as an ultimate prison instead. In this role it had two compelling advantages – it was uninhabited, and it was surrounded by a thousand-mile-wide moat.

Life on Norfolk Island during Tuki and Huru's visit in 1793 is well documented; the island and its buildings were surveyed during that year, and convict life was meticulously accounted for in King's letters, journals and reports. It was physically harsh – punishments of 800 lashes were meted out for theft, commuted to 250 lashes on a promise of good behaviour, and 300 lashes for idleness, commuted to 100. Women who cursed had their hair cut off for the first offence, their bodies shaved for a second, and were whipped at the cart's tail around the settlement for a third (King Journal, ANL, MS 70: 5). Clothing for the convicts was poor, rations were in short supply, and many of them (who had been transported in the horrific Second and Third Fleets to Botany Bay) were emaciated and unable to do much work. If this was civilization, it was of a curious kind.

By contrast with the convicts, during their seven months' sojourn on the island Tuki and Huru were well clothed, housed in Government House and fed at the Lieutenant-Governor's table. Tuki-tahua was a Te Paatuu priest's son from Oruru, a wealthy agricultural area, and Huru-koti's father was a high-ranking Ngaati Rehia chief from the Bay of Islands. Given their aristocratic backgrounds, they may have taken their privileged position for granted, and thought of themselves as chiefly visitors living with the most important family in the island, in a community composed largely of *toa* or warriors (the soldiers of the 102nd regiment), who acted as guards, and *taurekareka* or slaves (the convicts). On the other hand it is clear from King's account that their captivity (and perhaps that of others) greatly grieved them. They wept loudly for their loved ones every night, which in the confines of Government House, a small, two-storeyed building, must have been harrowing for King's family, and 'often threatened to hang themselves on very slight occasions and sometimes made very serious promises to putting it into execution, if they were not permitted to return to their own country'(King 1791–1794, Letterbook, ML, A1687: 187).

Lieutenant-Governor King had been largely responsible for Tuki and Huru's kidnapping. Frustrated by the inability of his convict flax-dressers to work the flax on Norfolk, he had advocated the capture of some New Zealanders (whose expertise with flax was well described by Cook and Banks) since the founding of the penal colony in 1788. As tribal accounts later reported, however, Norfolk flax was not the *tihore* (the best flax from which to make *muka* – flax fibre) and hence the *muka* broke in short lengths (White c.1850, ATL, MS 75, Folder B19: 90). As King ruefully observed,

> Every information that could be got from them, regarding their mode of manufacturing the Flax plant was obtained in One day . . . and which turned out to be very little, as this operation is the peculiar Occupation of the Women, and as Woodoo is a Warrior, and Tookee a Priest, they gave us to understand, that Dressing of Flax, never made any part of their studies.
>
> (King 1791–1794, Journal, ML, A1687: 135, 182)

King might well have considered this a bungled venture – the wrong people brought to work the wrong flax. Instead, it seems that he and his family became very fond of their involuntary guests. King wrote to Joseph Banks just before leaving Norfolk with Tuki and Huru, 'our intelligent and worthy friends, the two New Zealanders . . . have now been here seven months during which time they have lived with me and we are so much attached to each other that much real concern will be shown by every description of people here when they leave us' (King 1793, ANL, MS 9/95). When King finally farewelled Tuki and Huru off the north coast of New Zealand in November, according to William Chapman 'they cryed terribly and everybody on board was very much affected at the parting particularly the Governor who said he never parted with his mother with more regret than he did with those two men' (Chapman 1793, ML, MS 1974).

I am tempted to suppose that this was *mana* rather than magnanimity at work, but this may be unfair. Whatever forces drove King, however, they drove him very far. Shortly after he wrote to Banks, King commandeered the *Britannia*, a supply-ship en route to India with a profitable cargo of trade goods, to return Tuki and Huru home, and in doing so he jeopardized a hitherto unblemished naval career.

As for Tuki and Huru, they used their time on Norfolk well. Tuki taught some of the officers some Maori (King's 1793 journal included an extensive vocabulary), instructed King about a number of Maori customs and drafted an extraordinary political-genealogical map of the northern part of the North Island of New Zealand, on the floor of the study in Government House. He and Huru socialized largely with the civilians and the military on the island, learned from them 'not a little' English, something of the geography of the world and a number of practical skills associated with farming and the construction trades. When King dropped Tuki and Huru off near North Cape he left them with two green suits faced with orange, three swords, looking-glasses, handaxes, a selection of carpenters' tools, six spades, hoes, knives, scissors, razors, two bushels of seed maize, one of wheat, two of peas, a number of garden seeds, ten young sows and two boars (Fidlon and Ryan 1980: 367) – a magnificent array of European goods. And off Tokatoka Point King pressed noses and exchanged cloaks – and, it seems, names – with an eminent local *rangatira* (chief) 'Tokokee', and received two basalt *patu* (hand clubs) now held in the National Museum of Australia. As the canoes carrying Tuki and Huru left the *Britannia* the Europeans saluted them with three cheers, and at Tuki's direction the local people replied with three cheers of their own.

The most lasting consequences of Tuki and Huru's visit to Norfolk Island were three-fold. First, the manufacture of flax on Norfolk (despite its inferior quality) improved to the extent that some garments (including trousers and aprons), a foretopgallant sail, ropes and a long-line (afterwards tested on the *Daedalus*), were made. This kept alive the hope that a flax industry on Norfolk or New Zealand might eventually prove profitable (King 1791–1794, ML, A1687: 318–322).

Second, the effective introduction of pigs, maize and potatoes to Northland can be dated to 1793. According to a number of sources, including the one summary surviving account of Tuki and Huru's adventures: 'the Europeans gave them some pigs, male and female, and some Indian corn and potatoes, these increased (*tupu*) and were distributed to the other tribes of Ngapuhi' (White c.1850, ATL, MS 17, Folder B19: 81, 90). In Northland, at least, Tuki and Huru's kidnapping led to a local agricultural revolution.

The third consequence of Tuki and Huru's stay in Norfolk Island was a close and lasting relationship between Northland Maori and 'Kaawana Kiingi' (Governor King). When the *Fancy* visited Tokerau in 1795 and asked for Tuki, the people exclaimed 'My-ty Governor King! My-ty Too-gee! My-ty Hoodoo!' (Millington 1964: 135). *'Maitai'* is an ancient word for 'good' and King's reputation in this part of the North had evidently become widespread and excellent. Furthermore when Samuel Marsden met Huru in the Bay of Islands in 1819, he reported that,

> The great kindness of Governor King towards [Tuki and Huru] made the most favourable impression on all the natives who heard of it, and to the present day they always speak of it with gratitude and pleasure, and make enquiries after Governor King's oldest daughter, whose name is Maria, and who was only a few years [six-months] old when Hooratooki [Huru and Tuki] was at Norfolk. When [Huru] asked me about Maria, I told him that she now lived at Parramatta. He said he would go and live with her till he died.
>
> (Elder 1932: 155)

KAAWANA KIINGI AND TE PAHI

After he returned Tuki and Huru to Muriwhenua, King was long remembered in the North. Tuki and Huru were well connected in the local aristocratic networks (which must have conveyed many of King's gifts in subsequent redistributions), and they told others of his chiefly generosity. In 1805 the Ngaati Rehia chief Te Pahi, from Te Puna in the Bay of Islands, fulfilled a promise to his father Wharerau to go to Port Jackson to visit Governor King. King was now Governor at New South Wales, and he had sent gifts of pigs and potatoes via the whalers *Adonis*, *Argo*, and *Venus* to Te Pahi, in recognition of his friendly care of visiting European ships.

Te Pahi boarded the *Venus* with his four sons and an entourage in November 1805, and went with Captain Stewart to Norfolk Island. At Norfolk Stewart demanded payment for their passage, and would have detained Te Pahi's youngest son in lieu of payment if Captain Piper, the commandant at Norfolk, had not intervened.

Te Pahi was contemptuous of Stewart's behaviour, later telling King that he was no better than an *'emoki'* (*he mokai*, servant, slave). Captain Piper treated Te Pahi and his sons kindly, and housed them until they got a passage to Port Jackson. After a brief visit to the Derwent, Te Pahi arrived at Government House in Port Jackson, where he presented King with a number of 'mats' (dress garments) and a stone *patu* (war club), and saluted him with a *hongi* (ceremonial pressing of noses). He placed himself under the Governor's protection, saying that,

> If I [King] wished him to remain here, go to England or return to his own country, he was resigned to either, and in the most manly confidence submitted himself and his sons to my directions. All this was said in such an imposing manner that no doubt could be entertained of his sincerity.
>
> (McNab 1914 [1908]: 264)

Once again, King found himself impressed and disarmed by Maori chiefly behaviour. He invited Te Pahi and his eldest son Tuki (probably named after the Tuki who had stayed with King at Norfolk) to live with him at Government House, and arranged comfortable lodgings for his other three sons. Te Pahi, by his demeanour and acute intelligence, won general respect from the Europeans in Port Jackson. The *Sydney Gazette* (1 December 1805: 1) which reported his visit, described him as 'commanding', and King's account of him shows both admiration and liking.

> Tip-a-he is 5 feet 11 inches high, stout, and extremely well made. His age appears about 46 or 48. His face is completely tattooed with spiral marks, which, with similar marks on his hips and other parts of his body, point him out as a considerable chief or *Etangatida Etikitia* [*Rangatira Tiketike*?] of the first class. To say that he was nearly civilized falls far short of his character, as every action and observation shows an uncommon attention to the rules of decency in his every action, and has much the airs and manners of a man conversant with the world he lives in. In conversation he is extremely facetious and jocose, and, as he never reflected on any person, so Tip-a-he was alive to the least appearance of slight or inattention in others.
>
> (McNab 1914 [1908]: 264)

Te Pahi's visit to Port Jackson was no idle journey. He had come to see Governor King but also to investigate Governor King's society, and to assess its strengths and weaknesses. He met Samuel Marsden, whom he quizzed about the Christian God, and who spoke of his 'Clear, Strong and Comprehensive mind'. He studied European carpentry, gardening (particularly the cultivation of potatoes), spinning and weaving techniques, and social institutions. He collected seeds fanatically, and also young fruit trees. But if Te Pahi impressed the Europeans, not everything he saw at Port Jackson impressed him. He was scathing about the Aboriginals, regarding their methods of warfare as trifling and their way of life abhorrent. Some Europeans he regarded as ill-mannered and gauche. An officer's wife had given him some gifts, including some earrings which he redistributed in chiefly fashion to a young woman. The officer's wife reproached him for this, and took the earrings back from the hapless recipient. Te Pahi was furious. He packed up all the gifts she had given him, sent them back to her and refused to speak to her or see her again. As King commented,

> [He] constantly expressed his disgust at hearing of the presents he had received being in any way mentioned except by himself; and to do him justice, he always took every opportunity to speak of the donors with the most grateful respect.
>
> (McNab 1914 [1908]: 268)

Above all, Te Pahi was appalled by European ideas of punishment, regarding these as excessive and barbaric. While he was at Port Jackson, two soldiers and a convict were brought from Port Dalrymple, and tried for stealing pork from the King's store. One of them was sentenced to death. Te Pahi was horrified when he heard this, and went to visit them in jail, later taking a petition for clemency from them to Governor King. According to King

> He came into the room where I was writing, and in a very earnest manner, and I believe from the full force of conviction, he endeavoured to reason with me on the injustice of slaying men for stealing pork, and at the same time showing the severest sorrow and grief for their fate, which he concluded by taking the petition out of his pocket and giving it to me, at the same time shedding tears. He threw himself prostrate on the ground, sobbing most bitterly. Observing that I did not give him any answer or hope other than by saying I should consider of it he left the room and did not make his reappearance until the hour of dinner, having taken off the dress he had made here, and appeared very violent, exclaiming in the most furious manner against the severity of our laws in sentencing a man to die for stealing a piece of pork, although he admitted that a man might very justly be put to death for stealing a piece of iron, as that was of a permanent use; but for stealing a piece of pork, which to use his own expression, was eat and passed off, he considered as sanguine [*sic*] in the extreme.
>
> (McNab 1914[1908]: 264–265)

Te Pahi was asked by King about cannibalism, which he said his people did not practise but those about Thames did; he explained about Maori spiritual beliefs and chiefly polygamy, telling King he had several wives and fifty-two children, although he had killed one wife 'for having a troublesome tongue, nor could he help testifying his surprise that many of the women here did not suffer the same fate' (McNab 1914 [1908]: 267). He told King to control the whalers, and agreed that some of his people might come to Port Jackson, to look after the local flocks. King, who had long aspired to become the first Governor of New Zealand, began to plan a five-month expedition under the command of the surgeon of the *Buffalo*, 'for the purpose of making such observations on the inhabitants, their manners and customs, with the formation of the country, as the time and their situation might admit of' (McNab 1914 [1908]: 268). Te Pahi was enthusiastic about the project and promised to protect the expedition, but the plan was cancelled when King heard that he was about to be relieved as Governor of New South Wales. Te Pahi stayed with King for three months in all, and when the time came for his departure in February 1806 King had a silver medal struck (engraved on one side: 'Presented by Governor King to Tip-a-he, a chief of New Zealand, during his visit at Port Jackson, in January 1806'; and on the other 'In the reign of George The Third, by the Grace of God King of the United Kingdom of Great Britain and Ireland'). King hung this medallion around Te Pahi's neck on a silver chain, and he and his officers gave Te Pahi iron utensils, tools, a box of fruit trees, and bricks and the framework for a prefabricated house, to be erected for Te Pahi on his arrival back at Te Puna. One of Te Pahi's sons,

Matara, who had been sent a year earlier by his father to 'see the English at their settlement'(Banks, MS 9/139) and had learned some English on board various ships, accompanied his father and brothers on the journey home.

TE PAHI, GEORGE BRUCE AND ATAHOE

Lieutenant Symons of the *Lady Nelson*, armed tender, had been ordered to take Te Pahi and his companions back to the Bay of Islands. During the month-long voyage from Port Jackson Te Pahi became ill, and was nursed on board by a young man named George Bruce (or Joseph Druce, according to the ship's log) (Lee 1915: 293). Bruce was a pickpocket who had been transported when he was 12 years old for stealing two handkerchiefs; he had had a chequered career in New South Wales (including several years as an escapee in the outback) which he later recounted in a maudlin and not always accurate memoir (Bruce, ML, MS 3608). In March 1806 when the *Lady Nelson* finally anchored off North Cape, Tuki (King's friend from Norfolk Island) came on board, and George Bruce ran from the ship (Lee 1915: 293).

Three weeks later the *Lady Nelson* brought Te Pahi back to Te Puna, in the Bay of Islands. According to John Savage (1807), a colonial surgeon who had visited Te Pahi's settlement during his absence, Te Puna had about a hundred houses, each with its own garden, but Te Pahi himself lived on an adjacent island citadel. There he had a fine dwelling, a 'large collection of spears, war mats and other valuables', and a small elevated storehouse where he had imprisoned one of his daughters for several years for wanting to marry a commoner. As soon as the *Lady Nelson* anchored, the ship's carpenter set to work erecting Te Pahi's new prefabricated house nearby.

After the departure of the *Lady Nelson*, George Bruce made his way south. Within a few months he was married to Te Pahi's youngest daughter Atahoe, and tattooed as a warrior. His memoirs say little about his time in New Zealand; more detail survives in later newspaper reports of his adventures. Te Pahi was obviously a genealogical strategist, for having married Bruce to his daughter he immediately put him to work as an interpreter and advisor in his dealings with European whalers. He may also (as Bruce claimed) have gained useful information about European weaponry and fighting techniques from his new son-in-law.

From the time of his arrival back in the Bay, Te Pahi engaged in a flurry of entrepreneurial activities. He began planting quantities of maize and potatoes, and dispatched his son Matara on another journey, this time to England with Governor King to 'see the King [of England] and obtain from his Majesty and the English nation axes, Iron and musquets in order that they may be enabled to build houses and live as English men do'(Banks, NLA, MS 9/139). He had also evidently revised his ideas about British justice. According to Joseph Banks, shortly after his return Te Pahi introduced whipping as a punishment for theft in the Bay. Furthermore, some time in 1807 a group of convicts who had escaped from the Derwent in a schooner put into the Bay, and tried to capture a whaler. The convicts asked Te Pahi's people for help, but instead they told their chief who informed the whaler's crew. While the convicts were making their attack Te Pahi's men seized their schooner, and captured six of the crew. As King later reported sardonically to Banks,

> As this piratical attempt was regarded by His Majesty in a very different point of view from the Crime of stealing a piece of pork he *hung* the whole *six*, and desired the Captain of the whaler to tell King George and Governor King what he had done and was sure they would approve it.
>
> (King 1791–1794, ML, MS A83)

According to George Bruce's memoirs, he was happy in the Bay. During late 1807, the *General Wellesley* put into the Bay with Edward Robarts and his wife on board. Bruce arranged a cargo of spars for the vessel, and according to Robarts behaved well when the ship's boat, which had landed at the same spot where Marion du Fresne once set up his shore camp, was almost cut off by local warriors. The *General Wellesley* was still at anchor when a whaler came in with a warrant for Bruce's capture, dead or alive. Bruce begged Robart's wife to hide him. She put him under her bed and sat on it with her children while the ship was searched.

Perhaps in gratitude for his escape, Bruce told Robarts about a gold mine at North Cape, and guided the *General Wellesley* there with his wife Te Atahoe. The 'gold' proved to be fool's gold, and a storm blew up which carried the ship out to sea. To their great distress, Bruce and Atahoe were forced to stay on board and were carried off across the Pacific. At Fiji, when Captain Dalrymple tried to obtain a cargo of sandalwood, Bruce offered himself as an intermediary with the local people. According to Robarts,

> He said he understood them and began to speak some broken New Zealand words to them. 'O, Sir,' says he, 'I understand them perfectly.' 'Well,' says the Capt, 'you are the most proper person to go on shore and see if you can find any sandall wood. If you do, I will reward you handsomely when I reach India.'
>
> (Dening 1974: 190)

Bruce dressed himself in a Maori cloak, buckled on a sword and went ashore. The next morning, when the boat was sent to pick him up, he was found stripped naked on the beach. Despite his tattoos, the Pakeha Maori had not fooled the Fijians.

According to Bruce, after this Captain Dalrymple turned him and his wife out of their cabin, so that they were forced to sleep on the sandalwood logs. The ship was constantly becalmed and the food ran out; Bruce said that the white people on board, driven near to starvation, had made a plan to kill and eat the Lascar sailors when a providential wind carried them to Solo Island instead.

The ship then sailed to Malacca where Bruce went ashore. While he was off the boat the *General Wellesley* sailed to Penang with his wife. At Penang Captain Dalrymple traded Atahoe to another European, apparently as a servant, but Bruce followed her, and with the Governor's help eventually got her back. After a sojourn in Bengal, Bruce and Atahoe (who was by now pregnant) boarded a ship to return to New Zealand, and during the voyage Bruce delivered his 'princess of New Zealand' of a fine daughter. Upon their arrival back at Port Jackson, however, Atahoe contracted dysentery and died fourteen days later. Bruce abandoned his daughter in the Female Orphanage in Port Jackson and returned to England, where strangers on the streets, seeing his tattoos, jeered at him and made his life a misery. For the rest of his days, so far as we know, Bruce tried desperately to get back to New Zealand.

SELF AND OTHER ACROSS THE BORDERLANDS

The world of ideas has always been open to us; and we must travel that world and learn from it.

(Hirini Mead 1983: 345)

In the 'genealogy' I have briefly recounted in this paper, Maori and pakeha defined themselves in paradoxical mirror images that shifted over time, and epistemological boundary-crossing was commonplace. In a recent book *Two Worlds* (Salmond 1991), I thought it fair enough to echo the Maori metaphor of *Te Ao Pakeha* and *Te Ao Maori* (the Maori and European 'worlds'), for in the very first meetings between local people and Europeans – those short, sharp and often violent encounters – the boundaries (both phenomenal and cultural) between the European ships and the people on the beaches were only briefly breached. For the period that followed, however, as visits by European vessels became more frequent, the idea of 'borderlands' – of places on the edges, where new practices and patterns were negotiated out of contradictory circumstance – seems a better way of evoking what was going on. To my mind, 'borderlands' evokes the idea of the *pae* in Maori – that edge or metaphorical horizon, where people and ancestor gods or stranger groups enter into reciprocal exchanges which simultaneously separate, and entangle them.

Tuki, Huru and Governor King, Te Pahi, George Bruce, Matara and Te Atahoe were all boundary-crossers, each in their own way. They investigated the knowledge and practice of a strange society, and negotiated relationships across the edges. From the Maori 'side' of these negotiations, once they had decided that Europeans were human, Maori took an active and experimental interest in them. Sahlins (1985) claimed that Maori had a 'prescriptive cultural structure', a 'mytho-praxis' in which 'the world unfolds as an eternal manifestation of the same experiences'. Yet there is little enough of mytho-logical thinking in the history I have traced, and Sahlins's account seems fantastic when exposed to actual Maori historical practice. Genealogical thinking, on the other hand – a logic based on *whakapapa* – is everywhere evident, in the formation of aristocratic alliances, the cultivation of kin and quasi-kin ties and the diplomacy of reciprocity and gift exchange.

Maori epistemologies, far from being 'closed' and circular, appear to have been 'open' and entrepreneurial, quickly adapting to shifting circumstance as, out of uncertain edges between 'two worlds', a new society emerged.

Explorers and early colonial officers had no choice but to practise reciprocity with Maori; it was the only way they could obtain goods and information from them. Rather to their surprise, however, they often found themselves not only treating Maori as equals, but thinking of them that way. Despite European mythologies about 'savages', Maori men and women of *mana* were (and still are) quickly cosmopolitan, and impressive to Europeans. *Mana*, it seems, as ancestral efficacy, has power to operate not only at the ancient borderlands of the battlefield, the *tuuaahu* (shrine) and the *marae*, but also at the *pae* between Maori and Europeans.

'MAORI' AND 'PAKEHA' AS SELF AND OTHER IN CONTEMPORARY NEW ZEALAND

Ka whawhai tonu maatou, ake ake ake!
[We will fight on, for ever and ever and ever!]
(Rewi Maniapoto 1864 – oral history)

The fundamental error in anthropological thinking about the 'other' may not be, as Johannes Fabian (1983) has suggested, the creation of artificial distance between self and other in space/time, but rather the transformation of 'other' into anthropological object. For objects have these negative properties in western thought – they cannot speak, they cannot think, and they cannot know. 'Objectivity' creates an immediate epistemological privilege for the 'observer' – only he/she can truly know. This assumption has been much needed in anthropology, for difficulties with exotic languages, the brevity of most 'fieldwork', and the actual complexity of 'simple societies' might otherwise suggest that the observer knows little enough.

Zygmunt Baumann recently described assimilation as

a round-about confirmation of social hierarchy, of the extant division of power. It assumed the superiority of one form of life [/knowledge] and the inferiority of another, it made their inequality into an axiom, took it as a starting-point of all argument, and hence made it secure against scrutiny and challenge. It effectively reinforced this inequality through ascribing the discrimination of the 'inferior' sectors of the power structure to their own flaws, imperfections, and their very 'otherness'.

(Baumann 1990: 158)

It is possible that anthropology has been the specific mode in which western epistemology assimilated the knowledges of others, silencing them and converting them into curiosities that need not be taken seriously, even on the matter of their own experience of the world. In an earlier paper I described just such a relationship between western knowledge and Maori epistemologies in New Zealand (Salmond 1984). Such has been the insistence of Maori people on their *mana*, however, that they have refused to be permanently objectified. Over time, as Europeans defined Maori as 'savages', anachronistic stragglers in the march of history who would inevitably die out, or as 'natives', lower orders in the evolutionary scale who had to be 'raised up' and civilized, Maori have upheld their status as significant selves for whom Europeans are 'other', and have met Europeans wherever possible on their own ground, according to their own relational logic and their etiquettes of encounter.

The 'genealogy' I have investigated in this paper could thus well be carried on into the present. Relational logic helped to shape the Treaty of Waitangi, recognized today (at least rhetorically) as the founding document of a bicultural society, and crafted an enduring relationship between Maori chiefs and the British Crown. Relational logic helped to recruit Governor Grey and his imperial troops as mercenaries in the 1845–1846 inter-tribal wars in North Island (although Grey of course, did not see his role that way). Relational logic, in the end, could not overturn demographic domination, imperial bureaucracy or international capitalism, but Maori leaders have never ceased trying to persuade their European counterparts to behave with *mana* (i.e. honourably and well). This has led to a succession of petitions to the New Zealand Parliament over breaches of the Treaty, similar petitions to British monarchs, and during the two world wars, to the establishment of the Maori Pioneer Battalion and the Maori Battalion along genealogical lines. As Maori people migrated to the cities after World War II, relational logic led to the establishment of tribal and family associations and urban *marae*, so that Maori could continue to identify with ancestral descent-groups, and the founding of 'culture groups' to foster the performance of action songs, *haka* (chants of challenge) and *marae* rituals. Maori leaders fought for Maori to be taught in schools and universities, and in recent years for the establishment of *Kohanga Reo* or language nests (Maori-language pre-schools), *kura kaupapa* (Maori-language primary schools), *kura tuarua* (Maori-language secondary schools) and various kinds of *waananga* (schools of learning), to allow Maori ways of knowing to continue to evolve in a changing world.

The Waitangi Tribunal was established by a Maori Minister of Maori Affairs in 1975 to investigate breaches of the Treaty of Waitangi. The Maori Land March and the occupation of various disputed lands (Bastion Point and the Raglan Golf Course, for instance) led to an expansion of the Tribunal's powers, and its hearings, which were initially held in conference rooms, are now held on *marae*, where elders give their evidence orally in Maori (although this may be overweighted by the written evidence of historians and the requirements of a quasi-legal process). Tribal trusts established to disburse compensation payments for lands wrongly taken by the Crown, and an array of 'Iwi authorities' are gaining increasing commercial influence, particularly in forestry, fisheries and tourism; and political influence, particularly in welfare matters and resource management. Over the past five years the recently established National Maori Congress (a confederation of descent-groups), as well as the older New Zealand Maori Council have entered into direct negotiations with the Crown on the privatization of crown assets, including fisheries, forests, broadcasting frequencies, the railways and hydroelectric power.[7]

Not surprisingly, anthropology itself has been drawn into this 'history of struggles'. The right of non-Maori anthropologists to interpret Maori experience has been vigorously challenged (Walker 1990, Te Awekotuku 1991) and a generation of Maori anthropologists trained in the 1960s and the early 1970s at Oxford, in Auckland and elsewhere, are amongst the most prominent protagonists in current Maori–pakeha debates.[8] In 1991, when New Zealand sought to signify itself as a country to the world at the opening of the Commonwealth Games in Auckland, Sir Hugh Kawharu (anthropologist and leader of the local people, Ngaati Whaatua) delivered the opening *whaikoorero* (oration), while Dr Peter Sharples (anthropologist and leader of a multi-tribal *marae* in Auckland) led the 'culture group' which challenged a world audience in a spectacular televisual version of a *marae* encounter.

Every gain that Maori interests make in contestation with pakeha power, however, invites its bitter backlash. Maori leaders, especially those who argue for Maori self-determination, are castigated by politicians and the popular press. Maori projects which aim at economic independence invite unprecedented scrutiny, and any irregularities are seized upon. Health, education and economic statistics show continuing devastation among Maori people, and Maori advocates may become co-opted, or exhausted or demoralized. Still, the power of ancestral *mana* seems inexhaustible; as each generation has fought its battles, another generation takes its place.

Hinga atu he teetee kura	As one flax frond falls
Ara mai he teetee kura	Another rises

Perhaps this is why many Maori have no doubt about the continuing validity (and challenges) of ancestral ways of knowing in a modern world. As Eruera Stirling, eminent tribal expert and my long-time mentor and 'grandparent', once advised younger Maori,

> Knowledge [*maatauranga*] is a blessing on your mind, it makes everything clear and guides you to do things in the right way and not a word will be thrown at you by the people . . . . Maori-tanga (Maori being) is holding fast to the treasures of your ancestors – land, *marae*, the mountains – and returning in spirit to the minds of your forebears. It is not a light or easy thing but a difficult treasure, and heavy to carry.

On the conventions of being a 'knowing self', he added,

> *E tamariki ma* – study your *whakapapa*, and learn to trace your descent lines to all your ancestors . . . so that you can join yourselves together. Do

not use these treasures to raise yourselves above others – *ko mea, ko mea, ko mea, ko 'hau*! But if you are challenged, or if somebody throws words at you on the *marae*, then it is proper to stand up and reply. The old people said to us, be humble; work amongst the people and they will learn to praise you. That was the wisdom of our ancestors, brought from the ancient houses of learning in Hawaiki. The old men told us, study your descent lines, as numerous as the hairs upon your head. When you have gathered them together as a treasure for your mind, you may wear the three plumes '*te iho makauwerau*', '*te pare raukura*', and '*te raukura*' on your head. The men of learning said, understand the learning of your ancestors, so you can talk in the gatherings of the people. Hold fast to the knowledge of your kinship, and unite in the brotherhood of humanity.

(Stirling and Salmond 1980: 247)

RETHINKING SELF AND OTHER IN CONTEMPORARY ANTHROPOLOGY

Only if we can remember that 'the other' is never defined in intrinsic terms, but always in terms of its difference from the observer, will we have the epistemological basis for a differentiated understanding of the globe's societies. [And] this may be a pre-condition of any improvement in relations among the societies of the globe.

(Carl Pletsch 1981: 590)

The baskets of wisdom of our ancestors may be here with us, but be forewarned, they hold two types of knowledge, something bad and something of beauty. The fruits of beauty – seek them and nurture them, for your livelihood. But the evil fruits, trample them underfoot. Nowadays we have two sources of knowledge, that belonging to the Maori and that belonging to the Pakeha. The fruits of these are the same, both good and bad, but you must seek that which is good.

(Unnamed elder, quoted in Barlow 1991: 159)

In Maori epistemologies, the knowing self is constituted in relationship with ancestors and kinsfolk. The purpose of knowledge is to advance their interests and uphold their *mana*. Maori tribal thinkers view knowledge as practical and ethical, to be used to find good pathways for their people. Yet most of my Maori anthropological teachers and contemporaries no longer identify themselves as anthropologists. Perhaps this is (in part) because the ethnographic 'I', which sees 'other' as object, means for anthropologists' being and resource for anthropology's projects, comes too quickly into conflict with the relational self, which sees other Maori as kinsfolk, means for ancestral being and resource for descent-group projects.[9] When anthropological and Maori interests diverge, a choice is necessary. Usually, in such a circumstance, anthropology doesn't stand a chance.

It is possible that in anthropology, ideas of 'self' and 'other' must be rethought from the roots. Western European thinking, and the scientific–technological world it engendered and the knowing self proper to that world, seem increasingly fragile. A 'world civilization' confronts disorder as others resist the dictates of western reason. The academy is confused by unpredicted responses – insurgent ethnicities which confound the march of social logic, burgeoning populations which demand democracies of consumption, an environment exhausted by 'progress' defined as efficiencies of extraction. In anthropology, as elsewhere, the reaction has often been alienation and despair, a retreat into narcissism or struggles to retain control by definitions such as 'the world system', 'globalization' and 'localism', 'world culture as a structure of differences'.

The great anthropological questions – what is it to be human? What do we have in common as human beings and what divides us? – have lost none of their compulsion in a post-colonial order. What is needed, perhaps, are practical and ethical epistemological attitudes which give up the West's attempt to control the Rest; which seek answers to these questions (which are not just western questions) in ways that allow other knowledges to speak. If anthropology is to become a world, rather than just a western discipline, it must define its 'others' differently, as selves who also speak, think and know.

In New Zealand, at least, ideas of the relational self and anthropology as a collaboration between knowledges offer one possible pathway. It may lead, eventually, to accounts of cross-cultural encounters which do justice to the ancestors on both sides, and to the potent, perilous *pae* – the borderlands between them.

NOTES

1 Todorov's formulation sums up the matter precisely. There is no real reciprocity in the relation between self and other. 'We' (i.e. westerners) control the 'knowing' and reap the benefits. It is unclear what the 'other' has to gain, if anything, from this process.

2 Foucault defines a 'genealogy' as 'the union of erudite knowledge and local memories which allows us to establish a historical knowledge of struggles and to make use of this knowledge tactically today' (Foucault 1980: 83); this understanding is very close to Maori notions of *whakapapa*/genealogical accounts of the past.

3 There are moments in his analysis when Sahlins seems to acknowledge a genealogical structure in Maori thinking (e.g. 1985: 57–59) but his constant collapse of *whakapapa*/genealogy into mythology is fatal. Presumably, however, his argument that Maori always grasped events as replications of some mythic original was necessary to make a sharp contrast between prescriptive (i.e. 'cold') Maori and performative (i.e. 'hot') Hawaiian cultural structures.

4 *Pae* in Maori covers a range of meanings pertaining to ritual boundaries of various kinds – on the *tuuaahu* (shrine) where ancestor gods and people engaged, on the battlefield between one hostile group and another, on the *marae* in peaceful meeting, and in the exchange of gifts between descent-groups:

Pae	threshhold, hill ridge; ropes for hauling nets; any transverse beam
kai paepae	return present of food between one tribe and another
pae o te riri	resting-place of a war-party on the march

paepae hamuti	latrine beam
pae arahi	one who leads visitor onto a marae
paepae tapu	sacred threshhold
paepae	place where orators sit

5 See, in different ways, Sahlins (1985: 54–72; cf. Binney's devastating 1986 critique) and Obeyesekere (1992).
6 The correspondence was published in issues of *Te Pipiwharauroa* in November 1910 (p.7), December 1910 (pp.2–3) and January 1911 (pp.4–5).
7 For a more extensive account of many of these developments, see Walker (1990).
8 Among the names to conjure with in New Zealand, as leaders in the reassertion of Maori and tribal *mana* are: Sir Hugh Kawharu (D.Phil. Oxford, leader amongst Ngaati Whaatua, member of the Waitangi Tribunal, former Professor of Maori Studies at the University of Auckland); Dr Tamati Reedy (Ph.D. Auckland, leader amongst Ngaati Porou, former Secretary of Maori Affairs); Professor Hirini Mead (Ph.D. McGill, leader amongst Ngaati Awa, former Professor of Maori Studies at Victoria University); Professor Patu Hohepa (Ph.D. Indiana, former Chairman of Runanga o Ngapuhi, Professor of Maori Language at the University of Auckland); Professor Ranginui Walker (Ph.D. Auckland, former Chairman of the Auckland District Maori Council, Professor of Maori Studies at the University of Auckland); Dr Robert Mahuta (D.Phil. Oxford, Director of the Maori Research Centre at the University of Waikato, leader in the Kiingitanga or Maori King Movement); Dr Ngapare Hopa (D.Phil. Oxford, Maori Research Centre, important in the Kiingitanga); Apirana Mahuika (M.A. Sydney, leader amongst Ngaati Porou, Chairman of the National Maori Congress); Graeme Smith (M.A. Auckland, Senior Lecturer in Maori Education, University of Auckland); Dr Ngahuia Te Awekotuku (Ph.D. Waikato, Senior Lecturer in Women's Studies and Art History, University of Auckland); and Dr Peter Sharples (Ph.D. Auckland, former Race Relations Conciliator, leader of Hoani Waititi Marae in Auckland and the Manutaki Culture Group, Associate-Professor of Education at the University of Auckland).
9 To define 'other' as object, deprives 'other' of *mana*. Maori anthropologists have generally come into the discipline to uphold *mana Maori* and to advance Maori interests. If both 'self' and 'other', as Maori, are defined as anthropological object, and thus deprived of *mana*, Maori anthropologists are placed in an impossible double-bind.

REFERENCES

Manuscripts

Banks, J. 'Letter', MS 9/139, National Library of Australia.
Bruce, G. MS 3608, Sydney: Mitchell Library.
Chapman, W.N. 'Letter of 19 November 1793', Letters 1791–1838, MS 1974, Sydney: Mitchell Library.
Hohepa, P. (n.d.) 'A Note on *Mua/Muri/Tua*', Maori Studies Department, University of Auckland, typescript.
King, P.G. (1791–1794) 'Journal of transactions on Norfolk Island with copies of all correspondence', A1687; 'Letter to Banks' MS A83, Sydney: Mitchell Library.
—— (1793) 'Letter to Sir Joseph Banks 10 November 1793, Norfolk Island', MS 9/95; 'Journal', MS 70, National Library of Australia.
White, J. (c.1850) MS 75, Folder B19, Alexander Turnbull Library.

Published works

Asad, T.(ed.) (1975) *Anthropology and the Colonial Encounter*, London: Ithaca Press and Humanities Press.
Barlow, C. (1991) *Tikanga Whakaaro: Key Concepts in Maori Culture*, Auckland: Oxford University Press.
Baumann, Z. (1990) 'Modernity and ambivalence', *Theory, Culture & Society* 7: 143–169.
Binney, J. (1986) 'Review of Marshall Sahlins *Islands of History*', *Journal of the Polynesian Society* 95: 527–530.
Dening, G.(ed.) (1974) *The Marquesan Journal of Edward Robarts 1797–1824*, Canberra: Australian National University Press.
Elder, J.R.(ed.) (1932) *The Letters and Journals of Samuel Marsden, 1765–1838*, Dunedin: Coulls Somerville Wilkie.
Fabian, J. (1983) *Time and the Other: How Anthropology Makes its Object*, New York: Columbia University Press.
Fidlon, P. and Ryan, R.J.(eds) (1980) *The Journal of Philip Gidley King: Lieutenant, R.N. 1787–90*, Sydney: Australian Documents Library.
Foucault, M. (1980) *Power/Knowledge: Selected Interviews and Other Writings 1972–1977*, Sussex: Harvester Press Ltd.
Hansen, A. (1989) 'The making of the Maori: cultural invention and its logic', *American Anthropologist* 91: 890–899.
Heidegger, M. (1978) *Basic Writings*, London: Routledge & Kegan Paul.
Historical Records of New South Wales (1892) Volume I, Part 2 *Phillip 1783–1792*, Sydney: Charles Potter, Government Printer.
Johansen, J.P. (1954) *The Maori and his Religion*, Copenhagen: Munksgaard.
Lamb, W.K.(ed.) (1984) *George Vancouver: A Voyage of Discovery to the North Pacific Oceans and Round the World 1791–1795*, Volume 1, London: The Hakluyt Society.
Lee, I.(ed.) (1915) *The Logbooks of the Lady Nelson, with the Journal of her First Commander Lieutenant James Grant, R.N*, London: Grafton & Co.
McNab, R. (1914) [1908] *Historical Records of New Zealand*, Volume I, Wellington: John Mackay, Government Printer.
Mead, S.M. (1983) 'Te Toi Matauranga Maori mo Nga Ra Kei Mua: Maori Studies Tomorrow', *Journal of the Polynesian Society* 92: 333–351.
Millington, R.R.D. (1964) *The Map Drawn by the Chief Tuki-Tahua in 1793*, ed. J. Dunmore, Mangonui: the Estate of R.R.D. Millington and J. Dunmore.
Obeyesekere, G. (1992) *The Apotheosis of Captain Cook: European Myth Making in the Pacific*, Princeton: Princeton University Press.
Pletsch, C. (1981) 'The Three Worlds, or the division of scientific labour, circa 1950–1975', *Comparative Studies in Society and History* 23: 565–590.
Sahlins, M. (1985) *Islands of History*, Chicago: University of Chicago Press.
Said, E. (1978) *Orientalism*, London: Penguin Books Ltd.
Salmond, A. (1978) 'Te Ao Tawhito: a semantic approach to the traditional Maori cosmos', *Journal of the Polynesian Society* 87(1): 5–28.
—— (1982) 'Theoretical landscapes', in D. Parkin (ed.) *Semantic Anthropology*, London: Academic Press.
—— (1984) 'Maori epistemologies', in J. Overing (ed.) *Reason and Morality*, London: Tavistock Press.
—— (1991) *Two Worlds: First Meetings Between Maori and Europeans 1642–1772*, Auckland: University of Hawaii Press.
Savage, J. (1807) *Some Account of New Zealand, Particularly the Bay of Islands*, London: J. Murray.

Stirling, E. and A. Salmond (1980) *Eruera: The Teachings of a Maori Elder*, Auckland: Oxford University Press.

Strathern, M. (1992) *Reproducing the Future: Essays on Anthropology, Kinship and the New Reproductive Technologies*, Manchester: Manchester University Press.

Te Awekotuku, N. (1991) *He Tikanga Whakaaro/Research Ethics in the Maori Community*, Manatu Maori.

Todorov, T. (1982) *The Conquest of America*, New York: Harper & Row.

Walker, R.J. (1990) *Ka Whawhai Tonu Matou: Struggle Without End*, Auckland: Penguin (NZ) Ltd.

3   As I lay laughing

Encountering global knowledge in Bali

Mark Hobart

Knowledge is a coffin we carry around looking for a decent place quietly to bury. The image might seem surprising. It is common to imagine knowledge as something immortal which carries on growing remorselessly. There are other ways to think of knowledge however. Even were knowledge on the increase, what of those who are barred from enjoying it, although they are entwined in its snares? There is a darker side to knowledge: the fear of failing to master it, of being excluded from it, of becoming its object. How knowledge appears, indeed what it is, depends on how you are situated in respect to it. Here academics are in principle in a unique position to reflect upon their own practices. After all, is it not we who discover, advance, teach, disseminate and even control the growth of, knowledge? Yet we rarely talk about knowledge as such, except to outsiders. And new ways of thinking about something as often destroy previous knowledge as add to it. In anthropology such thinking makes a mockery of its most cherished creations: society, culture, human nature, reason and, I suspect soon, anthropology and knowledge itself. Each intellectual generation owes its being to its forebears and repays the debt by burying them.

THE ARGUMENT SUCH AS IT IS

Every few years an idea which has usually been rumbling away for years somewhere else momentarily convulses the little world of anthropology and threatens to upset the calm progress of research, writing and teaching. The latest tremor is the discovery that we may have been living through a process of incipient globalization for some time. A problem with much globalization theory though is that it is an exercise in retrenchment in the aftermath of post-structuralism and postmodernism. How convenient it would be were the unsettling suggestion unfounded that the modern world and its paraphernalia of nation-states and political economies did not exemplify the epitome of western rationality and was but a thing of shreds and patches. The fear that knowledge of that world might turn out more fragmented, closed and contingent than presumed in academic spin-doctors' accounts could then be allayed by focusing on how effective that knowledge could be shown to be in the globality of its reach. The west, whatever that is, had won. (The malleability of the notion of 'the west' contributes to the apparent success of western, or global, knowledge, which I take not to be one single coherent essence, but the heterogeneous product of a long history of practices.) Globalization theories celebrate the spatialization of history, get on with the cartography of the new world order (a.k.a. hypermodernity) or, with a nod to the pessimists, worry about how to alleviate the unfortunate side effects of the triumph of late capitalism. The argument looked more convincing in the mid-1980s with the impending signs of collapse of the Soviet Union than it does a decade later. As a seismic event to mark the end of history, it is reminiscent of Cyril Connolly's immemorial headline in *The Times*: 'Small Earthquake in Chile, Not Many Dead'.

Although it is still badly needed, this is not the occasion for an extended critique of globalization theory (on which see, for instance, Archer 1990). I shall confine myself simply to a few remarks relevant to this paper. Much of the apparent applicability of the notion of globalization relies on the play made of a fan of connotations (see Appadurai 1990; Featherstone 1990a; Robertson 1992). In particular, globalization suggests totality, which always gives academics a *frisson* of delight. A total problem suggests a total, indeed totalitarian, solution. The notion of globalization is hegemonic, because the globality is that of western civilization, variously imagined. Appeal to the self-evident phenomenon of globalization distracts attention from the contrary process of decivilization, by which the world is becoming in many ways a distinctly nastier, more polluted and dangerous place, not least the metropolitan centres which promulgate the Utopia. Like its predecessor, world-systems theory, globalization theory's descriptions of the world simplify complex and underdetermined events by imputing to them teleological and systemic properties, such that 'the local' becomes hypostatized as opposed dichotomously to 'the global'. (Whatever happened to regions, attention to which would vitiate simplistic oppositions?) This leads in turn to an endless and vapid play on their 'meanings' in an attempt to escape the reified and spatialized intellectual *cul-de-sac* created.

The account of knowledge that underwrites ideas of globalization is, unsurprisingly, deeply conservative. It reverts to a representational idea of knowledge as more or less accurately and definitively reflecting the world as it is, independent of those doing the knowing and describing. Its appearance of offering something *more* comes from the promiscuity by which 'global', and its shadow 'the total', refer to a process, an object, a universality and range of purported access, and a totality of scope. Accounts of knowledge are agentive. They define the objects, or subjects, of that knowledge, empower some people as being able to know but others as not and determine what counts as knowledge itself. In this chapter I wish therefore to consider critically the implications of ways in which Europeans and Americans, whose global knowledge is at issue here, have imagined knowledge and set out to constitute the world accordingly. This is emphatically not an exercise in epistemology in the sense of a search for timeless conditions of truth and privileged access to it. On the contrary, I take assertions about, and uses of, knowledge to be social actions with far-reaching consequences. The supposed neutrality of the knower in representational models underwrites a subtle hegemony. In a post-colonial, or global, world, epistemology has become the means to a new imperialism. For example, constituting much of the world as 'underdeveloped' defines those concerned as lacking, determines what they lack – the preordained goal which they have failed, but must struggle, to achieve – and specifies outside expert knowledge as the appropriate means to this end. A consequence of apotheosizing western knowledge is the dismissal of existing knowledges. One person's claim to knowledge is all too often another's condemnation to ignorance. Whatever knowledge is it is not neutral.

Among the problems in discussing knowledge is the fact that it is arguably not a unitary phenomenon and, in most representations, it is abstract. So knowledge is talked about using widely diverging constitutive metaphors. These metaphors are not 'dead' insofar as they have consequences. I sketch out below several partly incommensurable, but often amalgamated, forms widespread in popular and academic usage. I then consider the consequences of imagining knowledge in particular ways, notably for both knowers and what, or who, is known. Knowledge, on these accounts, emerges as some kind of mental object, state, residue or commodity, usually anchored in the human subject as a fixed, ultimately private, disposition. The following survey of metaphors of knowledge verges at moments on the comical, but their presuppositions are far from innocent or their consequences innocuous.

Treating knowledge as some kind of mental entity has the effect of denying the historically and culturally specific situations in which it is invoked and foreclosing reflection on the purposes, agents, subjects and objects imputed on particular occasions. For this reason I choose to consider knowledge as a range of situated practices, an approach which I have developed elsewhere (1993a). Recourse to practice does not miraculously solve the problem of knowledge, whatever that might be, not least as we have, *pace* Bourdieu (1977, 1990), no satisfactory account of practice. Reconsidering knowledge as various kinds of practice has several advantages though. So doing situates different uses of knowledge, instead of postulating it as a timeless essence, and highlights the consequences of such uses and of claims to knowledge. Not least for my present purposes, treating knowledge as practice articulates well with how Balinese have publicly represented their own knowledge to themselves and how they deal with their increasingly frequent encounters with global knowledge and its purveyors, which is the theme of the second half of this paper. For Balinese rarely speak of knowledge as a state, but of knowing and remembering as the acts of agents. Considering knowing as a situated public practice requires revising many of our presuppositions about knowledge. For a start laughing and dying seem to be implicated in knowing in ways I only partly understand at the moment. I intend the effect to be partly counter-hegemonic, in that it allows us within limits to reflect critically on our own ideas through the practices of people who are normally the objects of our knowledge. More immediately, treating knowledge as practice invites us to engage in a little ethnography on ourselves; to think about how, as anthropologists, we discuss and get on with our work. It suggests that what we actually do is engage in highly specific and diverse practices from talking to informants and writing publications to lecturing and marking essays, attending conferences and gossiping. Grand terms like 'knowledge' sit uneasily on such practices, which vary even between disciplines.

THE DISCIPLINING OF METAPHOR

Despite, or perhaps because of, the lucubrations of epistemologists, what western or global knowledge *is* sometimes seems fairly self-evident. Ideally it is potentially all-encompassing, systematic and abstract. Because it is abstract, it must be depicted catachretically, that is be instantiated through metaphors which are, awkwardly for a systematic vision, in part mutually contradictory. Three distinct, but overlapping, metaphors often surface in academic writing and casual talk about knowledge, which I designate as territorial, horticultural and capitalist. Two others occupy a more peripheral place: the revolutionary and the dialogic. The publisher's word limit precludes my giving detailed examples. So I must leave it to readers to exercise their agency in drawing upon examples from their own experience.

My starting-point is the representational model, which relies upon a visual metaphor of knowledge as mirroring nature (Rorty 1980). The world-to-be-known is spatially extensive and knowledge of it conceived as a landscape to be explored, conquered, mapped, controlled. As Anne Salmond has noted, spatial and visual metaphors elide in much anthropological usage. So 'understanding is essentially a way of *looking at things*', such that facts appear as objects, given, data (1982: 73). A recent variant is knowledge as flowing (see Appadurai 1990, who also uses the landscape metaphor exhaustively). Process, here, though is simply how a static model is made to cope with change and indeterminacy. In either case, the greater the superiority of the observer, the more objective and rational the surveilling gaze. By contrast, Maori, on Salmond's account, speak of knowledge as a scarce resource which should not be squandered.

The play of metaphors is less merely decorative, a simple way of speaking, than constitutive of the argument, and of the world. 'Much of the richness and piquancy of theoretical talk, and many of its new departures seem to arise from the flexibility and ambiguity of such non-literal language' (Salmond 1982: 81). The result may be flexible, but it creates closure. The image is static, timeless, ahistorical. History is just an extra, pseudo-spatial dimension: the time taken to explore the landscape or chronicle phases of development. Consider how Robertson, a major proponent of globalization, defines the problem in a piece entitled 'Mapping the global condition'. The

job is systematically to indicate and *explore* 'the major phases of globalization in recent world history' (1990: 15). History is reduced to the
compilation of phases: what Collingwood described as the 'scissors-and-
paste' method (1946: 33). It involves no critical questioning which requires
reevaluating our thinking about the past, and so changing our understanding.
Most accounts of knowledge sideline understanding, which I take to be
dialectical (Hobart 1991) and incompatible with the prevailing models. As a
landscape is something to be seen, it does not answer back. In fact no
questions are asked of it. Perhaps geologists, say, can get away with this; but
its implications for anthropologists, who work with people, are disturbing.
Even where anthropologists recognize that the kinds of facts we deal with are
fictions – in the sense of 'something made' (Geertz 1973a: 15) – they are
something which *has been*, not *is being* made.

Questioning and answering are activities which are the exclusive prerogative of the researcher. Things wait to be discovered. They are passive:
the activity belongs to the explorers who discover, map and master them. It
is the dream of globalization theory 'in which the other culture is largely
mastered' (Featherstone 1990b: 9). The model spatializes and objectifies
everything in sight, including discourse and meaning into determinable fields,
structures, institutions. So 'the general field of globalization must lay the
grounds for . . . the structure of any viable discourse about the shape and
"meaning" of the world-as-a-whole' (Robertson 1990: 17–18). In anthropology the corollary of this objectification is that people are still often treated
as passive subjects. They are to a degree aware of the collective representations and structures that determine their actions. They depend on anthropologists to frame, comment on and analyse their actions for them. There is
little recognition that people engage in critical thinking themselves and so
change the conditions of their own existence, which would require a radical
revision of the object (sic) of anthropological inquiry. People are still
informants, from whom we extract *information*. That is knowledge in its most
static, timeless, commodifiable form.[1]

The visual or territorial metaphor underwrites much of the idealized
activities of the natural and social sciences. The landscape need not be
outside, as it is, for instance, when societies are ethnographed. You can
explore inside: within the atom, the body or the psyche. There is a progression
however, from the landscape – female-like nature, there to be explored and
represented – to the masculine activity of intervening, to strip away and
expose, under the *controlled* conditions of the laboratory and, prometheanly,
to create. As Hacking has noted, there are fewer phenomena in nature than
are created by human intervention (1983: 227). When the natives have been
suitably (intellectually) pacified, anthropologists turn societies into field
laboratories to test hypotheses systematically, as Bateson and Mead did in
Bali (1942:xi–xvi, a work significantly subtitled 'a photographic analysis').
From this it is an easy transition through the hermeneutic theme park, where
we wander at will and admire the differences (Geertz 1973b) to ethnographic

museums (Baudrillard 1983: 13–23) and tourist resorts, where the terminally tranquillized natives enact tableaux of their former selves.

Uses of the territorial metaphor emphasize the object to be known, controlled and exploited rather than the nature of the knowledge involved. Attacking the idea that discovery and experimentation precede inductive generalizations, Popper argued,

> on the contrary the theoretician must long before have done his work, or at least the most important part of his work: he must have formulated his questions as sharply as possible. Thus it is he *who shows the experimenter the way.*
>
> (1934: 107, my emphases)

The shift from an inductive to a deductive view of knowledge parallels a switch of metaphor, neatly encapsulated in *Criticism and the Growth of Knowledge*, the critique by Popper's successors of Kuhn's revolutionary image of knowledge (of which more shortly). Knowledge is represented as a kind of organism, firmly rooted but continually growing.[2] With the landscape now domesticated, knowledge becomes a massive tree which grows to dominate the garden. The image is no longer of a static world of objects, but of the process of emergence of knowledge itself. There is an implicit entelechy in this image: the evolution of the organism is somehow pre-ordained and inexorable. Knowledge, like a growing tree, is powerful. It can, and will, displace whatever stands in its way. It is not just 'the *domination* of experiment by theory' (Hacking 1983: 167, my emphasis), but that images of the power of knowledge come to dominate.

This evolution of knowledge is not entirely without human intervention. The philosopher's job is to manure the tree and prune back adventitious branches, although they are not averse to a little intellectual topiary. They are, in the end though, glorified gardeners, servants of a force with its own direction and destiny. We must submit to injunctions: 'don't talk about things, talk about the way we talk about things' (Hacking 1983: 167), in order to achieve the 'semantic ascent' (Quine 1990: 81) to an arboreal eyrie from which to gaze from a superior, rational viewpoint. Meanwhile mere scholars of the humanities and some social sciences are the botanists, painters and guides to the garden who describe and celebrate the tree's stages of growth and particularities. In anthropology, the shift is exemplified in the work of writers like Clifford (1988) and Boon (1990), who have renounced ethnography for meta-commentary on the nature of anthropological knowledge itself as the significant object of study. The wonder of knowledge calls for suitable paeans.

Knowledge on this account derives much of its power from its being systematic. Notions of system, like stages of growth, are central to globalization theory and its precursor, world-systems theory. 'As systems move towards their natural demise they find themselves in "transition" to uncertain futures' (Wallerstein 1990: 38). Such naturalization first conflates knowledge and its objects, then by a reverse colouration of metaphor turns knowledge as an organism into a knowing organism. The stated aim of Wallerstein's world-systems analysis is 'with the degree to which this system became *conscious of itself* and began to *develop* intellectual and/or ideological frameworks which both justified it, and impelled its forward movement' (1990: 35, my emphases). Scholars emerge less as agents than as the instruments or immanent intelligence of knowledge itself as a transcendental agent endowed, in the more extreme versions, with its own consciousness.

According to the territorial metaphor, the discoverer or master of the world appears to be the proximate agent. However, as with the colonial conquest of the further expanses of the globe, this depends upon an image of knowledge which gerundively posits the world as investigable, and so to be explored, and singles out the appropriate willing subjects of such discovery. Professionalizing knowledge distances the knowers from their agency. The texts in which this knowledge is inscribed 'are authorless, so that their truths seem bigger than the authors, transcendent and revelatory. In this way, it is not only agency which is diminished, but also causality, and hence responsibility' (Vitebsky 1993: 109). As the tree of knowledge effloresces triumphantly and globalizes, it metamorphoses tropically into a banyan, overshadowing everything else.

Once knowledge has expanded so vastly, it becomes increasingly hard to describe as a unitary system or to decide who controls and owns it. As knowledge becomes progressively alienated from its erstwhile producers, it undergoes a further metaphorical transformation into symbolic and financial capital, a capital which itself has the capacity to transform. Capitalism itself often comes to be treated as a transcendental organism and the market as its mind. Organicity moves from knowledge to the object of that knowledge. This leaves the question of whether capitalism is still in its spotty adolescence, strapping adulthood or in its dotage. In any event, growth becomes transformation and division. 'What is occurring now is, in all likelihood bigger, deeper, and more important than the industrial revolution . . . the present moment represents nothing less than the second great divide in human history' (Toffler 1975: 21). Toffler's future was a world 'where science and technology were utterly synonymous with knowledge and knowledge was completely conflated with the structure of the new Information Society' (Archer 1990: 107). However, in late capitalism, as the emphasis has shifted from production to consumption (Baudrillard 1975) so knowledge has become a commodity which may be bought and sold democratically. Its most packageable form is as information, which in much globalization theory forms the vital commodity, generated by the new information technologies. This commoditized knowledge-as-information heralds apocalyptically the advent of a homogenized global culture at precisely the point that culture itself has been commoditized (as experience) and trivialized for mass consumption as tourism.[3]

In late, disorganized capitalism, so much information is generated that it is not possible to speak of particular groups of individuals as 'owning' knowledge any more. As knowledges proliferate and, like transnational companies, diversify, they need to be managed and marketed. (Significantly, in struggling to find a suitable term to talk about knowledge for the title of the original conference section, *Counterwork: Managing Diverse Knowledges*, my colleague Richard Fardon found himself forced *faute de mieux* into using this image.) Unreflective governments have even taken the metaphor literally. For instance, British universities have been told, in the words of successive prime ministers and secretaries of state for education, that they 'must enter the marketplace'. In the business of marketing a knowledge which nobody owns any more, it should come as no surprise that universities, including my own, have started to dispense with academics as vice-chancellors in favour of businessmen and bankers, who exhort us to think of students as consumers, to maximize turnover and increase efficiency and productivity.

Where does that leave the people we fondly thought of as in charge of knowledge? The academic as discoverer or producer, like the tree and its surgeon, are endangered species. If professionalizing knowledge distanced its creators from their agency, deprofessionalizing them ushers in the era of Weber's intellectual proletariat. As the market takes over the function of deciding what it is important to know about, academics become its instruments. And, as images of knowledge have changed, so have the ideas and practices of self-discipline which qualified knowers to become expert in their academic 'discipline'. What, in the territorial metaphor, was once the discipline required of the (typically male) explorer in order to survive the harsh conditions of the wild (honed in England by the privations of public school) became, in its later forms, the discipline of the controlled, white-coated figure in the laboratory. According to the horticultural metaphor, the world of knowledge reveals itself to the disciplined mind of the scholar, who is no longer the lichen-festooned ethnographer, but the commentator, teacher and professor: the disciplinarians at once of the subject and its disciples. What happens as the capitalist image of knowledge transforms? I suggest that discipline changes from the determination and frugality of the entrepreneur or the skill and industry of the craftsman to the surveillance and disciplining of the new proletariat through endless reviews of productivity, excellence and customer satisfaction. There is less need for self-discipline: the increasingly impersonal subject must respond to the dictates of the market.

As the supermarket emerges as the exemplary form of late capitalism, the superstore manager becomes the instrument of the new knowledge. As universities ape supermarkets, degrees increasingly resemble shopping expeditions among the competing delights of conveniently modularized, enticingly advertised courses. Teaching is consequently being transformed. For instance, my job over the last two years has changed to become largely about planning courses and organizing packaged course materials (including recording lectures for clients' convenience), managing teaching assistants (who, like checkout assistants, actually deal with the customers), handling complaints and, of course, filling in forms and submitting to surveys.[4] The role of academics as critical thinkers becomes not just irrelevant, but actually subversive of efficient marketing and management. (It is helpful to distinguish management from administration. I take administration to be the kinds of activity for instance in which colonial rulers engaged in a past imperial form of government.) The post-structuralist cliché of 'the death of the author' may be not just a conceit of the textualization of the world, but the product of the new imperatives. Maybe I have grown disabused, but my impression is that academia is rapidly replicating commerce, as output geared to instant ideas or easily assimilable thought-bytes, with short shelf-lives and sell-by dates, supersedes the less marketable critical scholarship. How much work published in the last decade (including this chapter) has actually contributed anything to human understanding, or will be worth reading in a few years? If knowledge is market-driven, will the books which sell in supermarkets and airport kiosks become the sources of knowledge – no longer Mill or Kuhn, but Mills & Boon?[5]

How convincing this sketch is I leave to the reader to judge. I am not arguing that there is anything inherent in such metaphors which determine human thinking, nor that people in any particular situation are necessarily constrained by such images. The test of the relevance of my argument is if it helps to explain practices to do with knowing and if it makes sense of the consequences. Sometimes, indeed, the metaphors appear to be adopted quite literally. For instance, the idea that the kind of knowledge needed to run a supermarket is directly applicable far more broadly is instantiated in Mrs Thatcher's decision to delegate key aspects of government policy-making to the executive heads of two foodstore chains. Selling baked beans qualifies you to decide how to determine the fate of patients in mental hospitals. If it were not so terrifying, it would be funny.

TOWARDS A REVOLUTIONARY DIALOGUE?

There are two other metaphors of knowledge, which fit less easily in the progression outlined above. The first is Kuhn's explicit image of knowledge as a revolution (1970 [1962]) and Feyerabend's endorsement of nihilism or dadaism as its method (1975), which are too well known to need belabouring. The revolutionary metaphor, perhaps inevitably in the social sciences – which are far more hidebound than their practitioners care to admit – becomes watered down and sanitized ('argument is war' (Lakoff and Johnson 1980: 4–5)). In anthropology there is supposed to have been an equivalent revolution, from the armchair disciplinarians of collated facts (now in vogue again) to participant-observation, a visual image which overlooks how much fieldwork depends upon talking and questioning. Were we to take the image of revolution seriously, it would imply that, far from being heirs to a glorious tradition, most existing knowledge is obsolete, if not downright dangerous. If knowledge is not something you accumulate, a great deal of what has been written about, say, Bali is not so much dated as useless or at best seriously misleading.[6] Such an insight threatens to put too many people out of business. So revolutionary fervour, which may burst out in the sporadic warfare of seminars or articles, but rarely conferences, is headed off into the set-piece battles fought out in journals and monographs, and is dissipated by the morass of committees which decide who gets hired and who gets the research grants, tenure and promotion.

The obverse face of the revolutionary image is knowledge as dialogue.[7] There is an important difference though. The previous metaphors are all great intellectual undertakings *en clé de mort* (Lévi-Strauss 1966: 194). To view knowledge as a landscape requires objectifying it first: turning people into specimens to be pinned to boards. Organisms die: and their growth requires others to. Commoditizing critical thinking as anodyne information leaves it murled and moribund. Revolutions are rarely bloodless. Dialogue, by contrast, is *en clé de vie*: it points to a future, however uncertain. It presupposes someone else with a mind of his or her own who is likely not to agree with you. Dialogue as an image also has the virtue of specifying some of the different kinds of practice in which we actually engage, like teaching classes, discussing in seminars, talking with colleagues and people during fieldwork. It treats knowing as a diverse set of situated practices. Kuhn's latter formulation of his paradigm (1977) as an exemplary way of solving problems suggests that knowledge is less an abstract mental entity than culturally and historically changing kinds of activity. The revolutionary and dialogic metaphors suggest in different ways that there is a case for considering knowledge as different kinds of practice which are more contested, confused and fragmented than is implied in the more authoritarian claims of knowledge to be an abstract conceptual system.

KNOWING AS A PRACTICE OR EVENT?

What does it involve to talk of knowledge as a practice?[8] Negatively, it requires us to pause before assuming knowledge to be a reified, ahistorical abstract entity, a tendency in anthropology which includes depicting local, or indigenous, knowledges as inherently systematic (Brokensha *et al.* 1980). Although doing so may encourage us to take local knowledges seriously, it invites in a Trojan Horse, because the effect is to impose alien categories and to ignore the case for taking knowledges as historically situated practices. Not just local knowledges, but also expert knowledge, may be more about 'knowing how' than 'knowing that'. Even academic writing is in no small part a craft. Local knowledge often exists as rival versions, which are not separable from the social conditions of their being known (Cohen 1993). It does not follow that such kinds of knowledge are irrational. They are subject to testing and modification, and involve theory and presuppositions (van der

Ploeg 1993). Knowing, in this sense, requires evaluation by some measure like appropriateness to particular circumstances or adequacy, rather than by its being true as such. Talk of truth is often meaningless, when what one is dealing with may be more like a performance (as in agriculture (Richards 1993)), or is so local that it could not authentically be codified as knowledge (Burghart 1993). To encrypt such a pullulation of practices in the coffin of knowledge barely leaves a skeleton.

To turn at last to Bali, the island has been the refractory object of western knowledge for centuries (Hobart 1990a). Indeed it already had a place in western knowledge before it was discovered according to Boon (1977: 10–34), because somewhere on earth paradise was thought still to exist. The problem was just to find it. Balinese and Europeans have a long history of mutual gazing and misunderstanding (Wiener 1995). Dutch colonization, the Japanese invasion, Independence, the massacres which followed the abortive coup of 1965, development and finally mass tourism are among the indices of Balinese encounters with the modern world. The relationship is not all one way. Leaving aside the impact of Balinese music on western music, more prosaically the silver for *Les Musts de Cartier* is now worked in Bali, as in the eighteenth century were rifle barrels (Vickers 1989: 18), because Balinese have turned out to be more skilled at working metals than Europeans in the respective periods. The book on how Balinese used Europeans (such as Walter Spies) to further their dealings with outsiders still remains to be written.

Such accounts however tell us little about Balinese practices of knowing, teaching, learning, questioning, criticizing and so on. Treating knowledge as a social practice also links rather nicely with Balinese discursive usage. Balinese whom I know commonly explained what we often call states of the world and mind in terms of action, *laksana*, or as work, *karya*.[9] The roots for 'know' in daily usage, *tawang* or *uning*, apply to both knowing and being conscious or aware. Interestingly, the words are rarely used in noun forms. I am not proposing that Balinese usage has no recourse to metaphor. Balinese themselves on occasion relate *uning* to *ening* 'clean (of water), transparent', and *nerangang* 'to explain' to *terang* 'clear, bright'. Nor am I advancing the crude Whorfian argument that Balinese cannot conceive of knowledge as an abstraction: they have available a range of Old Javanese (ultimately Sanskrit) words. The term most widely used, *pramāna*, suggests however '"ways" of knowing' (Matilal 1986: 97), the 'means of acquiring right knowledge' (Zoetmulder 1982: 1392). And the Old Javanese (and Sanskrit) term for knowing or knowledge, *jñāna* in Balinese becomes *pradnyan*, 'clever, knowledgeable', which like the other word often employed, *kawikanan*, implies a demonstrated ability to be able to do something. To start off an analysis by ignoring Balinese usage is peremptory and unwarranted.

Balinese stress on knowing rather than knowledge has parallels in Indian Nyāya accounts of perception and knowledge. Knowing is a process which, is set in motion by doubt and ends in a decision. . . . The end-product takes the form of a mental episode called *pramā*, 'knowledge' (a knowledge-episode). It is such a cognitive episode (*jñāna*) as hits the mark!

(Matilal 1986: 100)

Indeed Matilal's example is the same as the one Balinese used to me: seeing something in unclear light. (In passing, Balinese words for what we call 'meaning' imply hitting a target or reaching an objective.) By contrast to much western philosophical thinking, which emphasizes knowledge as 'a more stable, inter-subjectively communicable item' or disposition (Matilal 1986: 101), Nyāya philosophers and Balinese stressed believing and knowing as momentary episodes, which are recalled in subsequent acts of remembering.[10] As Matilal put it, 'Indian philosophers viewed a world or constructed a world of a series of cognitive events rather than collected a mass of true propositions' (Matilal 1986: 105–106). Is knowing an act or an event though? Matilal compared Nyāya accounts with Geach's theory of mental acts (1957) and opted for knowing as a mental episode rather than a mental act on the grounds that acting 'in ordinary language is ambiguous', as it applies 'primarily to physical movement and observable physiological behaviour' (Matilal 1986: 112). At this point, I prefer to suspend judgement as to how far his argument applies to Balinese. As they speak cheerfully of thinking, knowing and remembering as *laksana*, there is little point in doing unnecessary violence to their practices by over-interpreting them.

HEALING OR DOCTORING PATIENTS?

Among the ways of knowing, *pramāna*, to which Balinese give serious attention is the speech (*sabda*) of the dead, who do not lie. Unfortunately the mediums (commonly *tapakan*, literally 'those who are impressed upon') on whom they must rely are all too capable, in their view, of dissimulation. As doctors and health clinics purveying western medical knowledge have proliferated, become more affordable and less likely to kill patients than before, Balinese healers have had to take account of them. One response has been the rise of highly sophisticated local practitioners, to whom people travel from all over the island. Although most Balinese have now made use of western medicine at some point, the local healers have an epistemological edge over their rivals. Like many of their British counterparts, Indonesian doctors do not explain what they are doing or why. They treat the patient as passive and ignorant. By contrast, the local healers with whom I worked involved their clients as co-agents in inquiry into the causes of their condition.[11] Healing is a public exercise in knowing, of moving from doubt to deciding whether what was said hits the truth.

Let us consider brief extracts from one case treated by a celebrated healer, who was so popular that clients came to obtain numbered tickets, sometimes days in advance. Her sessions took place before a large audience, anywhere from thirty to seventy-five waiting patients and their families. During the boring parts those waiting watched television. When the healer was in séance, they listened and commented, sometimes in horror or sympathy, more often with much amusement at the sorts of mess peoples' lives got into. The session, like others, began and ended with the question of responsibility, and so agency, being discussed explicitly. (In the translation that follows, the clarificatory parentheses are mine. Italicized English words have been translated from the Indonesian; the remainder of the text is translated from Balinese.)

Healer: Now whether you will get advice or not is not yet sure. Whether you will be successful or not, we share [responsibility for what happens] together. Is that acceptable?
Clients: Yes.

The session concluded:

Healer: The *risk* [responsibility for deciding the validity of what was said] belongs to you, the petitioner. If you think it appropriate, write down what follows.
Clients: It is.

In several of her cases, the healer explicitly questioned the efficacy of Indonesian doctors. She began the séance by indicating that an unnamed forebear wished to speak. (Later to their suitable astonishment she named, apparently correctly, the clients' father who wanted to speak to his children.) The forebear described the (absent) patient's symptoms in detail: she was confused, she failed to hear what was said, her heart pounded, her joints were numb and she felt pain in her bone marrow. Worst of all she, and the other people in the compound, had terrible dreams every night. The healer continued:

Healer: What is more the ill person is unaware of being confused. It is no use referring this to a doctor, the doctor will be at a loss to work out what is the problem [i.e. the doctor will be as confused as she is]. The reason is that there are no clear *symptoms* . . . . When she is out in public, she is quite capable of sorting out East from West [to be muddled over directions in Bali is the acid test of deep confusion]; but as soon as she *enters* the compound, she is worse than a chicken under a clay water pot. If you say she is mad, do not think this is sent from God, if so she would be mad both in the streets and at home. She is not mad, but ill. However, this is not an ordinary illness; it is different; it is called 'not well, not ill'.[12] So, those are the *nature* of the signs [of something unusual] in your compound now. Have you understood?
Clients: Yes.

She then went on to explain, apparently speaking as a dead family member, that it was the collected forebears who had sent the illness as a warning that a dangerous device (*pakakas*) had been placed by ill-wishers within the compound.

Healer: If I can illustrate, it is like a *guided missile* [which has almost reached its destination] because it is about to explode [literally, 'it is on your *doorstep*']. In order that it doesn't *reach the point* of your being *blown up*, I, together with the purified dead and the recently cremated dead, have let loose my servants [*bebutan*, Balinese, invisible followers] to visit you with disturbances which would make you quickly seek clarification. This was in order that you would not be just *convinced* by a doctor. If you had been *convinced* by a doctor [i.e. doctor's diagnosis], you would now be dead. Now what is the use of dead followers to Me? This is why I sent bad dreams, even to the smallest toddlers. Have you understood?

Clients: We have.

Balinese had been greatly taken with television footage of missiles pursuing aircraft around the sky during the Falklands war. And the healer made use of such 'modern' images in her diagnoses. (On another occasion she likened the form of attack on a victim to a radio-controlled device.) She also showed that she was familiar with Indonesian and the basics of clinical terminology, which she encompassed as part of Balinese healing practice. (In Balinese terms, it was the deity who knew about all this. In Bali the dead too can learn.) Here the healer set up a confrontation which pointed to the limits of western medical knowledge. Where there are no clear symptoms or they fail to fall into pre-set categories, western medicine cannot cope. Its symptomatology is fixed, inflexible and unsituated, a dead monologic code. Doctors could not recognize an unusual sign, because they are bound by the straightjacket of received textbook knowledge. By a juxtaposition (known in Balinese as *masesimbing*),[13] she elegantly linked the patient's confusion with the doctor's inability to make sense of the symptoms. The picture she drew was of mortal danger impending, as real as a missile just metres from its target, while the doctor ran around in circles clucking furiously, blind to what was going on. Granted the calm, self-important gravitas and superiority to which most Indonesian doctors pretend, especially when dealing with villagers, the alternative image is delightfully ridiculous.

This was only the start. The deity explained that it had to send illness, including dreams, of a kind which doctors could not explain. It was crucial that the clients would be unsatisfied with any western medical diagnosis and would have to inquire further. Otherwise they would have been killed by the planted device. The deity's whole strategy depended on the limitations of western medical knowledge. Significantly, the healer made the logical crux of the argument hinge upon the doctor not succeeding in *convincing* the patient. Here she contrasted the authoritative, monologic voice of the putative doctor, which aimed at convincing an intimidated patient, with her own – or the forebear's – combination of sinuous logic, practical reason (a deity needs followers and so has a quite different concern for the patient from a doctor who is ultimately only interested in money) and dialogue. Action and signs were closely linked in the healer's speech. The dead had taken the action of sending a sign in the form of an action (making the victims have nightmares), which the victims had to think about to realize it was a sign requiring action. As they did not know the significance of the sign, the action was to seek advice. On this account, hermeneutics is not a limp-wristed preoccupation with textual meaning (it is the doctor who is tied to a closed system of signification determined by textual authority), but a sensitive ability to consider actual events critically and devise an appropriate response to them.

ALTERNATIVE POSITIONS

My second example is from a play performed in the research village in March 1989 by members of the Indonesian State Radio Company, before an audience of over a thousand people. The plot does not concern us here. I take two short extracts. The characters on stage were an Old Retainer, *Panasar,* [14] a Young Retainer who was his younger brother *Wijil*, and the low-caste wife of the Prince of Nusa Penida, an island off Bali. This last role, the *Liku* (played here incidentally by a man) is the stock part of a slightly mad and spoiled princess, who breaks polite conventions by saying what is normally left unsaid in public. Only the outlines of the plot were fixed, the rest was extemporized in the light of how the spectators reacted.

The first extract is from the opening scene, in which the Old Retainer entered alone and addressed the audience. (As in the previous example, the clarificatory parentheses are mine, the original was in Balinese, and translation from Indonesian is in italics. Performers drew on two other languages: Old Javanese, represented in bold, and English in bold italics.)

Old Retainer: . . . **All of us** living on this island cherish our *artistic and cultural life.* . . . How do we ensure it flourishes? What's the way to bring it about? [For a start] it's kind of you to put on this play. Also, Ladies and Gentlemen, it's good of you to come and watch, **because** if we aren't going to appreciate and look after our *arts*, who else are we to tell to do so? That's the reason that *guests* now come, that *tourists* come **from all over the world**. What are they really looking for? Is it not **solely because of** your *arts*, your *skill* [at crafts], your wisdom and expertise at making **all sorts of** *art objects*? That's the reason then that *tourists* come. What's this? Two of them have turned up. '***Welcome, good afternoon, thank you. I hope you glad see here.***' I know a couple of words to string together to start up a conversation. Well, now people *from overseas* enjoy watching, but we've all grown *indifferent*. Don't let it be like that. If things are as they are here, I feel happy and proud to address you. Isn't that so? I hope that we may succeed in looking after [what we have] **for ever**, so we can even improve on it . . .

As a highly skilled professional, the man playing the Old Retainer ranged across four languages even in this brief extract. The effect was to show the capacity of Balinese in theatre to encompass not only the past (in the use of Old Javanese), but the immediate present (Indonesian and English).[15] He started by referring to Balinese artistic and cultural life, for which he used a recently invented Indonesian expression (*seni budaya*). This framing of practices as 'culture' is part of the Indonesian state's drive to re-present ethnic differences, in Bali's case with the tourist market in mind. What people in a particular part of Bali previously just did is coming increasingly to be constituted self-consciously as 'culture'. The problem, as Balinese often complained, was that the opportunities for making wealth by working in the local tourist and handicraft economies have made people less willing to take time off to keep this new-found culture going. The retainer praised the audience for turning up to watch and noted that what brought tourists to Bali is their *knowing how* to do all sorts of things. (The sentence neatly combined the verb form of being expert, *wikan* (see *Kawikanan* p. 59 above), with the new Indonesian vocabulary of 'skill' at making 'art objects'.) Conveniently we were on hand in the audience to point to as an example and for the actor to suggest how important speaking English had now become in Bali. The very indifference Balinese had towards their own cultural heritage was implicitly linked to the new Indonesian order by his use of an Indonesian word, instead of several available vernacular ones. Ironically, his hope that Balinese would continue their past practices had already constituted culture in a moribund museological mode.[16]

Immediately before the following extract, the princess had been expatiating upon why the prince married her although she was ugly, and pronounced on what a woman must do these days to become a good wife. She continued:

Princess: If I *did not fulfil the specifications*, no one would have wanted to take me. I wouldn't have looked for a man. Do you know what *the first requirement is*?

Young Retainer: Indeed.

Princess: *Submit a letter of request!*[17]

Young Retainer: Huh!

Princess: *Second: be prepared to submit to a trial period of three months.*[18]

Old Retainer: It's very severe to apply for a job with the condition that one must *submit to a trial period of three months*.

Princess:	*Be prepared to take up any possible position.*[19]
Old Retainer:	Carry on.
Princess:	Do you know [the significance of] *be prepared to take up any possible position*? Did you think it was *in the whole of the archipelago*?
Old Retainer:	Doesn't it indicate *in the whole of the archipelago*?
Princess:	No.
Old Retainer:	What then?
Princess:	'*Be prepared to take up any possible position.*' It means: '*on the right, on the left, on top or underneath.*'
Old Retainer:	Oh dear! I thought it was to agree to go wherever one was posted.

Here the princess made fun of Indonesian bureaucratic protocols by applying them to the sexual attraction between couples. Instead of young people meeting in the many venues available to them, they should submit a formal letter of request. Starting from there she developed an implicit sexual theme to the hilarity of the audience by a play on the Indonesian word 'position' (*tempat*). Finally she subverted the ostensible theme completely by detailing sexual postures. As several spectators pointed out, it was all the more amusing because it was a man who was pretending complicity with the female members of the audience. (Barry Humphries, as Dame Edna Everage, did something similar.) Like the healer, the actor juxtaposed two themes and left it to the audience to infer how they linked. At various points in the play, the performers made it clear that how the spectators chose to understand what was said was up to them. The commentators with whom I discussed the play in detail said that most young people probably just enjoyed the double reference. However those who reflected more on what was said could interpret it as ridiculing the pompous, rigid procedures of the Indonesian bureaucracy. There was a third reading, which a commentator made (interestingly, a middle-aged man), namely a play on the desire for self-advancement through obtaining a government post – and the ordeals this might entail – and sexual desire, with the ordeals women have to go through to please men. It has become something of a cliché to describe theatre in Bali as didactic. To do so would be to miss much of the point as members in the audience I spoke to took it. Behind all this was an implicit, but sustained, mockery of the institutions of the Indonesian state by the repeated introduction of obscene themes which the actors wove together with quite different themes throughout the play. The humour moved easily between simple poking fun and obscenity to social criticism and to opening up alternative, sometimes deeply unsettling, possibilities. It suggested that there might be radically different understandings, not only about the conventions of behaviour being lampooned, but of the nature of the genres of representation themselves.

KNOWING AND LAUGHING

Knowledge among western academics is generally a very grave business indeed, to judge from the conferences of various anthropological associations I have attended over the years. The ponderous joke while delivering a paper, the occasional moment of levity during discussion just highlight how serious and important the occasion is. When visiting Balinese High Priests, textual specialists, healers and other experts, I have often been struck how often their conversation was interspersed with laughter, as were the healer's séances. When I tried to break the bad intellectual habits of a lifetime, I realized how important laughing was and a motley of occasions came to mind when laughing and knowing seemed linked in some way.[20] No one is above being laughed at under some circumstances. This is a theme familiar to Balinese specialists. In shadow theatre, the humble, fat servants routinely debunk one another, chaff their lordly masters, scoff at terrifying demons, make fun of the gods themselves and of members of the audience.[21] The people with whom I have worked in Bali stressed repeatedly to me that in theatre, as with other activities, you cannot learn or teach unless it is mixed with laughter.

One way to explain the healer's mockery of modern medicine or the fun poked at Indonesian institutions might be as a response to the fear of something beyond the capacity of Balinese to understand, let alone control. As the Old Retainer indicated, there is grave concern among an increasing number of Balinese over the effects of tourism and economic development. To reduce laughing to a mechanism for dealing with tensions and their psychic release (the tensions may even be inferred retrospectively from the catharsis itself) involves unnecessary over-interpretation. Appeal to the writings of Freud may not help, because too often they are invoked to underwrite a universalistic, closed and authoritarian theory of the human mind. The emphasis is on control, by which mind is made to mirror certain features of knowledge, of which mind itself is one object. The problem with such explanations, as with so much knowledge, is that they do not tell us very much. It does not tell us what Balinese do in fact laugh at, and what are the implications and consequences. A striking feature of genealogies of organized knowledge such as anthropology is quite how much they exclude rather than include. Human agents are reconstituted as ciphers of a narrow and exclusive anthropological imagination, such that not only are they alienated from their own actions, but the agents become largely unrecognizable, even to themselves on the few occasions they obtain access to ethnographic descriptions of themselves. The fact that laughter, fear, indeed so much of what people actually do and say, are so successfully eliminated or trivialized in most anthropological writings is a pretty damning indictment of our pretensions to knowledge.

The excerpts suggest that, unlike the use of the serial metaphors for knowledge outlined earlier, Balinese do not separate the knower from what is known, nor from the other participants. In theatre, the spectators are notably not passive, but are openly invited to reflect critically on what is being discussed. This hardly squares with the familiar stereotype of passive Asians by contrast with active westerners. Knowledge is still rarely commoditized and is not objectified in any simple sense. This is not to suggest that there are not specialized writings, which might appear to have objective authority or efficacy. However in my experience such as it is, Balinese paid less attention to the text as a source of objective knowledge than to the qualification of the person, and the study required, to master the practices necessary to realize the text's potential. Attaining such expertise affects your whole being: you do not just acquire texts and so knowledge. And part of knowing is knowing that such texts must always be used in a manner appropriate to *désa kala patra*, the particular place, occasion and circumstance.

Instead of prejudging what knowledge is, I prefer to start with situated practices: what people did and what people said about it. Ernesto Laclau has argued (1990) that social scientists have been preoccupied with the claims of structure for too long and have signally failed to take seriously the degree to which what happens is historical and contingent. Anthropologists' difficulties over unintended consequences are an obvious example. If we start to look at actual practices, then such unexpected themes as laughing and dying, for instance, seem to be linked in Bali to knowing in complicated ways. In the village where I work, there is a well-known story of a poor and illiterate man at a wake, who was teased by being asked to read a palm-leaf manuscript in Old Javanese. He fled in tears. On the way home he was summoned by giant figures who appeared, inscribed something on his tongue and told him to go back to the wake. On being taunted once again at his illiteracy, he astounded everyone by knowing how to read (and so to understand) the text. On Balinese telling, the story involves Balinese ideas of pleasure (*suka*) and suffering (*duka*). It also presupposes that, when matters reach an extreme (for instance, being mocked to the point of despair), they transform (*matemahan*) into their opposite. To reduce this story to being about compensation or some such theme would be paltry. Asserting the superiority of western, or global, knowledge requires ignoring much of what people actually do and say, declaring them ignorant and incapable of commenting on their own actions. This seems rather silly, not to say narow-minded, when the presuppositions people work with affect what they do and how they understand one another's actions.

One theme, I hope, is clear from the examples. Knowing is not the exclusive prerogative of some superior knowing subject. Both the healer and the actors assumed that the audience also knew what they knew. What was at stake rather was the significance of what everyone already knew and the importance of thinking critically about its implications. Knowing commonly takes place as part of a dialogue, which is how Balinese mostly study and read texts. (Actors deeply dislike appearing on television, because there is no audience, and they are reduced to working off one another.) What has all this to do with laughter?[22] Laughter is equally dialogic: you laugh with, or at, someone in company. Laughing to yourself is a sign of madness, not only in Bali. Knowing is directed at a target as, in a different way, is laughter. They are both about doing something in and to the world. If we insist on being dazzled by the apparition of global knowledge, we shall miss noticing practices which might tell us something, if only, like the doctors of the healer's image, we could stop running around under clay jars while unbeknown to us trouble looms. Above all, imagining or stating that you have knowledge all too easily justifies not inquiring too carefully or critically, lest it upset the illusion. The greater the claim to global dominion, the more such knowledge is likely to ignore what people are actually doing somewhere in the world.

Academic practices to do with knowledge are often *en clé de mort*: grave rehearsals of the traces of our presence. Dialogue with the people with whom we work offers no panacea. At most it is a warning against vacuity. The brief examples may have hinted at the complexities of Balinese commentaries on their own rapidly changing lives. One woman leaving the theatre performance remarked:

Pragina kaliwat duweg, tiang atenga mati kedèk
The actors were so clever, I half died laughing.

To claim I knew what she meant would be laughable.

NOTES

1 I am, incidentally, neither advocating a return to subjectivism or 'intersubjectivity', the loyal opposition to objectivism, nor to constructivism. It is the anthropologist who all too often defines the terms for other people's subjectivity. And the idea that humans invent, construct or constitute culture veers close to voluntarism. Nor am I proposing the fantasy of an access to true knowledge, unencumbered by metaphors and presuppositions. I am interested in how representations are *used* in practice and their consequences, a quite different concern.

2 Popper's sometime image was of leaping from one bobbing ice floe to another – a sardonic epitaph on the vision of territorial conquest.

3 The trumpeted convergence of previous differences as part of global compression (Robertson 1992: 8) is hardly original. Similar arguments were touted in the 1960s with the thesis of industrial covergence, but hardly achieved their millenarian expectations.

4 As electronic technology develops, presumably the Open University will soon have close to a UK monopoly as producer of courses based on videos, computerized coursework and examination in a market dominated by the US and no doubt in due course the Far East. I would like to thank Margaret Wiener and Ron Inden for their comments on the draft of this paper and Ron Inden for first suggesting the supermarket as the paradigm of late capitalism.

5 I jest not. The *Guardian* of 24 January 1994 reports that Barbara Cartland may actually have inspired the current British Prime Minister, John Major, to his 'Back to Basics' campaign.

6 Except, that is, for retrospective intellectual histories. It is interesting to see how authors cope with the rival demands of constructing genealogies to authorize their work and denying their antecedents. Much innocent fun is to be had watching, for instance, how Malinowski lecturers search around for some acceptable link between their argument and the thoughts of the master.

7 As Collingwood noted, the difference between these last two metaphors depends on whether one is prepared to recognize the need for divergence in argument. 'In a dialectical system it is essential that the representatives of each opposing view should understand why the other view must be represented. If one fails to understand this . . . [one's interlocutor] becomes . . . a combatant in an eristical process instead of a partner in a dialectical process' (1942: 211).

   The relationship of dialogue and dialectic is complex. Bakhtin argued against a Hegelianism which would monologize dialogue by locating it in a 'unique abstract consciousness' (Pechey 1990: 24). Instead he suggested 'dialectics was born of dialogue so as to return again to dialogue on a higher level' (Bakhtin 1986a: 162).

8 As the contributors to Hobart 1993b have written at length about the relationship of local and global knowledge, and tried to show ethnographically the case for treating knowledge as practice, I shall not repeat the arguments here. I merely note a few points because I assume them in what follows.

9 Significantly *laksaṇa* in Old Javanese is glossed as both 'action, doing, taking action, proceeding, operating, performing, practice' and 'mark, sign; that by which something is distinguished from other things . . . way of being or appearing . . . having the particular form of' (Zoetmulder 1982: 958). The connection, as Balinese put it, is that signifying is an action, as is one's way of being. Incidentally, I take signifying, like other practices, to be public acts, the agents of which need not be individual humans, but may be complex such as groups, public meetings, etc. (Collingwood 1942; Hobart 1990a).

10 On the significance of remembering and its implications for representations of agency in Bali, see Hobart 1990b: 327–330.

11 As everyone is aware that the ill are easily persuadable, one always takes along an independent person, whose job is to use their critical judgement. To a determined materialist, all this might seem peripheral to the central question of whether the treatment works. According to an old friend and ethno-medical specialist, Ivan Polunin, Balinese pharmaceutical expertise is remarkably broad-ranging. In a chemical idiom, you may pay many times more for a remedy in the form of pills from a clinic than for much the same as plant extracts from a healer. Knowledge once again is underdetermined, in the sense that different explanatory practices may achieve similar results. For Balinese specialists, the healer referred to below was a *balian tapakan* from Br. Lantang Hidung, Sukawati, in Gianyar.

12 This is a way of talking about 'illness of the thoughts' which is considered quite different from insanity, which may now be referred to psychiatrists.

13 *Masesimbing* is ostensibly to refer to one subject, but the real target is another, which is either indicated in the utterance or made clear by the circumstances under which the utterance is made. The significance of her juxtaposing the patient, doctor and chicken was lost neither on the onlookers nor on villagers to whom I played the recording later.

14 The root is 'base, foundation'. 'Anchorman' is the nearest English equivalent which comes to mind. The piece was in *Prèmbon* style. That is it resembles *Arja*, 'opera, or rather musical comedy' (de Zoete and Spies 1938: 196), except that the actors playing retainers wore masks.

15 The non-Balinese words were known to many adults in the audience, except for the English which was known to only a few.
16 Apart from this last sentence which is my own commentary, it was clear from a long conversation with the actor that the other nuances were deliberate.
17 This was a side swipe first at the formal protocols which are so striking a feature of Indonesian bureaucracy. It also suggested writing a love letter.
18 It has become practice in some organizations to engage staff on a trial basis in the first instance. The statement also referred to the increasingly common practice, especially in towns, of a couple sleeping together fairly openly before marriage.
19 There were two senses: (1) Be prepared to go on a posting anywhere within Indonesia. This is a common requirement of official postings; (2) Be prepared to have to adopt unusual sexual positions.
20 My debt to Bakhtin in both his studies of Rabelais (1984) and of dialogue (1986b) should be obvious.
21 Vickers (1984) and Worsley (1984) have noted the contrast drawn in traditional Balinese paintings between the energy, noise and – I would add – the laughter of the common people at work by contrast with the relatively cool restraint of the aristocracy, who hold themselves aloof. Knowledge seems to be set apart here as self-mastery. I have discussed the conjunction of laughing and knowing (and death) with several specialists on Balinese and Javanese. Each of them agreed they were somehow connected, and some gave examples, but none of us knew how to link it to our 'knowledge' of the societies in question.
22 Balinese, inevitably, have a word for my essay's title: it is *nyedèdèg*, to lean right back while sitting, a distinctive posture they often adopt when laughing heartily.

REFERENCES

Appadurai, A. (1990) 'Disjuncture and difference in the global cultural economy', in M. Featherstone (ed.) *Global Culture: Nationalism, Globalization and Modernity*, London: Sage.
Archer, M. (1990) 'Theory, culture and post-industrial society', in M. Featherstone (ed.) *Global Culture: Nationalism, Globalization and Modernity*, London: Sage.
Bakhtin, M.M. (1984) *Rabelais and his World*, trans. H. Iswolsky, Bloomington: Indiana University Press.
—— (1986a) 'Towards a methodology for the human sciences', in C. Emerson and M. Holquist (eds) *Speech Genres and Other Late Essays*, trans. V.W. McGee, Austin: University of Texas Press.
—— (1986b) 'The problem of speech genres', in C. Emerson and M. Holquist (eds) *Speech Genres and Other Late Essays*, trans. V.W. McGee, Austin: University of Texas Press.
Bateson, G. and Mead, M. (1942) *Balinese Character: A Photographic Analysis*, New York: Academy of Sciences.
Baudrillard, J. (1975) *The Mirror of Production*, St Louis: Telos Press.
—— (1983) *Simulations*, New York: Semiotext(e).
Boon, J.A. (1977) *The Anthropological Romance of Bali 1597–1972: Dynamic Perspectives in Marriage and Caste, Politics and Religion*, Cambridge: Cambridge University Press.
—— (1990) *Affinities and Extremities: Crisscrossing the Bittersweet Ethnology of East Indies History, Hindu-Balinese Culture, and Indo-European Allure*, London: University of Chicago Press.
Bourdieu, P. (1977) *Outline of a Theory of Practice*, trans. R. Nice, Cambridge: Cambridge University Press.
—— (1990) *The Logic of Practice*, trans. R. Nice, Cambridge: Polity Press.

Brokensha, D.W., Warren, D.M. and Werner, O. (eds) (1980) *Indigenous Knowledge Systems and Development*, Lanham, M.D.: University Press of America.

Burghart, R. (1993) 'His lordship at the cobblers' well', in M. Hobart (ed.) *An Anthropological Critique of Development: The Growth of Ignorance?*, London: Routledge.

Clifford, J. (1988) *The Predicament of Culture: Twentieth-Century Ethnography, Literature, and Art*, London: Harvard University Press.

Cohen, A.P. (1993) 'Segmentary knowledge: a Whalsay sketch', in M.Hobart (ed.) *An Anthropological Critique of Development: The Growth of Ignorance?*, London: Routledge.

Collingwood, R.G. (1942) *The New Leviathan or Man, Society, Civilization and Barbarism*, Oxford: Clarendon Press.

—— (1946) *The Idea of History*, Oxford: Clarendon Press.

de Zoete, B. and Spies, W. (1938) *Dance and Drama in Bali*, London: Faber.

Featherstone, M. (ed.) (1990a) *Global Culture: Nationalism, Globalization and Modernity*, London: Sage.

—— (1990b) 'Global culture: an introduction', in M. Featherstone (ed.) *Global Culture: Nationalism, Globalization and Modernity*, London: Sage.

Feyerabend, P. (1975) *Against Method: Outline of an Anarchistic Theory of Knowledge*, London: Verso.

Geach, P.T. (1957) *Mental Acts*, London: Kegan Paul.

Geertz, C. (1973a) 'Thick description: towards an interpretive theory of culture', in *The Interpretation of Cultures*, New York: Basic Books.

—— (1973b) *The Interpretation of Cultures*, New York: Basic Books.

Hacking, I. (1983) *Representing and Intervening: Introductory Topics in the Philosophy of Natural Science*, Cambridge: Cambridge University Press.

Hobart, M. (1990a) 'Who do you think you are? The authorized Balinese', in R. Fardon (ed.) *Localizing Strategies: Regional Traditions of Ethnographic Writing*, Edinburgh: Scottish Academic Press and Washington: Smithsonian Institute.

—— (1990b) 'The patience of plants: a note on agency in Bali', *Review of Indonesian and Malaysian Affairs* 24 (Winter): 90–135.

—— (1991) 'Criticizing genres: Bakhtin and Bali', in P. Baxter and R. Fardon (eds) *Voice, Genre, Text – Anthropological Essays in Africa and Beyond*, Manchester: Bulletin of the John Rylands University Library of Manchester 73 (3): 195–216.

—— (1993a) 'Introduction: the growth of ignorance?', in M. Hobart (ed.) *An Anthropological Critique of Development: The Growth of Ignorance?*, London: Routledge.

—— (ed.) (1993b) *An Anthropological Critique of Development: The Growth of Ignorance?*, London: Routledge.

Kuhn, T.S. (1970 [1962]) *The Structure of Scientific Revolutions* (second edition), Chicago: University of Chicago Press.

—— (1977) 'Second thoughts on paradigms', in *The Essential Tension: Selected Studies in Scientific Tradition and Change*, Chicago: University of Chicago Press.

Laclau, E. (1990) 'New reflections on the revolution of our time', in *New Reflections on the Revolution of our Time*, London: Verso.

Lakoff, G. and Johnson, M. (1980) *Metaphors We Live By*, London: University of Chicago Press.

Lévi-Strauss, C. (1966) *The Savage Mind*, London: Weidenfeld & Nicholson.

Matilal, B.K. (1986) *Perception: An Essay on Classical Indian Theories of Knowledge*, Oxford: Clarendon Press.

Pechey, G. (1990) 'Boundaries versus binaries: Bakhtin in/against the history of ideas', *Radical Philosophy* 54 (Spring): 23–31.

Popper, K.R. (1934) *Logik der Forschung*, trans. and expanded as *The Logic of Scientific Discovery*, New York: Basic Books.

Quine, W.V.O. (1990) *Pursuit of Truth*, London: Harvard University Press.

Richards, P. (1993) 'Cultivation: knowledge or performance?', in M. Hobart (ed.) *An Anthropological Critique of Development: The Growth of Ignorance?*, London: Routledge.

Robertson, R. (1990) 'Mapping the global condition: globalization as the central concept', in M. Featherstone (ed.) *Global Culture: Nationalism, Globalization and Modernity*, London: Sage.

—— (1992) *Globalization: Social Theory and Global Culture*, London: Sage.

Rorty, R. (1980) *Philosophy and the Mirror of Nature*, Oxford: Blackwell.

Salmond, A. (1982) 'Theoretical landscapes: on a cross-cultural conception of knowledge', in D.J. Parkin (ed.) *Semantic Anthropology*, London: Academic Press.

Toffler, A. (1975) *Future Shock*, London: Pan.

van der Ploeg, J.D. (1993) 'Potatoes and knowledge', in M. Hobart (ed.) *An Anthropological Critique of Development: The Growth of Ignorance?*, London: Routledge.

Vickers, A. (1984) 'Ritual and representation in nineteenth-century Bali', *Review of Indonesian and Malaysian Affairs* 18 (Winter): 1–35.

—— (1989) *Bali: a Paradise Created*, Ringwood, Victoria: Penguin.

Vitebsky, P. (1993) 'Is death the same everywhere? Contexts of knowing and doubting', in M. Hobart (ed.) *An Anthropological Critique of Development: The Growth of Ignorance?*, London: Routledge.

Wallerstein, I. (1990) 'Culture as the ideological battleground of the modern world-system', in M. Featherstone (ed.) *Global Culture: Nationalism, Globalization and Modernity*, London: Sage.

Wiener, M.J. (1995) *Visible and Invisible Realms: The Royal House of Klungkung and the Dutch Conquest of Bali*, Chicago: University of Chicago Press.

Worsley, P.J. (1984) 'E74168', *Review of Indonesian and Malaysian Affairs* 18 (Winter): 65–109.

Zoetmulder, P.J. (1982) *Old Javanese–English Dictionary*, (2 vols), with the collaboration of S. Robson, The Hague: Nijhoff.

4 Against syncretism

'Africanizing' and 'Cubanizing' discourses
in North American *òrìsà* worship

Stephan Palmié

My paper concerns the politics of representing the relationship between, what Herskovits (1937) called, 'African Gods and Catholic Saints in New World Negro Belief' in two, related, African-American religions:[1] Afro-Cuban Santería (properly: *regla ocha*),[2] and the 'American Yoruba Movement' (also known as Yoruba-Reversionism, or Oyotunji-Movement). Both are 'creole'[3] phenomena characterized by the prominence of elements traceable to the religious cultures of several Yoruba-speaking ethnic aggregates in contemporary southwestern Nigeria, most specifically the worship of a class of beings or powers known among the Yoruba as *òrìsà* (*oricha* in Cuban spelling conventions, *orisha* among the American Yoruba). Despite such similarities, what set them apart, most ostensibly, are the place, time, and historical circumstances of their respective origin. *Regla ocha* emerged among transplanted Africans in nineteenth-century Cuba;[4] the American Yoruba Movement was created – virtually singlehandedly – by an African-American cultural entrepreneur of US-origin in the course of the 1960s. Thus, while the Cuban *regla ocha* might be thought of as a 'spontaneous' development[5] explicable by the 'unintended' carryover of African religious knowledge, the American Yoruba Movement was deliberately founded as an attempt to reclaim what its adherents think of as a 'lost' cultural heritage.

Despite their different histories, multiple ties exist between these two religions and are the source of endemic ideological conflict. Frequently, such conflicts focus upon differently conditioned understandings of a concept anthropologists introduced into what Bateson (1958) might have called an incipient schismogenetic process. This concept is 'syncretism', and what it seems to drive apart are discursive formations underwritten, to a large extent, by a previous history of the differentiation of peculiarly Cuban and North American objectifications of cultural legitimacy and authenticity.

I will not debate the merits of syncretism as a descriptive or analytical concept, though I would argue that its relation to its purported empirical referents – certain processes and/or results of religious change – remains notoriously obscure.[6] Yet as problematic an intellectual tool as 'syncretism' may be, anthropologists have no monopoly on its use. On the contrary, as a global mode of knowledge production, anthropology has little means to guard its epistemological infrastructure against attempts to harness it to local agendas. Accordingly, I will examine some consequences of the instrumentalization, by religious practitioners, of notions about 'syncretism' (and its presumed opposites, such as 'purity') for the purpose of launching contrasting images of what the religions they profess are 'all about'. In particular, I will show how the ongoing interaction between several heterogeneous strains of discourse about the nature and history of these religions spawned a congeries of representational devices geared towards controlling definitions of the linkage between a putatively unitary and authentic African body of 'tradition', and its reproduction in divergent, and partly contradictory New World practices.

IN SEARCH OF THE REAL McCOY: TRADITIONS AND THEIR POLITICAL HISTORIES

As Roy Wagner (1981) pointed out, the perception of something – an instance of behaviour, a verbal utterance, a manifestation of belief – as 'cultural' presupposes the diacritical marking of previously unmarked human activity, in other words, the creation of a sense of distance from the 'thing' done, said or felt. This obviously circumscribes a good part of the dilemma of the 'anthropological gaze', and Wagner surely is not alone in criticizing the discipline's dual tendency towards 'inventing' and 'objectifying' the Rest for a West that defines its subjectivity against the foil of a residual 'savage slot' (Trouillot 1991) where 'things' are done, said or thought in a different (perhaps 'oriental', but in any case 'cultural') manner (cf. Abu-Lughod 1991). By the same token, however, the West does not go unmarked (or 'unothered', if you will), and there are good grounds for arguing that the past few centuries have seen the rise of elaborate (and no less totalizing) 'occidentalisms' on the periphery of the so-called western World.[7] None of this is particularly new or theoretically challenging. More problematic, perhaps, are the epistemological consequences of a realization that such processes of objectification occur within and not only between different cultures. People, at times, disengage themselves from the routine business of 'living their cultures', step back and assume a 'theoretical stance' (Schütz 1984) *vis-à-vis* their own doings and sayings, thus transforming them from what the outside observer might read as 'symptoms' of culture into a symbolic artefact accessible to conscious manipulation – a 'way of life', a 'tradition', 'custom', etc. What was previously naively practised (or even continues to be so practised by some people), can now be honoured or revamped, rationalized or defended.[8] Local moments of 'self-reflexiveness, in which peoples externalize their cultures' (Keesing 1982: 298), raise genuine problems once we consider that such instances of cultural awareness – as well as the attempts at 'managing' or 'engineering' one's own culture which tend to flow from them – rarely (if ever) occur spontaneously, but are themselves embedded in histories of much wider scope: histories that involve a confrontation with something which is perceptibly discontinuous with one's way of life, customs or traditions, and therefore allows for what Thomas (1992) calls their 'reactive objectification'.[9]

In that sense, those bearers of any given culture whom Shils (1971, 1981) would term 'tradition-seekers' face a predicament rather similar to that of the salvage ethnographer and the diffusionist anthropologist of the turn of this century: their chore is not only to recover a pristine, though seemingly vanishing cultural past, but to retrace – largely by morphological inference – histories of, presumably allogenic (and therefore inauthentic, or, at best irrelevant), materials added to the 'real McCoy'. Still, the question Shils fails to address is whence exactly the impetus for such quests derives, and why at some times people regard their perpetrators as butterfly collectors, while at others they join them in mortal combat over what we complacently relegate to the realm of reification and invention. The answer, of course, is history – though not only in terms of the *res gestae* of processes of change and confrontation, but also in terms of those *historiae rerum gestarum* (whether of indigenous or external derivation) that allow for comparative evaluation of past and present, self and other along moral lines.[10] Such 'stories' (and their behavioural consequences), however, do not simply arise as 'functional responses' of single definable units – individuals, societies, cultures – to change and attendant imbalances.[11] These 'stories' are themselves 'historical', and they unfold in dialectic articulation with ideas and forces both intrinsic and extrinsic to their 'tellers'' social and cultural 'units of allegiance', situated as the latter are within wider historically structured 'arenas of differentiation' (Thomas 1992: 226).[12]

In what follows, I will try to delineate two such 'political histories of tradition' (Lindstrom 1982: 317) with particular attention to those larger, encompassing discourses which – to my mind – provided a good part of the stimulus towards the 'historicization' and 'politicization' of their (putative) cultural content. Limitations of space will not allow me to elaborate on the fact that these larger discourses have, at least partly, built upon historically divergent anthropological traditions – including national schools and a division of intellectual labour which, to an extent, runs parallel to fault lines of political economy and language[13] between the US and Latin America. This, however, should not detract from my general argument, that the incorporation of anthropological theories about 'syncretism' into public discourses about 'Africa' and 'Europe' and their respective roles in shaping New World national cultures not only gave rise to different forms of 'cultural awareness' among Cuban and US-African-American *oricha/orisha*-worshippers, but to a large degree predetermined the schismogenetic process currently obtaining between Cuban-American Santeros and African-American 'Yoruba Reversionists'.

THE AFRICAN CONTRIBUTION: CUBAN AND
NORTH AMERICAN DISCURSIVE TRADITIONS

'Even though he may come to call himself a Catholic,' the 25-year-old Cuban lawyer Fernando Ortiz wrote in 1906,

> the Afro-Cuban remains a fetish-worshipper. It would be naive to claim that the native African black, who reached Cuba with fetishist aberrations firmly imprinted on his primitive brain, would have stripped himself of his proper religious beliefs in order to don the vesture of Catholicism.
>
> (Ortiz 1973: 23)

Himself a member of the Cuban elite, steeped in the intellectual traditions of European positivistic social reformism, Ortiz[14] was to modify drastically – though essentially never abandon – the gist of this statement during his long scholarly and political career. In 1921, he still bemoaned the fact that the Cuban state had missed the chance to convert the ancient, and meanwhile largely defunct, Afro-Cuban '*cabildos de nación*'[15] into an institution of scientifically engineered moral reform.[16] Yet some sixteen years later Ortiz announced the first public presentation of *batá* drum-rhythms and sacred *lucumí*[17] chants at the University of Havana as an integral element of Cuba's national cultural heritage which a history of slavery, colonialism and racial prejudice had unfortunately driven underground. One year later, Ortiz founded a Department of Afro-Cuban studies, and in 1940 he published perhaps his single most influential work, *Contrapunteo cubano del tabaco y el azúcar*. In this book he propounded, with the endorsement of Malinowski, a theory about the paramount role of a process he called *transculturación* in the shaping of Cuba's national ethos. Emphasizing the transformation, mutual interpenetration, and eventual blending of uprooted Old World cultures, as well as the essentially innovative character of the resulting amalgam or *ajiaco cultural* (cultural stew), Ortiz meant to counter current theories about 'acculturation' as a unidirectional process of cultural flow parallelling the gradient of power in colonial settings or racially divided societies (such as the US). Yet similar to (though independent of) its Latin American pre-cursors, such as José Vasconcelos' concept of *la raza cósmica* and Gilberto Freyre's ideas about *miscibilidade* or *luso-tropicalismo*, Ortiz's trans-culturation concept was *also* designed as an ideological device for the objectification of a Cuban national identity to be defined in contradistinction to the exclusionary racialist discourses flourishing in Europe and the US since the turn of the century.[18] If Cuba was – as Castro would later say – *un país latinoafricano*, then investigating Afro-Cuban religions meant less a search for ultimate origins, than the reconstruction of a process Ortiz's sister-in-law Lydia Cabrera (herself a prolific amateur ethnographer) was to call *mestizaje psíquica* (Cabrera 1980a: 239).[19]

In contrast to such Cuban attempts to incorporate creolized manifestations of African culture into the project of building a synthetically conceived national identity, the study of African-American cultures in the US developed along entirely different lines. Regardless of whether differences between black and white behaviour were relegated to a history of victimization, cultural loss and subsequent maladaptation, or explained as the consequence of African cultural retentions, the net result was the representation of African-American cultures as thoroughly divergent from what Americans tend to label the 'cultural mainstream'. The eventual outcome of this debate is well known and need not be detailed here.[20] Suffice it to say that the rediscovery of Herskovits's key monograph, *The Myth of the Negro Past* (originally published in 1941), by African-American intellectuals occurred at precisely the moment when the integrationist agenda of the early Civil Rights Movement in the US was giving way to more aggressive dissimilationist tendencies associated with the so-called 'cultural nationalist' wing of the black Movement. To put it bluntly, 'Africa' suddenly made sense – and has increasingly done so – for black Americans in search of a 'usable' cultural past. For it provided historical anchorage for a 'tradition' sufficiently 'deep' and autonomous not only to impart a sense of legitimate cultural identity (by the standards of a society sporting institutions such as the Daughters of Liberty), but to be flaunted in response to the options thrown up by a political system ever more sensitive to symbolic markers of ethnic distinction.

Although these directions of ideological drift on the part of Cuban and American intellectuals do not coincide neatly with tendencies observable within either Santería or the American Yoruba Movement, nevertheless, their adherents have not been able to avoid the influence of these larger ideological currents.[21] Since Castro's rise to power, the flow of emigrés from revolutionary Cuba has not only given rise to – by now well-consolidated – Cuban exile communities in several major urban centres of the US, it has also engendered a flourishing Afro-Cuban religious diaspora. This 'second' transplantation of Yoruba deities, who had earlier reasserted their presence in nineteenth-century Cuba, had two important consequences. On the one hand, it brought their Cuban (or, by now, Cuban-American) worshippers into contact with peculiarly North American conceptualizations of the African and European ingredients of their faith. On the other hand, it also (at least indirectly) provided the stimulus for the development of a rival form of worship of these powerful beings – one whose aggressive politics of re-Africanization of 'syncretistically adulterated' Cuban beliefs and practices runs counter to an understanding of 'tradition' still at the very heart of North American variants of Afro-Cuban religious practice.

THE 'WHITE MAN'S CLOTHES'

Though individual practitioners of *regla ocha* seem to have resided in the US since at least the 1940s, the establishment of functioning cult groups capable of initiating new personnel seems to have occurred in New York in the early 1960s, and in Miami some eight to ten years later (cf. Palmié 1991: 184–205).

By the latter date, however, the example of Afro-Cuban worship patterns had already resulted in the foundation of a native African-American offshoot of the Black Nationalist movement whose origin A.L. Kroeber would have welcomed as an instance corroborating his theories of 'stimulus diffusion' (Kroeber 1940). This is how the Detroit-born founder of the American Yoruba Movement, His Royal Highness Oba Ofuntola Adelabu Adefunmi I (né Walter Serge King), recalls what led up to his initiation into *regla ocha*,[22]

I think that it was mainly because [of my] desire to become an African priest. When I arrived at that conclusion in 1956 or '57 it was . . . I thought I would go to Haiti, because Haiti is more popularly known as a place for the preservation of the African religion. So I went to Haiti, but somehow there – that was not for me. *Obatalá* [the *oricha* into whose cult he was to become initiated] felt that I should go, in time, to Cuba. So about a year later was when I finally found out about Cuba, and I found it out in a very interesting way. I used to conduct ceremonies for Dambada Hwedo [a Fon deity also worshipped in Haiti under the name of Danballa]. I [had] started an organization called the Dambada Hwedo Ancestor Priests in Harlem [prior to this King, who had been raised as a Protestant, had already passed through an Islamic phase]. That organization went on for about two years, and then I began to receive some very interesting criticism from a friend of mine who . . . was Chris Oliana [a black Cuban then living in New York]. Chris Oliana knew about Santo [i.e. *regla ocha*]. He told me I should get into Santo, and he told me . . . I should get a statue of St. Barbara. But, of course, at that time I was deeply involved in the Nationalist Movement of the 60s. So the mention of a thing called Santo which, of course, translated into English means saint, [and for us] who are raised in the Protestant religion and have no knowledge of Catholicism, to tell you that you must get a statue of St. Barbara, a saint, means that you are going to become a Catholic. So quite naturally I objected to this and refused to get involved with it and told him: no, I'm interested in African [religion]. But he say: well, it *is* African! I say: how can it be African? And he wants me to get a statue of St. Barbara! This is not an African name, this is not an African saint. And from the picture you [i.e. Oliana] showed me, this certainly is not an African lady. This is not an African god. This is white woman! And so I refused to get involved in it for a whole year. Finally . . . he explained to me: this is *just called* Santo. This is a Spanish name. It's got an African name. The African name is *ocha*, he explained. And all of the ceremony in it is all purely African. And he said that the Catholicism [in it] is just a bunch of . . . well . . . you can imagine what he said. But in any case, it was at that point when I said: do you *mean* that if I got initiated into this Santo – in what you call Santo – I would be an African priest? And he says: yes, you certainly would! . . . so I said: wow, if that is the case, I will go to Cuba within a month. 'Cause he told me you can go to Cuba and get the pure African religion. So I said: well, I'm going to Cuba then in a month!

I said: I've got $800 and I'll take that. So he says: well, if you go, I will go.

(Oba Ofuntola, June 1977)

And so they did. King and Oliana were initiated in Matanzas on the eve of the Cuban revolution in the autumn of 1958. After their return to New York, they initially seem to have collaborated on a Cuban-African-American religious joint venture. Yet their relations did not remain amicable for long. King/Ofuntola's ambition to purge the religion of spurious 'Cuban admixtures' eventually drove them apart. Though the Cubans could not question the legitimacy of Ofuntola's initiation into the priesthood of *regla ocha*, they resented what must have appeared outrageous deviations from their conception of '*la tradición*'. Starting out with the refusal to use Catholic imagery, and the advocacy of African-style attire on a daily basis, [23] Ofuntola and his growing African-American following quickly exploded the limits of Cuban tolerance by advocating a return to 'African style' initiations, [24] instructing uninitiated persons in secret knowledge, and performing sacred chants on television, thus breaking important barriers of esotericism. In addition, they introduced the crucial element of racial dichotomization into what – to the Cuban understanding – had for long (too long to be more than dimly remembered) become a religion in which the *oricha* themselves chose people to become members of *regla ocha* irrespective of their ethnic or racial origin.[25] This is how Ofuntola viewed this matter in 1977,

by the time I left New York, the Cuban priests and myself were worlds apart. Our whole life-style had changed, we had introduced a racism into the religion that didn't exist among the Cubans. They didn't have the race problem that we had in the United States, and, of course, they couldn't understand my extremely severe racial attitudes at that time. So that naturally alienated a lot of them.

(Oba Ofuntola, June 1977)

Indeed, when, in October 1970, Ofuntola and his following left New York to found the theocratic community of Oyotunji[26] in rural South Carolina, what he had on his hands was a 'new' religion.

A more recent American Yoruba pamphlet contains passages unmistakably addressed to Cuban adulterators of the 'true faith'. The *Igbimolosha* or priestly council – 'brain trust', the author calls them – of Oyotunji ruled as follows with regard to the 'astrological calendars of Orisha festivals [in Oyotunji] which departs so radically from the Orisha calendars used in Brazilian Candomble and Cuban Santería which are based on the celebration day of corresponding Roman Catholic Saints which was necessary during slavery times' (Ofuntola 1982: 28):

such practices are obsolete and should be discontinued since the need for them has passed. It has [been] ruled that such practices are cultural abominations on the free and enlightened Afro-Americans – it is thoughtless and dangerous. Dangerous, the Igbimolosha has ruled, because it tends to Europeanize and 'whiten' the Black Gods of Africa as was done by the Syrians, Greeks, and Romans after their conquest of Egypt and their penetration into the ancient Egyptian religion and their opulent priesthood.

Forbidden also by the Igbimolosha is the use of images of the Roman Catholic Saints to represent African Gods and Goddesses. This is tantamount they argue, to the old slavery process of alienating Africans from their true identity by dressing them in the 'white man's clothes' and giving them 'slave' names.

(Ibid.: 28–29)

Four years later, Chief Ajamu, head of the Yoruba Temple of Miami had even fewer qualms when it came to the subject of 'slave names' and the 'white man's clothes' in the Cuban tradition. 'And when they dress these people!' he exclaimed in the course of a conversation on the *ropa de santo* – elaborate possession garments reflecting a combination of African-derived ideas about the *oricha* as well as colonial Spanish imagery related to royalty and exalted social status (such as gilt paper crowns):[27]

Like when a person is . . . as they say, 'saint' – and that's right, it's saint, it's not *orisha* – when the saint descends upon them, on his horse, and they rush 'em off to dress them, they come back with these little early English outfits on them, they look like the Three Musketeers with the little knickers, knickerbockers coming up to here [pointing to his knee] and the little . . . almost like a beret to one side with a feather in it . . . ah, it's disgusting!

(Chief Ajamu, December 1986)

These examples should suffice to demonstrate the American Yoruba, or Yoruba-Reversionist, position on the issue of 'syncretistic' forms. How do Santeros view the 'syncretistic nature' of their religion?

SYNCRETISM SANTERO-STYLE

The saints are the same here as in Africa. . . . The only difference is that ours eat a lot and have to dance.

(Statement by the Cuban Santera 'Oddedei', alias Calixta Morales, reported by Cabrera 1983: 19.)

No less than anthropologists, Santeros depend on post-hoc rationalizations to account for the emergence of what outsiders have labelled 'syncretistic' forms. Just how, for instance, Catholic statuary found its way into the *oricha* shrines Santeros erect in their homes is simply not known. Nor is it commonly reflected upon. Brandon's experiences in this respect closely parallel my impressions:

There is considerable variability here in the answers one gets from questioning people about this [i.e. the relation between Catholic Saints and

African gods]. Sometimes you get the impression, when pursuing this line of questioning that you are forcing people to think about something they rarely think about. It is as if you were asking people to rationalize something which simply exists as a vague background to their religious activities.

(Brandon 1983: 180)

Nevertheless, the saints are there in the form of plaster statues, sometimes approaching life-size, towering over altars and shrines that harbour the objectivations of the *oricha*'s presence and power – sacred stones (*otanes*) contained in receptacles known as *soperas*.[28] Nor is it difficult to elicit support from Santeros for conceptions about the thoroughly 'syncretistic' nature of this religion. Many of them will be quick to point out to an *aleyo*[29] that 'yes, San Lázaro is *Babalu Ayé* in person', or 'Santa Barbara represents *Changó*'.[30] Indeed, the 'classic' method (pioneered by Herskovits in the course of his Haitian research) of presenting believers with chromo-lithographs of Catholic saints and asking which African deity they depict, might well yield the impression that a thorough identification between *santos* and *oricha* obtains in the minds of the majority of Santeros. This is reflected in the general tenor of academic treatments of this issue. The following statement by a Cuban-American scholar has a genealogy traceable to a plethora of similar pronouncements by Cuban ethnographers such as Ortiz (1938, 1940, 1973), Lachataneré (1938, 1942) and Cabrera (1983),

Santería is the product of the identification between the gods of the slaves and the Catholic saints of their masters . . . . El santo is the divinity born of the syncretism between the Yoruba god or *oricha* and the Catholic saint. The process of syncretism that gave birth to the *oricha*/santo was the result of the associations and projections that the slave and his descendants found between the saint that his master wanted him to worship and the divinities that he and his ancestors had worshipped all their lives.

(Sandoval 1979: 138)

The standard explanation for this birth of the Cuban santo/*oricha* out of the spirit of Europe and Africa assumes that the slaves 'discovered' a match between the attributes of specific African deities and those of particular saints in Cuban folk Catholicism (such as colours, spheres of influence, martyrio-logical and hagiographic details, etc.). This, in turn, is said to have led the slaves to the realization that the saints could be used as a kind of 'disguise' under which the worship of the old gods could be continued while projecting the outward appearance of Catholic observance. Eventually, the story goes, a gradual conceptual 'merging'[31] occurred, the results of which are observ-able today: saints and *oricha*, Africa and Europe, blend into a hybrid unit, heterogeneous in character, though increasingly 'unmarked' in terms of the genealogy of its ingredients.

Perhaps unsurprisingly, an American scholar first voiced doubts about this reasoning. A mere three months of fieldwork in Cuba apparently sufficed to convince Bascom (1950) that the ritual significance of the *otanes* (sacred stones) as a focus of sacrificial action overrode the comparatively negligible ceremonial role of Catholic statuary. Bascom was right. Santeros observe a relatively clear-cut 'praxeological' distinction between 'African' and 'Catholic' cultural forms which – to a certain extent – corresponds to metonymical and metaphorical modes of representing the sacred. The *otanes* and those other objects which go into the making of what Santeros refer to as the *fundamento* (foundation) of an *oricha* are often talked about as containing the deity's powers, or serving as its abode. Catholic images, however, are generally regarded as images symbolizing its attributes. As one of my informants succinctly stated the matter: 'when you see a saint in church, you only see an image created by man', the *fundamentos*, however, are 'a part of the power that lives with the person [who owns it]. It is the power of the *oricha* himself' (Natividad Torres, March 1988). While few Santeros will be as explicit about the matter as this, none of them would think of sacrificing an animal to a statue (and this despite the fact that Cuban folk Catholicism shares in the Mediterranean tradition of miraculous images (cf. Ortiz 1975)). The *fundamento*, however, provides a point of privileged access to the *oricha*, allowing for communication and interchange between humans and the divine. This is where these beings or powers 'live', 'eat' or 'speak' (through divination). Most obviously, perhaps, an *oricha* may ask his devotee to put up a statue of the corresponding Catholic saint as a pleasing adornment to his shrine – much as he would ask for a bunch of flowers (see Palmié 1991: 258–270, 317–340).

Nevertheless, until very recently, Bascom's 'discovery' hardly affected the general scholarly consensus on the santo/*oricha*-equation. Nor has it – again, until very recently – inspired closer investigations of the ways in which Santeros themselves understand this *liaison*.[32] As Cabrera's informant Calixta Morales happily seems to have stated, African gods and Catholic saints had fused into a 'transculturated' conceptual compound differentiable, at best, by the eating habits displayed by one of its representational modes: while the *oricha* thrive on animal blood, tasty food preparations and succulent fruit, the santos content themselves with an occasional whiff of incense and a sprinkle of holy water.

FROM THE NATIVE'S POINT OF VIEW

Whatever the truth of the matter may be, one cannot help but notice that the 'natives' are well aware of the conceptual and narrative constructions scholarly producers of knowledge about their religion have foisted upon their beliefs and observances. Indeed, they have begun to talk back. While written 'compendia' of ritual knowledge seem to have circulated among Santeros since the second decade of this century (León 1971; Hesse 1977), in recent years tracts and pamphlets expounding the 'real' nature and history of *la religión* have begun to proliferate. This has given rise to a novel discourse which, though overtly resisting 'outside' typecasting, is nevertheless informed by, or at any rate cannot free itself from, previous histories of objectification. Directed both at the religious community *and* the general public (including scholarly 'experts') such programmatic statements almost invariably contain a harangue over popular misconceptions – including ideas about the origin and essence of the relation obtaining between Catholic saints and African gods, an issue few of the authors seem to be willing to let pass. 'Many [people] hold different views and preconceptions about the origins of this religion', reads a typescript[33] authored by Gilberto Zayas, a priest of *Changó*:

> Many believe it is Catholic. Many are confused to such a degree that they do not know the difference between this cult and the spiritist cult which is indirectly mixed with this religion on account of the great influence Spiritism had in Cuba.
>
> I am going to begin to tell you what I have told to so many people who still remain in this confused state. Almost certainly I will be condemned for expressing my opinion, as has been the case in the past. This religion is not Catholicism, and it has nothing to do with it. The origin of this religion is in the forests of the country previously called Yorubaland, better known today as Nigeria. From there comes what we today know as Santería.
>
> With the importation of slaves to the New World, many African cults were imported. Many different cults arrived which, in one form or the other, were classified as witchcraft or black magic. [Yet h]owever much they brutalized the African black, he was still more alive than the white and, thanks to Catholicism (for if I say one thing, I also say the other), this cult grew strong roots in Cuba, and today has expanded to the United States and other parts of Latin America. Thanks to Catholicism, this cult was not nipped in the bud. Therefore, we need to say *maferefun* [a *lucumí* phrase meaning 'thank you'] to Catholicism, though there is no need to continue calling our orichas by the name of their Catholic camouflage. So let us begin to try calling them by their [real] names more often, rather than saying 'Sta. Barbara Bendita' to Changó.

While Zayas's plea for conceptual unpacking seems to evoke a narrative deliberately reversing standard anthropological plottings of the syncretistic process (not the believers, but their enemies failed to mark the distinction between saints and *oricha*), some Santeros would go even further. Advocating the replacement of the term 'Santería' – which he denounces as misleading and derogatory[34] – by that of '*lukumí*'[35] the *italero* (specialist in cowrie shell divination [*diloggun*] and ritual expert) Ernesto Pichardo, in his publication *Oduduwa Obatalá*, explicitly addresses not only 'the general public', but specifically 'the scholarly "experts" . . . and those lukumí priests who serve as their "informants"' (Pichardo 1984: 76). For although 'the primary function of the anthropologist is to objectively report what he is informed about by them [, w]e cannot say that this has been entirely the case'. Instead, Pichardo feels, such professional *aleyos* have unwittingly added untruth to injury – excluded as they are by rules of esotericism, not only from legitimate access to 'true' inside knowledge, but consequently also from any valid means of telling facts from mistaken impressions.[36] Hence their rash generalizations about 'syncretism', derived from their incapacity to distinguish between what Pichardo (1984: 26ff.) calls 'visible' and 'invisible' syncretism'. Having focused their interpretations merely on formal aspects of religious practice, anthropologists and other 'experts' failed to differentiate levels of understanding pertaining to stages in religious socialization marking the careers of individual believers and priests in 'lukumí religion'. The question, he claims (quite rightly, to my idea) is not whether objects identifiable as pertaining to the symbolic repertoire of other religions grace the altars of priests of *regla ocha*, *but what their owners themselves think they represent.*[37]

Although Pichardo's analysis comes close to a call for a (hitherto non-existent) sociology of Afro-Cuban religious knowledge, it is nevertheless both a self-conscious attempt to counter previous objectifications of Santería, and, ironically, yet another instance of essentializing discourse; this time launched by an 'insider' unusually knowledgeable about the signs of the times. It is hard to tell whether such attempts at wresting control over the production of essentializing narratives from outside observers antedate the North American diaspora of Afro-Cuban religion.[38] Yet it is tempting to attribute such tendencies to 'deconstruct' the trope of syncretism to the influence of a discursive milieu favouring the analogy of biological speciation as the hallmark of cultural authenticity and legitimacy. 'Multicultural' America is not a breeding ground for ideologies defusing purportedly primordial ethnic distinctions in the service of 'transcultural' political denouement, and Miami is no exception. There, the rise of an economically powerful and demographically dominant Cuban enclave has been paralleled by the increasing politicization of 'native' ethnicities, both white and black. Though language is clearly a central issue, a wide variety of emblematic differences – some readily available, some tailored on the spot – have come to enter the discourse on cultural legitimacy. As Cubans in the US, Santeros *per force* participate in such discourses – and not just because the immigrant experience has problematized their *Cubanidad* ('Cubanness') with respect to conceptions of 'purity' and 'hybridization'.[39] Members of Miami's Afro-Cuban religious subcultures face more than the antagonism of unsympathetic Anglo-Americans. The most vicious attacks come from upwardly mobile, avowedly Christian 'white' Cuban-Americans intent on salvaging their reputation as a 'model minority' by dissociating themselves from what their host society perceives as an atavistic, and thoroughly 'un-American' Latin/African cult.[40] Yet apart from the peculiar 'transethnic' coalition between 'Anglos' haunted by the spectre of cultural displacement, and Cuban-

Americans achievers fearing stigmatization, Miami's Santeros face a less obvious, though perhaps even more excruciating, dilemma. Especially for the large number of Santeros hailing from Miami's culturally well-adapted white Cuban-American middle class, the existence (and rhetoric) of the American Yoruba Movement poses a threat of a different order: a threat not so much to their self-conception as the true 'keepers' of an essentially African tradition, as to their control over the public projection of such an image.[41]

If preempting academic (or other) 'outsider representations' of *regla ocha* as a syncretistic religion has become a cottage industry of sorts, another stream of discourse targets those who would accuse Santeros of having 'Cubanized', 'Americanized', 'whitened' or otherwise adulterated the 'true' African religion. Viewed superficially, the net result of this is a process of symmetrical schismogenesis proceeding largely, though not exclusively, on a rhetorical level: both Yoruba-Reversionists and certain self-styled spokes-men-priests of *regla ocha* reactively cast and recast the public image of their respective creeds in ever more 'African' terms. At the same time, it is tempting (though probably wrong) to read a complementary sociological dynamic into this process: the 'whiter' the constituency of *regla ocha* gets, the more its objectifications take on an African appearance.[42]

Yet whether such generalizations hold water or not, and regardless of the fact that most Santeros are inclined to try to curb aspirations to leadership (including 'spokesmanship') within their fold (cf. Palmié 1987), there remains the question: whence do the 'raw materials' for such manipulations of objectified traditions derive? What do American Yoruba and entrepren-eurially inclined priests of *regla ocha* draw upon, in support of their inversions of prior 'outside' (anthropological or other) objectifications of their religions? And if by now they have learned to heed Durkheim's famous recommendation 'de considérer les faits sociaux comme des choses' (Durk-heim 1973: 15), where – if at all – do they draw a line between practice and its representations?

BEYOND POLITICS I: MANAGING TRADITIONS

Given the not so recent self-reflexive turn in the social sciences, the question of whether the syncretistic conundrum might be yet another instance of a reification exploding in the analyst's face does not seem far fetched. The representations of 'Africa', 'Cuba' and 'Europe' rampant among the practi-tioners of North American varieties of *oricha/orisha*-worship are hardly autonomous developments. Likewise, the notion of 'syncretism' – whether evaluated positively (i.e. 'Cuban-style') or negatively ('American-style') – quite clearly is borrowed (or should we say 'pirated'?) from a discourse originally extrinsic to *regla ocha* (though perhaps not to the American Yoruba Movement for which the conflict over the santo/oricha relationship seems to have played a constitutive role right from the start). Not so, however, a certain notion of 'purity' or 'traditionality' which is very much at the heart of Santeros' reflections upon the state of their beliefs and practices. Yet the concept of 'traditionality' that practitioners of *regla ocha* gloss when referring to *la tradición* – as a matter of religious, rather than political concern – is salient not so much in terms of 'content' as of 'continuity'.

Irrespective of public squabbles over projections of 'Africanity' or 'Cuban-idad' measurable in terms of morphological correspondence to a standard of 'Yoruba-ness' established, by now largely through reference to the ethno-graphic literature, there is a very real sense in which Santeros feel – and represent to each other – the threat of cultural loss and debasement. This fear relates to complex, and seldom clearly articulated, notions about *la tradición* as an original body of sacred knowledge (*conocimientos*) that was once transferred to Cuba *in toto*, but has since been subject to erosion through amnesia and deliberate deviation.[43] Since the concept of *conocimientos* is intimately linked to conceptions of sacred (as well as social) power, [44] this seemingly entropic process has devastating implications. Still, Santeros are quite aware that it is fundamentally predicated upon what Barth (1990) would call the 'economy of information' peculiar to their religion: like power itself, knowledge is hard to share, and since the initiation rites merely establish the novice's right of access to such knowledge – not, however, a corresponding obligation on the part of his or her elders to impart such knowledge to the novice – stories about recalcitrant *mayores* (elders in the religion) who would not share their secrets, ultimately taking them to their grave, abound among members of Miami's Afro-Cuban religious community.[45] Consequently, important knowledge has been lost: chants, drum rhythms, and ways of preparing sacrificial offerings have been forgotten; previously important ritual injunctions are no longer observed; certain *oricha* have stopped descending upon their devotees; the priesthood's discipline and morals have lapsed; commercialization has turned the religion into a racket.

However, contrary to such laments (including scholarly ones),[46] what Santeros perceive as a losing battle against cultural change and attrition is but a consequence of the reproduction of *la tradición*. This is so because *la tradición* itself is a hollow category, objectifying the passage of essentially underdetermined cultural matter along a temporal axis marked by historically contingent representations of 'traditionality'. The objective concatenation of events (a chant forgotten here, some relaxation of ritual discipline there), appears juxtaposed to, and sometimes is overwhelmed by symbolically bound 'relative time' (Smith 1982). Then the past, as Peel (1989) puts it, truly becomes a 'cultural work'. For in attempting to stem the tides of change Santeros resort to practices designed to recover or recompile (*recopilar*) lost, distorted or decontextualized knowledge, or rectify (*rectificar, arreglar*) corrupted aspects of ritual, while factually inducing change and innovation. Such 'rectificatory' practices are by no means a recent development, nor are they generally perceived as such. The reason for this is expressed rather clearly by the anonymous author of a pre-revolutionary divination manual claimed to be compiled from older handwritten *libretas*.

Over the course of the years we have had access to many of these already mentioned libretas. When we encountered discrepancies and notable antagonisms in them, we have exhaustively discussed these points with Olochas and Oluwos [*lucumí*-terms for priests of *regla ocha* and high-ranking specialists in *ifá*-divination] with known experience (some of whom pertaining to the past century), until a coincidence of opinions was reached. In addition, making use of their *aché* [sacred powers] as well as our own, we have many times gone before the oricha in order to attain a confirmation or negation of our doubts.

(Anonymous 1959: 4)

What the author glosses as 'going before the *oricha*' is divination: the ultimate source of legitimacy and authentication in a religion in which the deity of divination, *Ifá* or *Orunmila*, is regarded as witness to the creation of the world and is therefore believed to know all there ever was and will be. It is the single source of absolute knowledge. Likewise, reckoning from contemporary practice, the reference to discussions with priests 'pertaining to the past century' can be interpreted as relating to oracular communication with the spirits of deceased possessors of superior knowledge. The gods and the dead are the true arbiters of what *la tradición* can legitimately encompass, for only their injunctions can ensure continuity with, and rule out deviation from, an elusive sacred past against which contemporary 'authenticity' can be measured.[47] Chronological time, and the historical residues of cultural change it leaves in its wake, thus becomes partly reversible: compiling and recompiling an objectified body of knowledge always on the verge of crumbling away into oblivion, Santeros grope their way into a future which they create by bypassing, as it were, the present through hermeneutical acts designed to neutralize its impact upon *la tradición*. Hence it is possible that, in their *concejos* (oracular communications), the *oricha* themselves vacillate between differently plotted narratives of their cultural ties to their worshippers and the historical vicissitudes of their mutual interaction. In other words: the gods themselves may have 'rediscovered' their 'Africanity'.

An example may help to clarify this point: Bascom (1951) and Cabrera (1980b: 2) claim that the term 'Yoruba' (as opposed to the New World ethnonym '*lucumí*') was virtually unknown among Santeros in Cuba in the 1940s. If this were true, a number of interesting corollaries suggest themselves. Since it is highly unlikely that enslaved Yoruba-speakers reached Cuba after about 1875 – in other words before the final coming of the 'pax Britannica' to Nigeria – the term 'Yoruba' could not have been used by them as an ethnonym referring to their collective identity. For while it originally appears to have been a term used by the Hausa to refer to the subjects of the Oyo state, we know that its use as a linguistic-*cum*-ethnic classifier was pioneered by Christian missionaries, and did not attain its modern significance as a catch-all for the different pre-colonial polities of Yoruba-speakers until well into this century (Law 1977: 4f.; Peel 1989). At the same time, we have evidence that slaves designating their identity as '*lucumí*' in nineteenth-century Cuba distinguished among themselves a variety of 'ethnic' divisions (cf. Palmié 1993a). How then could their descendants (physical as well as spiritual) have found out that the religion they practised was 'genetically related' to that of an African ethnic group that had not even come into existence *as such* at the time *la tradición* was implanted in Cuba? Probably in the same way that Ortiz originally came to the conclusion that what he and his contemporaries used to regard as the indelible 'imprint of African fetishism' on the 'negro's primitive brain' was the result of an historical process of diffusion: by consulting Africanist texts.[48] The only difference would have been that while morphological correspondences and deviations compelled Ortiz and his successors to take recourse in the auxiliary notion of 'syncretism', for Santeros the solution may have been divination: no doubt – whatever the truth may be, the *oricha* would have confirmed it.

This, however, still leaves us with the problem of whether the discursive clashes between Santeros and American Yoruba have any saliency beneath the level of public rhetoric. If the American Yoruba Movement has its historical roots in *regla ocha*, and if their king is not an impostor – which he cannot be, since he was initiated in a 'legitimate' Cuban manner – why do the *oricha*, in the case of the latter, sanction ideas and ways of behaviour Santeros regard as *contra la tradición*?

BEYOND POLITICS II: HISTORICAL MISSIONS

In his preface to what remains the only monograph on Oyotunji (Hunt 1979), William Bascom expressed puzzlement over the fact that 'the Yoruba elements in Oyotunji's lifestyle had not been retained by Blacks in the United States. They have been recreated, and with surprising accuracy'. Though acknowledging the king's brief 1972 trip to Nigeria ('I do not even know how he could become a Babalawo during a short visit') he felt that '[m]uch was undoubtedly learned from the Cubans prior to his break with them'. Then again, Bascom noted significant changes from the Cuban pattern 'back' to modern Yoruba usage, and wonders 'what . . . the sources for these revisions' might have been. 'It would be very interesting to know what books were consulted in the research on Yoruba culture', he concludes,

> My own publications [on Yoruba culture] are readily available, but many others are not. The Yoruba names for worshippers of the deities could not have come from my works, e.g. Ogunyemi (Ogun suits me), Shangodele (Shango comes home), or Esubiyi (Eshu begat this one); nor could the name of the king himself, Adefunmi (Crown gave me), whose first name, Oseijeman, is of Akan origin.
>
> (Bascom 1979:vi)

By 1985, a visit to Oba Ofuntola's royal palace might have helped to resolve Bascom's queries. The king had amassed a rather impressive collection of ethnographic literature on the Yoruba as well as other Africana. The village's appearance ostensibly betrayed close study of the richly illustrated volumes on the shelves of the palace, so much so that – as its inhabitants proudly related – not only had Oyotunji in the meantime been covered by *National Geographic Magazine*, but a film crew had 'rented' the village as the stage for a movie set in Africa. Four years earlier, in June 1981, Obá Ofuntola had retraced the sacred journey of so many other Yoruba rulers to the holy city of Ifé, where His Divine Royal Majesty King Okunade Sijuwade, Olubushe II, the Oni of Ifé had ordered his chiefs to perform the coronation rites for him. As one of his publications states,

> Oba Ofuntola Oseijeman Adelabu Adefunmi I became the first of a line of New World Yoruba Kings consecrated at and to the Ooni of Ife. He was presented with a special Ceremonial Sword of State incised with the name of his Liege Lord the Ooni of Ife. It is his emblem and license to speak in the name of the King of Ife.
>
> (Ofuntola 1982:vi)

Walter Serge King had come a long way since his first decision to become an 'African priest'. While we can only speculate about the Ifé authorities' motives for legitimating a New World dependency in a traditional manner,[49] the motives of the American Yoruba seem obvious. Indeed, one is tempted to view this incident as the final bridging of a gap between text and life, a move from ethnography back to culture. For in a rather concrete sense, the king's official coronation transformed what cynical observers might view as a 'Yoruba theme park' into an authenticated kingdom.

But then again, this is merely one possible recension of the state of affairs in Oyontunji and, to conclude this essay on a personal recollection, the circumstances of my first trip to Oyotunji left little doubt about the ambivalent nature of this cultural project. In the summer of 1985 I was invited[50] by Ernesto Pichardo to accompany him and a delegation of white Cuban Santeros to Oyotunji where these ritual specialists had been commissioned to initiate one of the king's wives into the cult of *Babalu Ayé*, an *oricha* whose shrine (along with that of the goddess *Obá*) Pichardo and his religious associates had established in the village in 1977. Although they had initiated villagers into the priesthood of these *oricha*, none of them had yet acquired the qualifications to autonomously reproduce their cults in Oyotunji.

When we reached Oyotunji after a twelve hour drive in a rented van, the priests from Miami and their *aleyo*-entourage were formally received by the King and the highest title holders. The Santeros now faced four days of almost incessant, though probably well-paid, ritual labor. I, however, received a rather remarkable object lesson in what Herskovits would have called 'diffusion in process'. To give just one example, in a moment of slack time prior to the commencement of the public ceremonies on the second day of the initiation ceremony, the master drummer of Oyotunji used the opportunity to present three of his students to the Cuban *italero*. Patiently Pichardo joined them in their ceremonial round of the village shrines, commenting on their performance of drummed salutations to the gods. Yet only a few hours later, the village's master drummer had turned into an apprentice himself: properly clothed in beautiful Yoruba-style attire he stood next to Pichardo who – dressed in white jeans and a purple polo shirt – took the lead in the *lucumí* chants of the public parts of the initiation ceremony. Protruding from the luxuriously draped cloth of the drummer's robe was a tape recorder by means of which he salvaged the sacred 'African' texts emanating from the Cuban's mouth. Quite clearly, what I was witnessing was the emergence of tradition out a curious cross-cultural, but religiously mediated, encounter. For I have no doubts that the chants Ernesto Pichardo directed at the *oricha* in the sweltering heat of that summer afternoon in 1985 have, by now, become integral to the religious culture of Oyotunji.

Afterwards, nobody – not even Pichardo (who might have taken rhetorical advantage of the situation) – seemed too keen to comment on this incident. Comparatively rare as they probably are, such instances of religious 'collaboration' between Santeros and American Yoruba are not normally volunteered as topics of discussion by either party to an 'outside' interlocutor – unless the issue at hand is one pertaining to 'cultural policy'. Even if my questions might, on another occasion, have elicited derogatory comments, the *entente cordiale* in the aftermath of a major ceremony perhaps ruled out religious name-calling. For just as American Yoruba will otherwise be quick to point out the grossly 'syncretistic' Cuban deviations from 'the African way', Santeros at times show great amusement at the 'weird' antics of latter-day Yoruba, who forsake airconditioning, electricity and running water for a communal life based on what Cubans think are utterly spurious claims to an African cultural past. Nevertheless, there is an important reason why neither party can terminate the peculiar, ideologically tense relationship obtaining between them. On the one hand, for the Santeros, despite all their 'Africanizing' innovations, the American Yoruba are not only the offshoot of a prestigious Cuban religious lineage (linked to the rest of the community by the king's Cuban religious 'descent'), but interact with the same deities. Would the *oricha* have sanctioned (indeed, mandated, as he told me once) Pichardo's trips to Oyotunji if they utterly disapproved of the life-style and worship practices of the American Yoruba? On the other hand, for the American Yoruba, the Cubans – no matter how much their 'syncretistic' tendencies and 'white' life-style may be resented – still hold a key to a past that North American blacks seem to have lost.

As Chief Ajamu explained to me in 1986, given that American blacks had suffered a historically induced 'cultural amnesia', it now was the Cubans' historical mission – ordained by the *orisha* and *Ifá* himself – to return the culture they had managed to preserve to its legitimate black heirs. Statements such as these obviously go beyond mere political rhetoric: just as Ofuntola's coronation in the sacred city of Ifé, the very 'cradle of Yoruba states', has infused the sign at the village gate staking Oyotunji's claim to political/

cultural autonomy ('You are leaving the United States of America') with authority, so have the ministrations of Pichardo and other Cuban Santeros before him helped to breathe life into the bookshelves of Walter S. King's South Carolinian palace. Yet for the Santeros, this very fact, ironically, rules out their perception of Oyotunji as 'all sham'. Whether they like it or not, they have turned themselves into harbingers of the past: donors of cultural stuff which – once selectively purified of 'white admixtures' – serves as part of the sacred fuel propelling the American Yoruba into a traditional future.

ALL IN THE SAME BOAT

What, then, are we – who cannot take recourse to Ifá's apodictions – to make of all this? Implicated as anthropologists clearly are in the making of the syncretistic conundrum, what options are left to us other than the relatively trivial conclusion that our own pontifications have conjured up realities that no longer support 'conventional' ethnographic inscription?[51] No doubt, a parodic element looms large in episodes where the object of study takes 'his observers' for a ride into the never-never land of his or her own imagination. The sign 'African Village as Seen on TV' at the gate of Oyotunji, easily transmutes into 'Yoruba-religion as described by Bill Bascom', or 'Afro-Cuban syncretism as written up by major Cuban ethnographer', and *vice versa*. American Yoruba and Cuban Santeros do not invent and objectify themselves (and each other) under circumstances of their own choosing. We have been there before, so to speak, and we left traces. Hence the peculiar *déjà vu* effect. Only now we observe – as if in a time warp – elaborations upon the intellectual debris earlier generations of anthropologists left afloat in a variety of local and supra-local discourses.[52] But does this warrant privileging one type of narrative over the other? Must we resign ourselves to the choice between a denigration of the other's autonomy as producer of nothing but 'derivative discourse' (Chatterjee 1986), or an abdication of ethnographic authority that leaves us musing about the relativity of all knowledge? Yet to construe the problem in terms of 'authoritarian' ethnography versus ethnographic farce is to miss the point.

There is little question that the consumers of ethnography nowadays include both those for whom and those about whom ethnography has been written previously (nor any argument that this should be otherwise). Similarly, it is hardly possible any longer to disentangle the local 'foreground' of the fieldwork situation from a 'background' of ethnographic knowledge. They intermesh not only in our personal subjectivity, but in a total historical field within which the ethnographer is merely one actor in pursuit of a particular project that may well intersect with the projects of those he purports to study. Such projects as well as their products – however easily unmasked as 'inventions', 'reifications' and the like – are embedded in social contexts in which the 'struggle for the real' takes on eminently political dimensions. There is nothing inherently wrong with an anthropology locked in a mutually referential relationship with 'native' discourses. Both represent historically conditioned and deployed modes of interested symbolic practice, and both partake of specifically structured sets of resources available within what Wolf (1982) calls historically constituted 'ecologies of collective representations'.

Rather than merely providing a glimpse of the tribulations faced by representatives of 'contaminated traditions', the case at hand should therefore teach us to phrase our questions in a more appropriate way. The problem lies less in acknowledging anthropology's involvement in embarking Cuban-American Santeros and American Yoruba on their schismogenic course (far from being sorcerer's apprentices tampering with our magic wand, they – at least in a certain sense – know much better what is at stake). The question is rather why our complicity seems to matter to them. How and why, in other words, is intertextuality between these various discourses established and sustained? If 'syncretism' has gone sour for everybody involved, why do we all – Santeros, American Yoruba, and anthropologists – find it so easy to agree on this matter? Might this be because it all is – to explicate the Melanesian allegory underlying parts of this essay – merely a case of 'kastom' shared and unshared on different levels of articulation between 'culture' and 'society' (cf. Lindstrom 1982; Tonkinson 1982)? In which case, would we then have to count outside experts like ourselves among the kastom-champions? In the context of contemporary American society, this is by no means an academic question. As 'public experts in matters of culture', anthropologists occasionally (but perhaps more often than they themselves realize) act as mediators between those who produce emblematic practices and artefacts, and the kinds of institutions that bestow the benefits of 'legitimacy'. Our public identity (as well as our careers) in no small measure hinge upon our ability to represent certain social realities as 'authentically different' (and, if possible, traditionally so). Conversely, few anthropologists will veto state support for the preservation of whatever culture their textual products helped to enshrine as 'different', 'traditional' or even only 'interesting'.[53] At least in the case at hand, to suppose that the 'objects of study' were unaware of this meshing of projects would be more than naive. But so would the assumption that they would necessarily agree with our judgement about their culture and the ways in which they present it to us.

But this is not the whole answer either. Situational shifts in representational strategies – on whoever's part – correspond to differently structured venues for cashing in on symbolic capital, each productive, at the same time, of particular ideological contradictions.[54] Yet once evoked and objectified as '*la tradición*', 'the African Way', 'Yoruba Reversionism' or, indeed, 'Santería' and *regla ocha* (for, in linguistic terms, both arguably represent nominalized constructions), the aggregates of beliefs and practices thus marked acquire a double-edged quality as 'culture' enacted and ideologically projected, embodied and externalized, at one and the same time. One has to live with whatever results it engenders. Far from ruling out ideological estrangement, the schismogenetic proliferation of emblems of contrast between Santeros

and American Yoruba, is necessarily predicated upon their shared commitment to (and occasional co-operative manipulation of) a single set of sacred
resources. But there is nothing tenuous about the relation between these
'levels of articulation' (to speak of 'levels' at all may already be a distortion).
Neither does a rigid distinction between 'inside' and 'outside' discourse
adequately describe the situation. Men like Ofuntola or Pichardo do not
simply put on a show when in our presence, and get on with the real business
when among themselves. Several streams of discourse seem to flow together
in their lives and religious careers. Yet precisely because they literally
embody diverse knowledges, their agency in articulating different systems
generates processual consequences within a total historical field.

'When we speak of Afro-American cultures', Sidney Mintz (1989b: 14)
reminds us, 'we are speaking of disturbed pasts.' But we are also speaking
of self-conscious attempts to invest such pasts with continuity and moral
significance. Here the 'neotraditional culture' analogy (if not the whole
approach tied to this concept) becomes questionable. For there simply is no
unselfconscious 'aboriginal state' from which practitioners of an undisturbed
local 'tradition' were catapulted into confrontation with global modernist (i.e.
'colonial') ideology. Though perhaps attractive for its ironic potential,
drawing an analogy between anthropological interference and 'indirect rule'
will not do in the case at hand – and not because anthropologists are marginal
to the institutional realm where power is generated and resources are
allocated. Rather – and more obviously, perhaps, than in many other cases –
the very inception of American forms of òrìsà-worship (whether in Cuba or
the US) was predicated upon the opening up of social channels through which
a discourse on power (in both the secular and sacred sense) could flow. *La
tradición* had an 'objective' – though always precarious – existence right
from the start.[55] By the same token, as points of reference (or departure),
'Africa' and 'Europe', 'Cuba' and 'North America', are products of an
inherently historical discourse – and that, again, holds true for everybody
involved: Santeros, American Yoruba, and ourselves. The plot is the same.
What makes us gravitate towards each other or drift apart at different
moments are strategic choices of narrative which, in turn, partly circumscribe
our role requirements as characters in a complex unfolding story of much
wider scope.

We may thus find it relatively easy to explain how Cuban and North
American anthropologists, at a certain stage, came to perceive 'syncretism'
as a viable means of converting objectifications of African-American cultural
forms into (however differently conceived) cultural capital. Likewise, the
subsequent devaluation of such intellectual currency might be perceived as
a problem in the history of anthropology in its relation to American ideologies
about cultural legitimacy. Yet matters are different for those upon whose
ideas and practices we conveniently tag and re-tag our labels. They have gods
to tend to, and that may be the very least difference that makes a difference.
Although many Santeros (and perhaps some American Yoruba),[56] at times,

may acknowledge the fact that Ifá speaks with a thoroughly historical voice (else it would have fallen silent long ago), there is no relativism involved in such introspection. The management of tradition, in a very real sense, spells business. Cultural pasts – as well as futures – are never just a given, but must be produced, modified, contested and defended in line with the options and constraints perceived within a historically constituted present that needs to be 'chartered'. Different junctures in time and social space may offer different semantic and political tools to work with; different venues for alignment or opposition may appear linked to different rewards; but at the same time they may imply different dangers of loss, disfiguration, and atrophy of the bodies of knowledge upon which claims to identity and distinction are based. In the end, as 'managers of knowledge', we all wind up in the same boat. This is not an answer to all questions, but maybe to some. If Elegguá – the god who opens and closes the various roads of fortune – may engineer our spectrum of choice in this matter, the decision about which course to follow nevertheless remains ours.

NOTES

1 My thanks go to Richard Fardon, Bonno Thoden van Velzen and Sidney Mintz for the helpful comments and criticism they offered.

2 Following conventions in the anglophone literature on Afro-Cuban religions, I capitalize 'Santería', 'Santero', and 'Santera', etc., and avoid Yoruba-derived appellations for individual priestesses and priests (i.e. *iyalocha* and *babalocha*). As in much indigenous discourse, my use of the Spanish masculine plural 'Santeros' (rather than the gender-neutral *olocha*) has no implications for the sex of the persons designated.

3 I am not using the term 'creole' in the currently fashionable sense, to imply an analogy to linguistic phenomena and processes (cf. Drummond 1981, Hannerz 1987, or Brown 1993), but in reference to its older meaning: the indigenization in the New World of something of Old World origin (cf. Arrom 1951, Nègre 1966 and Perl 1982 for hypotheses about the etymology and history of the term). Close to my understanding is Breen's (1984) use of the term to differentiate between colonial 'charter societies' (New World social aggregates physically as well as ideologically dependent on Old World input) and 'creole societies' capable of autonomous reproduction of their social structures and cultural content under New World conditions.

4 The dating of its inception is problematic. We know that the beginning of large-scale slave importation into Cuba roughly coincides with the crumbling and eventual demise of the Oyo state, and that the illegal slave trade to both Cuba and Brazil fed off the disastrous wars that subsequently erupted between different Yoruba polities. (See Palmié 1991: 21–83.)

5 That is, it just seems to have come into being without any (known) premeditated effort on the part of its earliest practitioners to 'found' an Afro-Cuban religion. However, since oral traditions recall the names of several late nineteenth-century priests who are said to have 'rectified', 'reformed' or otherwise changed previous practices and tenets of belief, this may well be a reflection less of historical fact than of conceptions of *regla ocha* as not only a 'genuine' folk religion, but a linear descendant of what used to be called a 'tribal religion'.

6 See Peel (1968, 1990) for particularly stringent methodological criticism of typological approaches.
7 See, for instance, Southall (1979), Hamel (1987), Helms (1988), Comaroff and Comaroff (1988) and Kramer (1989).
8 Cf. Hobsbawm's distinctions between 'convention' or 'routine', 'custom' and 'traditions' as increasingly ideologically marked terms encapsulating conceptions of continuing practice (Hobsbawm 1983). The use of the term 'objectification' for processes invoking morally and politically charged representations of 'culture' seems to originate with Cohn (1987).
9 The telling misnomer of 'culture contact' obviously comes to mind here. Since Linton's first attempt at generalizing some unexpected outcomes – unexpected, that is, from the perspective of European imperialist ideology – of contact between technologically 'advanced', and relatively 'backward' social formations within a colonial arena, we know that 'conscious, organized attempts on the part of a society's members to revive or perpetuate selected aspects of its culture' (Linton 1943: 230) may, and indeed do, occur. The same, however, holds true, for example, for endogenous innovation, or the peculiarly 'western' pursuit of 'discovery'. Once one considers the enormous intellectual dislocations the 'discovery' of the Americas or the 'classical' Orient wrought upon European theological and anthropological discourse (see, e.g., Hodgen 1964; Van Kley 1971), the alleged incident (nicely re-imagined by De Bry) when Puertorican Arawak subjected a bunch of Spaniards to a 'drowning-test' in order to ascertain experimentally whether they were or were not immortal (Hanke 1959: 24ff.), appears a rather pragmatic exercise at fact finding.
10 This interdependence of variables relating to social time and space is well stated by Lindstrom with respect to Melanesian 'kastom',

> One needs a notion of *kastom* to compare present circumstances to those of the past, or to compare one's own culture with that of other people. The first comparison is thinkable only if there is a concomitant conception of the possibility of change in structure. The second comparison is possible only when a people comes in contact with cultures of a different order. The emergence of a history of tradition is a multiple process.
>
> (Lindstrom 1982: 316)

11 Typified by the plethora of functionalist studies of presumably 'acculturation'-induced social convulsions such as 'millennarianisms', 'crisis cults' or 'revitalization movements'. See, e.g., Wallace (1956) for a classic example.
12 Anderson's (1983) treatment of the variegated (and variable) historical requisites for processes of differentiation that led to the emergence of 'nations' as culturally compelling units of identification and allegiance is instructive here.
13 As well as some much more complex (and far less tangible) local alignments between scholarly and nationalist discourses, the local historical 'intertextuality' (and the supra-local oppositional elaboration of which) still awaits serious study. (But see Ekeh 1990 regarding the dialectical articulation of discourses on 'tribes' and 'tribalism' in anthropology and African political discourse.)
14 Who, one should add, penned these lines during a lengthy absence from Cuba, and before he had met a practitioner of an Afro-Cuban religion outside of a jail.
15 Apparently 'ethnically' organized associations of urban blacks whose institutional history dates back to the early period of colonization. As several scholars – including myself (Palmié 1991, 1993a) have argued – there are good evidential grounds for viewing the 'cabildos' as the 'breeding ground' for the modern Afro-Cuban religions.
16 A lament packaged, incidentally, in the single most important study of these institutions produced to this day (Ortiz 1921)! Quite clearly, Ortiz operated within

the classic nineteenth-century framework where sociological and cultural knowledge-production was geared towards the end of maximizing the rationality of state-control (cf. Linke (1990) for examples of European antecedents to this programme). In all fairness, one must say that Ortiz included Catholicism in the range of 'atavistic superstitions' he felt were hampering Cuba's social progress (cf. Ortiz 1973 especially ch. 5).

17 The esoteric cult language of *regla ocha*, the phonology and lexical content of which has been interpreted as genetically related to (what may have been) nineteenth-century Yoruba (cf. Olmstead 1953, Castellanos and Castellanos 1992: 290–301).

18 In this, Ortiz was clearly influenced by Martí's visionary anti-racism, most succinctly expressed in his famous dictum that to be Cuban meant to be *más que blanco, más que negro*. At the same time, Ortiz, who temporarily served as Minister of Education in revolutionary Cuba, provided a 'scientific' foundation upon which Castro and Guevara erected the ill-fated ideological edifice of their doctrine of the *hombre nuevo*. See Chase (1980) for an overview of the kind of intellectual agenda Ortiz was reacting against. By 1946 Ortiz had gone so far as to reject the concept of 'race' as altogether scientifically invalid (cf. Ortiz 1975). Still, it should not be forgotten that Ortiz's pre-1930 writings betray a strong attachment to the very intellectual mould out of which the so-called scientific racism arose (cf. Mullen 1987).

19 Although Davies and Fardon (1991) neglect the important dimension of Ortiz's patrician social background as well as the developmental dynamic of his thought (such as the astonishing intellectual *volte face* he performed between about 1920 and 1935), their comparison of Cuban and West-African ethnographic/literary genre conventions aptly illustrates the fundamental differences between Ortiz's programme of harnessing ethnography to the task of assembling a symbolic repertoire of 'national' representations, and the British structural-functionalists' project of inscribing discrete units of colonial others upon the ethnographic landscape of Africa.

20 See Mintz (1964, 1989a) and Szwed (1974) for more precise information on the so-called Frazier–Herskovits debate. As I argue elsewhere (Palmié 1993b), both positions may, ultimately, be traceable to Franz Boas' views on what then was called 'the Negro Problem'. For even though the two interpretative 'schools' that evolved in the course of the 1930s are localizable in terms of their institutional origins (Melville Herskovits at Columbia, Franklin Frazier at Chicago), Frazier's mentor Robert E. Park (a long-time associate of Booker T. Washington) shared in large part Herskovits's teacher, Boas's, ideas on the matter of 'Negro-uplift'.

21 I cannot pretend to do justice to the even more complex issue of the historical development and current phenomenology of Cuban versus North American constructions of 'race' – and the compounded nature of Cuban racism in exile. (See Aguirre 1976, Dixon 1988, Moore 1988, and Palmié 1989.)

22 The tape from which the following statements were transcribed has a curious history: it was given to me by the Miami-based Santero Ernesto Pichardo who had recorded a conversation he held with Obá Ofuntola upon Pichardo's first visit to Oyotunji village in 1970. Its recording marks the first of a series of contacts between Miami's Afro-Cuban religious community and the Oyotunji branch of the American Yoruba Movement. I am grateful to Ernesto Pichardo for allowing me to peruse this unique document.

23 Perhaps not coincidentally, by 1960 King/Ofuntola had begun to operate an African boutique – the Ujamaa African Market – in Harlem.

24 Initiation into the cult of a single *òrìsà*, instead of the Cuban pattern where novices 'receive' (*recibir*) five to seven oricha in addition to their *dueno de la cabeza* (that is, the *oricha* for whom they receive their primary consecration). Such

Oyotunji-style single-*oricha* initiations come closer to current Yoruba practice than the Cuban equivalent. Ofuntola claims initially to have justified this 'innovation' by reference to economics – the Cuban pattern involves costly sacrifices to as many as eight deities. This argument seems to make sense to some Santeros as well: during my fieldwork in Miami, one Cuban Santera told me that a friend of hers was going to get initiated in Oyotunji village because of the prohibitive costs of initiations in Miami.

25 To Santeros, the idea of proselytizing is utterly foreign. According to their understanding (which seems to come fairly close to what modern ethnographic accounts tell us about Yoruba ideas on such matters), each person's fate – including whether or not he or she is to be initiated into the cult of an *oricha* – is partly predetermined. Usually the *oricha* will indicate such a necessity by visiting persistent illness or bad luck upon the person in question. Once divination discloses that an *oricha* 'claims one's head', initiation becomes the single solution to such problems. In contrast, at least as regards the Oyotunji community, racial divisions are rationalized on a similarly 'theological' basis: while whites are allowed to visit Oyotunji, they cannot become members of the community for religious reasons. As was explained to me during my own visits to Oyotunji, the fact that villagers are obliged periodically to honour their ancestors would militate against this, since it would be offensive to the African ancestors to be 'fed' alongside the spirits of white slave holders.

26 The name means 'Oyo returns' in Yoruba.

27 See Brown (1989, 1993) for an excellent discussion of the synthesis of various strains of imagery of 'royalty' in the aesthetics and iconography of *regla ocha*.

28 Many of these receptacles are what their Spanish name suggests: china soup tureens painted in correspondence with the respective *oricha*'s sacred colour(s).

29 The term Santeros use for outsiders or uninitiated persons who meddle with their religion. It derives from the Yoruba word *àle'jò*, that is, 'stranger'.

30 Typical phrases are *santo x representa al oricha y*, or, *santo x es el mismo oricha y.*

31 Herskovits (1937) spoke of a 'confusion of theological concept' which comes quite close to the views expressed by various early Cuban students of the matter.

32 Murphy's pronouncement that '[i]f one looks at the beliefs of *santería*, one only sees a hodge-podge of African and Christian elements', whereas its practice gave evidence of 'a rather elegant system of complementary and reciprocal rituals appropriate to different social contexts and religious concerns' (Murphy 1980: 349f.) represents a case in point. In the past decade, however, several scholars – most remarkably Poyner (1982), Brandon (1983), and Brown (1989) – have gone beyond such facile reiterations of received 'ethnographic' wisdom. See Verger (1963: 213) for an early critique of conventional understandings of African-American syncretism, and Gonzáles Huguet 1968 for a notable attempt at empirical differentiation undertaken by a Cuban scholar.

33 The Spanish original was given to me by its author in 1985 for the explicit purpose of steering my research in the right direction.

34 Though commonly used by practitioners of *regla ocha* today, as its meaning suggests, 'Santería' is, in fact, a derogatory heteronym.

35 The use of '*lucumí*' as an ethnonym designating certain groups of slaves from the Bight of Benin was – to the best of my knowledge – first documented by Alonso de Sandoval in early seventeenth-century New Spain. We also know that by the middle of the eighteenth century, some Afro-Cubans employed it as a referent to an aspect of their own social identity. Its etymology has variously been traced to a 'kingdom of Ulkami or Ulkama' whose existence in the area of modern Nigeria was reported by Dapper in 1670, or the Yoruba salutation *oluku mi* ('my friend!'). See Palmié (1991: 479f.) for a survey of theories about the origin of this term.

Whether Pichardo's spelling of the term with a 'k' relates to the orthographic revisionism current among some black Americans eludes me. The American Yoruba, at least, prefer to designate themselves as 'Afrikans'.

36 Pichardo is not the first Santero to voice such criticism. In the 'prologo' to Nicolas Valentin Angarica's *Manual de Orihate* (1955) José Roque de la Nuez (alias Efún Yomí) denounced Lydia Cabrera's magnum opus *El Monte* (originally published in 1954) in no uncertain terms:

> What knowledge can modern writers acquire if they are neither 'SANTEROS', nor practise this religion? What ideas can they suggest to the public opinion, when the source of knowledge of which these writers avail themselves, are the comments of persons who likewise are neither santeros, nor practise this religion? This is what appears to be the case in the recently published work 'EL MONTE' . . . 'El Monte' definitively is a literary gem, but as far as the revelation of the secrets of lucumí religion is concerned, the [descriptions of] ceremonies are as confounded as the language used.
>
> (de la Nuez in Angarica 1955: 3f., capitalization in the original)

37 Pichardo thus concedes that the saints may help to bridge a conceptual gap for priests whose exposure to Afro-Cuban religious culture previous to their initiation has been slight, who entered the religion late in life, or who are generally uninterested in theological matters. The true *consciente* ('knower'), however, though he may likewise display such images among the objects that make up his shrine, would never dream of 'equating' them with the *oricha*. Interestingly, Pichardo's pronouncement on this issue parallels an educational strategy currently propagated by the archdiocese of Miami. On the basis of Vatican II, the Catholic priest Enrique Sosa (1983) argues that although Santería should be respected as an expression of popular faith, the object of catechetical endeavours should be to clarify the differences between the 'true' saints, and the Afro-Cuban counterparts with whom some members of the faith are wont to falsely 'identify' them. I have no doubt that Pichardo would wholeheartedly agree – if for rather different reasons.

38 We simply have too few indications of whether Santeros could, or even felt a need to, address a general public. Apart from the ritual compendia (*libretas*) mentioned above, very few documents written by Santeros during the republican period are known (a notable exception is Angarica (1955) which, however, comes close to a *libreta* format). For somewhat different reasons, a similar lack of evidence makes it impossible to compare the situation in revolutionary Cuba. If, as Moore (1988) claims, the revolutionary government has (until very recently) aimed at the 'folklorization' and 'museumization' of Afro-Cuban religious culture as an 'object lesson' in Cuban cultural history (thereby denying the relevance of its *practice* to contemporary Cuban society), one would certainly want to know whether and how Santeros responded.

39 Including – perhaps most painfully – the cultural background to what Hoetink (1967) termed their 'somatic norm image'.

40 See Palmié (1989, 1990) for discussions of these aspects of the Afro-Cuban religious diaspora in Miami.

41 This problem has become especially acute in the aftermath of the so-called Mariel-Exodus, when Miami's exile community received its first significant input of black Cubans. Perhaps not surprisingly, most black 'Marielitos' wound up in the lower socioeconomic ranks of Miami's Cuban exile community. Likewise, Miami's Afro-Cuban religious community (hitherto dominated by priests phenotypically 'white' even by American standards) evidenced little enthusiasm about integrating black priests claiming superior status. What aggravates this conflict (only too happily swept under the rug in conversations with *aleyos*) is the fact

that many black Marielitos cannot live up to the enormous ritual expenditures an active religious life in Miami demands. The following typewritten statement by a black Marielita (who preferred to remain anonymous) shows that Oyotunji-style initiations are fast becoming an economic (though, perhaps not religious) alternative. Claiming that the increasing costs of religious participation in Miami have virtually despoiled the 'legitimate heirs' of the Afro-Cuban tradition of their 'spiritual heritage', she goes on to relate the case of the 'González family':

> This family [of Afro-Cuban origin, and] traditionally affiliated with the religion told me in desperation that, although they needed to have their eldest son initiated [for reasons of health], the scarcity of their economic resources forbid this measure. 'How is it possible,' the mother told me desperately fearing for the life of her child, 'that although this is ours, we are barred from it?' I recommended to that person to stay calm and faithful, and promised her to make contacts with the community that exists in North Carolina [in fact, South Carolina] and which has dedicated itself to the life and practices of the Yoruba.

42 There is no question that *regla ocha* had made significant headway among Cuban whites long before the revolution (cf. Palmié 1991: 166–177). On the contrary, it seems quite likely that – irrespective of matters of socially contingent racial definitions – this trend is informed by larger shifts in American public discourse, viz. the increasing acceptance of 'Africa' as a point of reference for 'legitimate' cultural pasts in general and, in particular, the ascent of 'Yoruba culture', in the popular imagination, to a level of grandeur and antiquity hitherto only attained by Ethiopia.

43 See Brown (1989: 85–99) for a pathbreaking attempt to account for the emergence of this view. Brown's analysis of 'insider' narratives about the origins of *la tradición* in conjunction with divergent modes of ritual practice reveals the coexistence of competing 'parallel traditions' within *regla ocha*. At the same time, however, a convergence of such notions with older anthropological (or western commonsensical) theories of cultural stability and change should not be ruled out. In trying to explain the fact that the *ifá-* and *erindilogun*-texts collected by Bascom in Nigeria differ quite radically from those current in Miami, Cuban-American divination specialists are puzzled about who to blame for having 'introduced changes' (for shouldn't they really be the same?). My impression is that the explanation of choice is that the Africans simply 'didn't take care of their culture'.

44 The *hombre de conocimientos* is one who has come into possession of powerful esoteric knowledge which enables him or her to *trabajar* ('work') – that is, to communicate with, and participate in the power of the *oricha* in order to effect transformations that reflect upon the world of the living.

45 For example, Pichardo, who cautions scholars against generalizing from statements made by inadequately trained informant-priests, approvingly writes that

> In Cuba and in exile the [novice-] priest is permitted to learn [only] what he sees or hears without any reasoned explanation. Even when one attains priesthood, the profound secrets are not easily obtained; 'learn what you see and always do it in the same manner'. In exile, the priests who have had the chance to study with a master do not extend the religious profundities to the better part of novices. They only impart them to some of them, whom they think worthy of receiving such knowledge.

(1984: 76)

46 A characteristic example is Murphy's elegy for the traditionality and moral integrity of Santería in Cuba which he sees giving way to the values of a ruthlessly individualistic, secular and profit-oriented society in exile (Murphy 1987). More interesting, perhaps, is the fact that Lydia Cabrera – who, after emigrating to

Miami, announced that she would refrain from studying *regla ocha* there so as not to spoil her fond memories of what it was like in Cuba – in 1980 published a *libreta*-style compendium explicitly designed to help incorrectly trained novices to find their way back to the 'genuine tradition'.

47 See Brown (1989) for an extended discussion of this ideological moment in relation to conflicts over ritual practice.

48 de la Nuez writes approvingly that Angarica (who indeed claims Yoruba-origin for *la religión Lucumí*) had access to 'a dictionary and a Yoruba-translation of the Bible' and used them in compiling his *Manual de Orihate* (1955) so that 'the reader could acquaint himself with its legitimate and true orthography and correct pronunciation' (de la Nuez 1955: 4). In fact, however, Angarica's transliteration of *lucumí* words and phrases appears far more 'hispanicized' than in other comparable texts. The ongoing research of David Brown promises to shed light on the origins and nature of the 'Africanist connection'.

49 Some indications of a conscious 'internationalist' cultural policy on the part of the Yoruba are provided in Abimbola's account of a visit to Brazil, where he (as *babalawo-cum*-Vice Chancellor of the University of Ifé) had earlier installed the Candomblé priest-*cum*-scholar Deoscoredes dos Santos (alias *mestre Didi*) 'as *Baálè Sàngó* of Bahia on the instructions of the Federal Government of Nigeria' (Abimbola 1979: 620), and now assisted in dos Santos's consecration as *Alápini* (that is, high priest of the royal ancestor cult of *Oyo*).

50 Along with a few other *aleyos* – among them another anthropologist, a reporter from the *Miami Herald*, and an English professor from the University of Miami who had lived in Nigeria for several years. Quite clearly, the composition of this group of 'privileged outsiders' reflected strategic intent: we were to document and publicize the results of this journey (including the religious dependency of Oyotunji on Cuban Miami). I have no doubts that – in some form or other – all of us eventually complied.

51 Here I am not only talking about what Marcus and Cushman (1982) called the genre conventions of 'ethnographic realism', but more fundamental problems of epistemology and method. For the crux of the matter has less to do with the relation between rhetoric and plausibility than it does with the question of how to proceed analytically if 'our' solutions to problems posed by an ethnographic reality 'out there' *mutatis mutandis* turn into a part of the reality we set out to study. I am grateful to Richard Fardon for thinking my argument in this matter to its logical conclusion.

52 Richard Price's remarks (1983: 8–26) about this dilemma are well worth comparing, especially since the Saramaka he worked with have a conception of historical knowledge as a scarce commodity that, in many ways, parallels ideas about *la tradición* held by practitioners of *regla ocha*. Though I share Price's feelings about the moral responsibilities ethnographers face when 'interfering with alien knowledge systems', I think his conclusions ultimately evade the issue. Rather than worrying about the potential breakdown of a *cordon sanitaire* between 'our' and 'their' knowledge systems, we should ask ourselves *why* we perceive the appropriation of anthropological knowledge by our 'objects of study' as problematic. Could it be that this is – to speak with Mary Douglas (1966) – due to a fear of 'matter out of place'? (cf. Sjorslev 1989, Carrier 1992).

53 To refer to the Oyotunji episode reported above, there is no question that this kind of pay-off system was on the mind of everybody involved. Contrary to the usual self-perception of anthropologists as marginal participants in political discourse, the fact that we sometimes function as gate-keepers to such resources as state support (or, alternatively, might have functioned as handmaidens of official 'cultural policies' perceived as repressive) allocates far greater political (as well as cultural) significance to ethnography than many of us like to acknowledge.

54 See Asiwaju (1976) for a case that very nicely illustrates this point.
55 This is not to say that in this (or any other case) 'cultural objectification' is necessarily a result of 'western' interference (cf. Thomas 1992). There may well have existed different measuring rods before the 'Great Transformation' set in. The point rather is that in the case at hand it is impossible to ignore the fact that none of the bodies of 'traditional' knowledge and practice dealt with in this essay were ever 'spontaneous emanations' or 'unselfconscious doings'.
56 The qualifier simply refers to my inadequate ethnographic knowledge.

REFERENCES

Abimbola, W. (1979) 'Yoruba religion in Brazil: problems and prospects', *Actes du 42e Congrès International des Américanistes*, Paris: S.d.A.
Abu-Lughod, L. (1991) 'Writing against culture', in R. Fox (ed.) *Recapturing Anthropology*, Santa Fe: School of American Research Press.
Aguirre, B. E. (1976) 'Differential migration of Cuban social races: a review and interpretation of the problem', *Latin American Research Review* 11: 103–124.
Anderson, B. (1983) *Imagined Communities*, London: Verso.
Angarica, N. V. (1955) *Manual de Orihate*, n.p.
Anonymous (1959) *Los Oraculos de Biague y Diloggun*, Habana: n.p.
Arrom, J. J. (1951) 'Criollo: Definición y matices de un concepto', *Hispania* 34: 172–176.
Asiwaju, A. I. (1976) 'Political motivation and oral historical traditions in Africa: the case of Yoruba crowns, 1900–1960', *Africa* 46: 113– 127.
Barth, F. (1990) 'The guru and the conjurer: transactions in knowledge and the shaping of culture in southeast Asia and Melanesia', *Man* 25: 640– 653.
Bascom, W. R. (1950) 'The Focus of Cuban Santería', *Southwestern Journal of Anthropology* 6: 64–68.
—— (1951) 'The Yoruba in Cuba', *Nigeria Magazine* 37: 14–20.
—— (1979) 'Introduction', in C. M. Hunt, *Oyotunji Village. The Yoruba Movement in America*, Washington, D.C.: University Press of America.
Bateson, G. (1958) *Naven*, Stanford: Stanford University Press.
Brandon, G. E. (1983) 'The dead sell memories. An anthropological study of Santería in New York City', Ph.D. dissertation, Rutgers University, Ann Arbor: UMI.
Breen, T. H. (1984) 'Creative adaptations: peoples and cultures', in J. P. Greene and J. R. Pole (eds) *Colonial British America*, Baltimore: The Johns Hopkins University Press.
Brown, D. H. (1989) 'Garden in the machine: Afro-Cuban sacred art and performance in urban New Jersey and New York', unpublished Ph.D. dissertation, Yale University, Ann Arbor: UMI.
—— (1993) 'Thrones of the *orichas*: Afro-Cuban altars in New Jersey, New York, and Havana', *African Arts* 26: 44–59, 85–87.
Cabrera, L. (1980a) *Yemayá y Ochún*, Miami: Colección del Chicherekú en el exilio.
—— (1980b) *Koeko Iyawó: Aprende Novicia*, Miami: Colección del Chicherekú.
—— (1983) [1954] *El Monte. Igbo Finda Ewe Orisha Vititi Nfinda*, Miami: Colección del Chicherekú.
Carrier, J. G. (1992) 'Introduction', in J. G. Carrier (ed.) *History and Tradition in Melanesian Anthropology*, Berkeley: University of California Press.
Castellanos, J. and I. Castellanos (1992) *Cultura afrocubana III: las religiones y las lenguas*, Miami: Ediciones Universal.
Chase, A. (1980) *The Legacy of Malthus*, Urbana: University of Illinois Press.
Chatterjee, P. (1986) *Nationalist Thought and the Colonial World*, London: Zed Books.

Cohn, B. (1987) 'The census, social structure and objectification in South Asia', in B. Cohn (ed.) *An Anthropologist Among the Historians*, Delhi: Oxford University Press.

Comaroff, J. and J. Comaroff (1988) 'Through the looking-glass: colonial encounters of the first kind', *Journal of Historical Sociology* 1: 6–32.

Davies, C. and R. Fardon (1991) 'African fictions in representations of West African and Afro-Cuban Cultures', in P. Baxter and R. Fardon (eds) *Voice, Genre, Text: Anthropological Essays in Africa and Beyond* (Bulletin of the John Rylands University Library of Manchester 73: 125–145).

de la Nuez, J. R. (1955) 'Prologo', in N. V. Angarica, *Manual de Orihate*, n.p.

Dixon, H. (1988) 'The Cuban-American counterpoint: Black Cubans in the United States', *Dialectical Anthropology* 13: 227–239.

Douglas, M. (1966) *Purity and Danger*, Hammondsworth: Penguin Books.

Drummond, L. (1981) 'The cultural continuum: a theory of intersystems', *Man* 15: 352–374.

Durkheim, E. (1973) *Les règles de la méthode sociologique*, Paris: Presses Universitaires de France.

Ekeh, P. P. (1990) 'Social anthropology and two contrasting uses of tribalism in Africa', *Comparative Studies in Society and History* 32: 660–700.

González Huguet, L. (1968) 'La casa-templo en la regla de ocha', *Etnología y Folklore* 5: 33–57.

Hamel, G. R. (1987) 'Strawberries, floating islands, and rabbit captains: mythical realities and European contact in the Northeast during the sixteenth and seventeenth centuries', *Journal of Canadian Studies* 21: 72–94.

Hanke, L. (1959) *Aristotle and the American Indians*, London: Hollis and Carter.

Hannerz, U. (1987) 'The world in creolization', *Africa* 57: 546–559.

Helms, M. (1988) *Ulysses' Sail*, Princeton: Princeton University Press.

Herskovits, M. J. (1937) 'African gods and catholic saints in New World negro belief', *American Anthropologist* 39: 635–643.

Hesse, A. (1977) 'Eine *Libreta de Santería* – Beispiel für den Beginn schriftlicher Tradierung auf Kuba', in B. Brentjes (ed.) *Der Beitrag der Völker Afrikas zur Weltkultur*, Halle: Martin Luther Universität Halle-Wittenberg.

Hobsbawm, E. (1983) 'Introduction: inventing traditions', in E. Hobsbawm and T. Ranger (eds)*The Invention of Tradition*, London: Cambridge University Press.

Hodgen, M. T. (1964) *Early Anthropology in the Sixteenth and Seventeenth Centuries*, Philadelphia: University of Pennsylvania Press.

Hoetink, H. (1967) *Caribbean Race Relations. A Study of Two Variants*, London: Oxford University Press.

Hunt, C. M. (1979) *Oyotunji Village. The Yoruba Movement in America*, Washington, D.C.: University Press of America.

Keesing, R. M. (1982) 'Kastom in Melanesia: an overview', *Mankind* 13: 297–301.

Kramer, F. (1989) 'The otherness of the European', *Culture and History* 6: 107–123.

Kroeber, A. L. (1940) 'Stimulus diffusion', *American Anthropologist* 42: 1–20.

Lachataneré, R. (1938) *Oh, mío Yemayá!*, Manzanillo: Editorial 'el Arte'.

—— (1942) *Manual de Santería*, La Habana: Editorial Caribe.

Law, R. (1977) *The Oyo Empire, c.1600–c.1836*, Oxford: Clarendon Press.

León, A. (1971) 'Un caso de tradición oral excrita', *Islas* 39/40: 141–151.

Lindstrom, L. (1982) 'Leftamap kastom: the political history of tradition on Tanna (Vanuatu)', *Mankind* 13: 316–329.

Linke, U. (1990) 'Folklore, anthropology, and the government of social life', *Comparative Studies in Society and History* 32: 117–148.

Linton, R. (1943) 'Nativistic movements', *American Anthropologist* 45: 230–240.

Marcus, G. and Cushman D. (1982) 'Ethnographies as text', *Annual Review of Anthropology* 11: 25–69.

Mintz, S. W. (1964) 'Melville J. Herskovits and Caribbean Studies: a retrospective tribute', *Caribbean Studies* 4: 42–51.
—— (1989a) 'Introduction', in M. J. Herskovits, *The Myth of the Negro Past*, Boston: Beacon Press.
—— (1989b) [1974] *Caribbean Transformations*, New York: Columbia University Press.
Moore, C. (1988) *Castro, the Blacks, and Africa*, Los Angeles: Center for Afro-American Studies, UCLA.
Mullen, E. J. (1987) '*Los negros brujos*: a reexamination of the text', *Cuban Studies* 17: 111–129.
Murphy, J. M. (1980) 'Ritual systems in Cuban Santería', unpublished Ph.D. thesis, Temple University, Ann Arbor: UMI.
—— (1987) 'Lydia Cabrera and *La Regla de Ocha* in the United States', in I. Castellanos and J. Inclán (eds) *En Torno a Lydia Cabrera*, Miami: Ediciones Universal.
Nègre, A. (1966) 'Origines et signification du mot "créole"', *Bulletin de la Société d'Histoire de la Guadeloupe* 5/6: 38–42.
Ofuntola Oseijeman Adelabu Adefunmi I. (1982) *Olorisha: A Guidebook Into Yoruba Religion*, n.p.: Great Benin Books.
Olmstead, D. L. (1953) 'Comparative notes on Yoruba and Lucumí', *Language* 29: 157–164.
Ortiz, F. (1921) 'Los cabildos afrocubanos', *Revista Bimestre Cubana* 16: 5–39.
—— (1938) 'La música sagrada de los negros yorubá en Cuba', *Estudios Afrocubanos* 2: 89–104.
—— (1940) *Contrapunteo Cubano del tabaco y el azucar*, Habana: J. Montero.
—— (1973) *Los negros brujos*, Miami: Ediciones Universal.
—— (1975) *El engaño de las razas*, Habana: Editorial de Ciencias Sociales.
Palmié, S. (1987) '"La religion del chisme": Klatsch, Informationskontrolle und soziale Organisation in den afrokubanischen Religionen Miamis', *Lateinamerika Studien* 23: 197–207.
—— (1989) 'Spics or Spades? Racial classification and ethnic conflict in Miami', *Amerikastudien/American Studies* 34: 211–221.
—— (1990) 'Kulturkampf in South Florida: the case of the Church of the Lukumí Babalu Ayé'. Paper presented at the Second International Meeting of the Association for Caribbean Studies, Vienna.
—— (1991) *Das Exil der Götter. Geschichte und Vorstellungswelt einer afro-kubanischen Religion*, Frankfurt: Peter Lang.
—— (1993a) 'Ethnogenetic processes and cultural transfer in Afro-Caribbean slave populations', in W. Binder (ed.) *Slavery in the Americas*, Würzburg: Königshauser und Neumann.
—— (1993b) 'The Other within: American anthropology and the study of ethnic minorities in the 1920s', in W. Binder (ed.) *American Minorities in the 1920s*, Frankfurt: Peter Lang.
Peel, J.D.Y. (1968) 'Syncretism and religious change', *Comparative Studies in Society and History* 10: 121–141.
—— (1989) 'The cultural work of Yoruba ethnogenesis', in E. Tonkin, M. McDonald and M. Chapman (eds) *History and Ethnicity*, London: Routledge.
—— (1990) 'The pastor and the *babalawo*: the interaction of religions in nineteenth century Yorubaland', *Africa* 60: 338–369.
Perl, M. (1982) 'Los dos significados de la voz "crioulo/criollo". Consideraciones lingüísticas e históricas', *Islas* 73: 169–178.
Pichardo, E. (1984) *Oduduwa Obatalá*, Miami: Rex Press.
Poyner, R. (1982) 'Thunder over Miami', in *Thunder over Miami: Ritual Objects of*

Nigerian and Afro-Cuban Religion, Exhibition catalogue, Miami: University of Florida and Miami-Dade Community College.

Price, R. (1983) *First Time. The Historical Vision of an Afro-American People*, Baltimore: The Johns Hopkins University Press.

Sandoval, M. C. (1979) 'Santería as a mental health care system: an historical overview', *Social Science and Medicine* 13B: 137–151.

Schütz, A. (1984) *Strukturen der Lebenswelt II*, ed. T. Luckmann, Frankfurt: Suhrkamp.

Shils, E. (1971) 'Tradition', *Comparative Studies in Society and History* 13: 122–159.

—— (1981) *Tradition*, Chicago: University of Chicago Press.

Sjorslev, I. (1989) 'On the edge of the text: three books on Afro-Brazilian religion', *Culture and History* 4: 91–116.

Smith, M. E. (1982) 'The process of sociocultural continuity', *Current Anthropology* 23: 127–142.

Sosa, J. J. (1983) 'Religiosidad popular y sincretismo religioso: santería y espiritismo', *Documentaciones Sureste* 4: 1–14.

Southall, A. (1979) 'White strangers and their religion in East Africa and Madagascar', in W. A. Shack and E. P. Skinner (eds) *Strangers in African Societies*, Berkeley: University of California Press.

Szwed, J. F. (1974) 'An American anthropological dilemma: the politics of Afro-American culture', in D. Hymes (ed.) *Reinventing Anthropology*, New York: Vintage Books.

Thomas, N. (1992) 'The inversion of tradition', *American Ethnologist* 19: 213–232.

Tonkinson, R. (1982) 'Kastom in Melanesia: introduction', *Mankind* 13: 302–305.

Trouillot, M.-R. (1991) 'Anthropology and the savage slot: the poetics and politics of otherness', in R. Fox (ed.) *Recapturing Anthropology*, Santa Fe: School of American Research Press.

Van Kley, E. J. (1971) 'Europe's "Discovery" of China and the writing of world history', *American Historical Review* 76: 358–385.

Verger, P. (1963) 'Afro-Catholic syncretism in South America', *Nigeria Magazine* 78: 211–215.

Wagner, R. (1981) *The Invention of Culture*, Chicago: University of Chicago Press.

Wallace, A.F.C. (1956) 'Revitalization movements', *American Anthropologist* 58: 264–281.

Wolf, E. (1982) *Europe and the People Without History*, Berkeley: University of California Press.

5 Knowing the past
Plural identities and the antinomies of loss in Highland Bolivia

Olivia Harris

History, it could be argued, is local knowledge *par excellence*. The 'past' can only be an object of knowledge insofar as it is exemplified by, identified with, particular actions or events that have been played out in localities. Even attempts to conceive of a world history have to locate the narrative in places although, in such cases, the range of location may be unusually broad.

However, in the development of historiography in Europe, it is not locality as such that is the subject of historical narratives (except in the limited case of 'local history' itself) but civilizations, nations or peoples. By the late twentieth century, it can be argued that concepts of identity at every level are crucially derived from highly fashioned and coherent narratives about the past. This is very apparent in the case of national identity, which is invoked through well-established narratives of the origins, the continuous existence and historical vicissitudes of the people in question, and underwritten by museum displays, folkloric dances and so forth. It is also true of other kinds of groups such as the working class or women, for whom a crucial element in their constitution as collective political subjects has been the recovery and rewriting of a forgotten history.

The idea that people may have little awareness of their own past in the sense of well-documented narratives has come to be seen as almost scandalous. And given the fundamental place of written documentation to the constitution of knowledge of the past, one of the ways in which non-script cultures have long been marked as inferior is because they have no recorded past. In what follows, I wish to explore both aspects of this configuration: on the one hand, the implications of different ways of knowing the past and, on the other, assumptions involved in attributing identity on the basis of historical narratives.

NATIONALISM AND THE ANTINOMIES OF LOSS

The representation of the indigenous Americans as lacking self-knowledge because they had no writing is long established. This view is particularly explicit with regard to knowledge of history. Walter Mignolo, writing of the sixteenth and early seventeenth century, speaks of the 'complicity between alphabetic writing and history' found in the Renaissance view of knowledge (1992b). For the 'men of letters' (*letrados*) who sought to know the New World (they termed it 'new' because, of course, there was no reference to it in their books), the intelligence of the inhabitants was not in doubt, but they could not understand their own history because they did not have letters (Mignolo's citations from Torquemada and Acosta are particularly explicit on this point (1992a, 1992b)). Garcilaso de la Vega, the first great *mestizo* writer of the Americas, wrestles with the same problem:

> Inca, uncle, since your people have no writing, how is the memory of past events preserved? What information do you have concerning the origins of our kings? The Spanish and their neighbours have divine and human histories, from which they know about the origins of their kings. They even know how many thousands of years ago God created the heaven and earth. All this and much more they know from their books.
>
> (Garcilaso de la Vega 1609: Bk I, par. XV)

Four centuries later, a similar position is echoed by educated Bolivians. As a townsman said to me once: 'these Indians are ignorant. Why, they don't even know their own history!' The stuff of the past from which history is created has disappeared because it was not recorded. In this instance, the loss of the past is explained by a lack in the culture of the Indians, based on their ignorance of writing. However, the theme of loss is not restricted to this instance but recurs at all levels of Bolivian society. The metaphor of imperialism is mined for images of plunder and extraction. In the sixteenth century, it was the Spanish who looted and destroyed the treasures, the skills and the accumulated wisdom of Andean civilization. In the twentieth century, it is the gringos who steal, purchase or expropriate both archaeological pieces and historical knowledge, stored so often in archives across the ocean. Treasured items from the Gold Museum go missing, historical documents cannot be located.

In my experience of fieldwork in the *ayllu*s,[1] peasant communities in Northern Potosi (Bolivia), there is recognition of these kinds of loss but rarely a sense of anguish. When I have asked people to tell me of events that took place before their lifetime, the common response is 'if you had come before, you would have been able to talk to people who really knew. We no longer know these things, we did not witness them. Those who knew are all dead'.[2] Such statements are made out of robust realism. I could detect none of the pathos that I expected.

At the same time there are stories which reveal a recognition of the extent of their loss. Don Pedro Allqamamani described to me once how, long ago, the Indians knew the art of writing 'but then the Spanish landlords arrived and said "*carajo, indio*, you are ignorant savages, you don't know how to write", and since then we have lost the knowledge'. Some people tell tales of how it happened that the Indians came to be the most despised members of society through their own failing. Such stories articulate the generalized self-conception of Indians with reference to a past that is not tied to place. This is a 'constitutional' view of history, to use the concept developed by Carrier, in the sense that it refers to 'uncaused events that constitute or reconstitute the world' (Carrier 1987: 118).

Nationalists, by contrast, are particularly prone to dwell on loss. The knowledge in which nationalism is grounded is in many ways based on a sense of loss: the 'imagined community' is often the idealized one that is believed to have existed, or whose incipient demise must be mourned and challenged. Yet much of the recent writing on nationalism is at pains to point out the fictitious 'invented' element in such reconstructions of the past. Thus Handler writes of the attempts by Quebequois nationalists to construct bounded cultural objects, that they are 'a process that paradoxically demonstrates the absence of any such objects' (1988: 27). Hobsbawm has noted even more ironically that the historian is to the nationalist what the poppy-grower is to the heroin addict.[3] Both in different ways play upon the ambiguous dialogue between loss and continuity.[4] Anthropology too, especially in its modernist form, has often been founded on the premise of loss, its subject matter defined as tradition and community in contrast to the disenchanted world in which its practitioners perceived themselves to be living (Robertson 1990; Harris 1995b).

In Bolivia, a nationalist movement known as Katarismo[5] has emerged over the past twenty-five years among Aymara-speakers of the *altiplano*. Like so many other nationalisms, it grew out of the dilemmas and displacements of people whose childhood was spent herding sheep in monolingual peasant hamlets, who went to school and were successful academically, and whose educational achievements offered them a radically other way of experiencing the world that denied their own past. For the Kataristas, it is the state itself, and the creole-*mestizo* ruling classes who have repressed and destroyed the Indian past.

Their sense of loss becomes pervasive as modernization and ecological crisis force dramatic changes – typical contexts for the development of nationalist movements. In this the work of anthropologists and folklorists plays a part, since so often we seek to document living traditions, handed down from the past and authenticated by it. In many instances the populations that anthropologists have studied stand for the past; they are the mute bearers of history, the more so because they have so often been seen as incapable of knowing the past themselves.[6] This is typical of the nationalist view of peasants and informs the attitude of outsiders to Aymara-speaking peasants.

This complicity of anthropology, and of writing, in the creation of a lost object was brought home to me when I revisited the Laymi village in Northern Potosi where I lived during my first fieldwork in the early 1970s:

> August 1990: I return after an absence of six years to Muruq'umarka. The changes are palpable, partly the result of the prolonged drought which had

propelled people of all ages, but especially the young, to work in cocaine production in the tropical Chapare region. I have copies of a small book of my ethnographic essays published in Bolivia to present to them. I am filled with a trepidation that anyone who has done fieldwork in the region will recognise: how far is what I have learnt from them the product of their help and active collaboration, and how far is it in spite of their enduring doubts and suspicions, behind their backs as it were? Will they welcome the book I had told them I would write, or view it as a betrayal?

Don Alberto Kamaqi makes a speech of thanks in the crowded community house. The same age as me, twenty years ago he was awkward and somewhat disaffected; at that time he was the only person who was fully literate, since he had nearly completed high school in Challapata. Today he lives in the closest town, Uncia, where he is an active Katarista and works in rural development projects. His message is that they need my book, because the children growing up today live in such a changed world that only by reading it will they learn what their customs were.

Don Alberto's sense of loss, and his expressed need to preserve a sense of the vanished past, seemed not to be shared by the rest of the community. Most of the people I talked to interpreted the changes as being both the result of economic hardship, and also a form of progress, a mark of their increasing 'civilization'. By wearing factory-made clothes instead of their own colourful homespun, by shifting from Aymara to Quechua as their first language, by keeping more of the children in secondary school, by earning illicit dollars, they gain the approval of the local *mestizo* townspeople.

My little book may become an objectified repository of knowledge about the past of this community, rendering the Laymi Indians 'knowable' to themselves, as well as to others, in a new form. Memory is often said to be the cultural resource of the oppressed. And yet the particular narratives of the past recounted by nationalist historiographies, such as that which the Aymara Kataristas are developing, frame collective identity in a particular way. The Kataristas introduce an element of nostalgia: of a longing for what has been lost. Within the twentieth-century nation-state such narratives have become naturalized, and so we recognize their shape. They combine a lament for what has been lost with a hope for continuity with the past.

LATIN AMERICAN ETHNOGRAPHY AND PLURAL KNOWLEDGES

In the Latin American context the imagery of loss imposes itself in a particularly direct way. While the early European commentators frequently described the civilizations of the Americas in terms of what they previously lacked (alphabetic writing, true religion, history), today the narrative of European annexation of the great highland civilizations is more generally told as one of the coming of loss through destruction by the colonizing forces:

loss of life itself in the spectacular demographic collapse of some areas, and the attendant loss of skills, knowledge and identity.

In anthropology, this historical process of loss has often been portrayed as the elimination of otherness itself. My experience as a beginning post-graduate student in London in the early 1970s, when I was told that it would be 'boring' to study Andean peasants since they were so 'europeanized', is far from unique. The reality of course is more complex. They were certainly subjected to profound changes and pressures stemming from the Europeans, but as the white settlers and their descendants have repeatedly pointed out, the 'problem' is that they never became Europeans. When it did not result in direct genocide, the loss experienced in the Americas involved profound transformation, a process often identified as creolization.

Ulf Hannerz's essay on 'The world in creolization' defines creole cultures as 'those which draw in some way on two or more historical sources, often originally widely different. They have had some time to develop and integrate' (1987: 552). Like others, he uses the metaphor of water to evoke the fluidity of cultural forms, which flow into one another in such a way that their distinctive origins merge in a new 'stream'. The hydraulic imagery has the advantage of not reifying culture; however it suggests an unduly benign view of the ways in which 'widely different' cultures (the neutrality of the terms belies the political realities often involved) flow together in a cumulative process of growth and merging. Even in the case of rivers, distinct waters can flow together in a single stream for hundreds of miles without merging (e.g. parts of the Amazon); in the case of cultural forms, such imagery precludes consideration of how and how far issues of boundedness and incompatibility, of power and resistance come into play.[7]

In the Andean context instability and fluidity have historically been contained by an enduring set of racial/cultural classifications. In the first decades of Spanish administration a basic legal principle was established that separated the 'republic of the Spanish' from the 'republic of the Indians'. Europeans were forbidden to live on Indian lands, and the integrity of Indian social organization was protected, in theory at least, as a condition for their paying tribute. The distinction between 'Indians' and non-Indians was grounded in this fiscal obligation, which in turn gave it an enduring reality (Harris 1995a).

However, this principle of apartheid was undermined, particularly as the native population was obliged to accept the Christian faith of their rulers, and thus began perhaps the first great example of cultural globalization of the modern era. This was accompanied by a sustained and dramatic mixing of populations. With the erosion of native authority, the chaos of the early decades of Spanish rule and the growth of towns, new types of 'natives' began to emerge who were not affiliated to any particular group. Moreover, a profound mixing took place, most dramatically perhaps in the mining city of Potosi, where thousands of Indians from the whole of the southern highlands arrived each year by rotation to perform tributary labour. Large-scale processes of migration, too, meant that differences between ethnic groups became less marked.

However, when people refer today to the 'mixing' of populations that resulted from European administration of the Andean region, it is not the intermingling of the native populations that concerns them so much as the mixing of native and European, known by the Spanish term *mestizaje*. Sixteenth-century Spanish concepts of purity of blood or caste meant that in the New World a profusion of terms developed to refer to the new hybrids that resulted from racial intermarriage or breeding, and *mestizos* have typically been regarded as tainted, illegitimate, outside the law in a sense, for all their privileged position *vis-à-vis* the Indians (Demelas 1981; Harris 1995a; Bouysse-Cassagne 1994).[8]

Mestizaje is today the dominant ideology of national identity. Latin American nations espouse a political rhetoric which treats ethnic differences as a relic of the colonial past, and proclaims a new synthesis of diverse elements. And yet as leaders of the developing Indian movements are quick to point out, the neutral terminology of 'mixing' (*mestizaje*) denies political and social reality, which is one of an intensely hierarchical system of values, in which racism persists usually quite openly. A further consequence of the discursive insistence on *mestizaje* is that it indirectly reproduces precisely that category of the distinctively 'Indian' which it consciously negates. That is, since *mestizo* identity is necessarily glossed as a mixture of the native and the Spanish (sometimes also admitting the input of other European and non-European cultures), it necessarily presupposes the existence of 'the Indian' – and the 'Spanish' – as a guarantee of its own signification.[9]

At this global level, the 'Spanish' (or 'European') and the 'Indian' ingredients of *mestizaje* are both fictions. Neither is, or ever was, homogeneous or unified. The 'Spanish' is given coherence as a recognisable cultural set through being identified with the Castilian language and with Catholicism; Indians is a generic category created by colonialism, through which its members were variously transformed and caught up in exogenous economic circuits and systems of knowledge. Many exotic features which today mark out Indian communities as distinctive, such as clothes and music, and the open field system of highland agriculture, have been shown to derive in good part from European models. The complexity of the current situation can perhaps best be summarized by saying that everything is mixed but not everything is *mestizo*. And yet, again and again the idea recurs that the *mestizo* is inauthentic in comparison with the two traditions from which it is derived.

In educated discourse, the contrasts between Indian, *mestizo* and European (and *cholo*, the transitional category between Indian and *mestizo*) may be indexed by genotype, education, language use, or socioeconomic position, but ultimately they rely on arguments from origins and a particular historical narrative. To 'explain' *mestizaje* involves returning to the point of origin: the moment when American women began to bear the children of the conquistadores, when the pagan Indians became Christians, when the Inca was replaced by Charles V. Language too is used as a marker of distinctive points of origin: Spanish 'comes from' Spain, Aymara and Quechua 'are' indigenous languages. When these are mixed, they give rise to the hybrid of Andean Spanish, which is not yet recognized as a distinctive language.

Linnekin and Poyer have made a useful and enlightening contrast between 'Mendelian' and 'Lamarckian' models of identity. The former is a bounded, closed reproductive system determined by biological inheritance, while the latter is not bounded, but open to environmental influences (Linnekin and Poyer 1990). Mendelian identity characterizes European ideas of nationhood. In the central Andes, the history of state forms, and the organization of fiscal obligations, have ensured the dominance of the Mendelian model in public discourse. The conceptual space within which ethnic labels are ascribed is that of the apparently fixed poles of Spanish and Indian. And outsiders conceptualize Indian identity in this way even though the historical evidence indicates that it is actually far more 'Lamarckian'. *Mestizaje*, by contrast, is Lamarckian, constantly threatening the production of fixed meanings, even though it is forever defined by its two points of origin.

Andeanist anthropology has contributed to a Mendelian discourse in the way that it has characteristically juxtaposed early historical sources with twentieth-century fieldwork, as historians found insight in ethnographic accounts for interpreting early colonial documents, and fieldworkers increasingly recognized that present-day practices resembled the accounts found in chronicles and documents of the sixteenth century, or at least echoed them in interesting ways. The demonstration of continuities was a response to the constant claims that today's Indians have lost the glories of Inca civilization. However, in the process, long-term antecedents of present-day practices were overemphasized to the detriment of the ways that the Indian communities themselves represent their past (in terms of discontinuity) and their present (in terms of a particular morality tied to highland agriculture, more than to origins).

What are the modalities which have been used to express the varieties of self-conception and the knowledges that they entail? While anthropologists today generally accept the hybrid nature of cultural creativity, the problem remains of how to conceptualize different forms of cultural flow or transfer, if we are to move beyond vague generalities. After all, the process is often a quite self-conscious affair, and articulated as such by the agents of cultural transformation.

To talk of mixing, syncretism or creolization depends on the prior assumption of recognisable difference based on relatively stable identity. This in turn begs many questions, since contrary to the Mendelian concept of identity as a closed system of reproduction, all cultural traditions are open to outside influences and are constantly borrowing and adapting to new encounters. On the other hand, there are also limits and boundary mechanisms: well-established means of contrasting and evaluating knowledges, whether in terms of their origins, their effects, or their truth conditions.

Thus, any argument which depends on origins as a means of identifying difference runs up against the difficulties first that there are no autonomous cultural traditions, and second that it is bound to fix and reify the distinctiveness of the contrasted cultures. This is precisely the argument used so often by nationalist discourse.

There are a number of different ways in which different knowledges and the relationships between them may be conceptualized. At issue is a politics of interpreting the new knowledges arising out of European annexation and evangelization. I have identified six which presuppose very different ideas of the nature of historical actors as moral agents.

1 The model of mixing or creolization. In classical anthropology, concepts such as acculturation or syncretism were used. These often concealed a tacit Eurocentrism since, *de facto*, it was not the general principle of cultural mixing that preoccupied anthropologists so much as the transformations wrought on different features of European culture and knowledge systems through the process of creolization (this is clear, for example, in Herskovits (1967)). Today hybridity is more positively celebrated by anthropologists (e.g. Sallman *et al.* 1992). As already argued, it presupposes fixed points of origin for the cultures which then mix, and in Latin American social discourse it involves constant regress to the historical point of origin in 1492, or the conquest of particular regions by the Spanish.

2 Given the extreme inequalities of power, many prefer a model of colonization, rather than the politically neutral language of 'culture contact', syncretism and so forth. For example Mignolo writes of the 'colonization of Amerindian languages and memories' (1992a). In favour of a 'colonization' model is the fact that the knowledge brought by the Europeans to the New World was in many aspects bounded and absolute, defining other forms as inferior or wrong, or the work of the devil.

The politics of this position are obvious, and draw support from the history of European annexation of the Andean region, with the forced imposition of Christianity, writing and, gradually, the Spanish language too. In the Andes today, it is commonplace for anything that appears to be similar to something Spanish or Christian to be labelled as European in origin. The striking implications of such assumptions are that the European is powerful and the indigenous is weak. We know well enough that politically and militarily this was the case, but it does not thereby follow that 'indigenous culture' should be reduced to a residue for which no European antecedent has (yet) been unearthed.

3 An alternative is to attribute more agency to the colonized, and phrase the relationship in terms of borrowing. This is premised on the assumption of

relatively autonomous traditions of knowledge which can be identified even though they change. The often sophisticated intellectuals of the former Inca state confronted the challenge of making sense of the new knowledge system in the late sixteenth century (Salomon 1982). As Tedlock has argued for the Popol Vuh, the Maya sacred text, it has too often been assumed that any part of the creation story that resonates with the book of Genesis must have been influenced by the Christian narrative. However, the presence of allusions to the Christians, and overlappings of narrative, does not conflict with its being 'authentic Quiche' (Tedlock 1983: 265–266).

4 A somewhat different strategy is that of juxtaposition or alternation, where two radically different knowledge systems are both accepted without a direct attempt at integration. For example Frank Salomon's innovative reading of indigenous writers of the late sixteenth and early seventeenth centuries argues that these were 'chronicles of the impossible' because they confronted 'the problem of combining two drastically differing viewpoints about the nature and usefulness of the past' (1982: 9). The incompatibility resided particularly in meaning attributed to past events by Christian narratives of salvation, and in the teleological ordering of time.

5 Another conceptualization which attributes agency is that of imitation or direct identification. I am thinking here of the self-conscious adoption of alternative knowledge or cultural forms in place of one's own. It involves a basic change of identity, unlike borrowing which implies continuity of identity through change. In the Andes, social mobility from Indian to *mestizo* usually involves wholesale rejection of Indian identity, in favour of and identification with what is seen as white or Hispanic (e.g. by change of name, diet, clothing, language).

6 Finally, an alternative mode is that of innovation and creativity (see, for example, Salmond, Chapter 2 in this volume). Here the attention is firmly removed from contrasted knowledge systems and priority is given to autonomy and independent agency. Unlike the previous types, this one does not focus on origins.

In the late twentieth century these ambiguities of relationship between different knowledge systems apply particularly clearly to formal education. The Kataristas, whose politics often derive from the tensions between their educational success and their sense of exclusion from national society, frequently favour a creolization model. Others see the education system currently in operation as a form of cultural genocide, a deliberate attempt to eliminate Indian 'ignorance' in favour of the knowledge offered by civilization. This view corresponds to the colonization model. On the other hand, the Indian communities rarely resist education, and often actively seek to establish schools. In Muruq'umarka for example, Don Roberto Yujra, as community authority in the 1940s, arranged for the first schoolteacher to come, paid by quotas from each household, as soon as the law changed to allow Indians to receive primary education. This might be seen as imitation or direct identification (the fifth type of relation between knowledges in my earlier listing). However, in a recent article concerning the meanings of literacy in the Indian communities of Northern Potosi, Platt suggests that the incorporation of aspects of literacy should be seen as evidence of the Indians' capacity to modernize themselves (1992). In other words, a relationship of borrowing or of creativity (respectively, my third and sixth types).

The dilemmas raised by school education today are not dissimilar to those that arose in the first decades of Christianization. In both cases, there is little evidence that the indigenous populations refuse(d) these new sources of global knowledge. On the contrary they recognize(d) their power and importance and avail(ed) themselves of them. In both cases what has proved problematic is the exclusivity of the new form of knowledge, its denial of the possibility of adapting to the local environment and transforming itself in the process. It is the boundedness of the global, its incompatibility with the local that stands out. Christianity and science both apply rigorous exclusionary principles of truth which devalue forms of knowledge that do not meet these criteria. In the case of Catholic Christianity, evidence of adherence to pre-Christian practice was proof for the early evangelists of the Indians' associations with the devil.[10] Today schooling is seen by townspeople as a way of civilizing the Indians who, once saved from their ignorance, will leave their state of savagery and become integrated into the nation. *De facto*, this contains an element of truth: those who have completed most of secondary school rarely stay to work the land, but try to join the ranks of the urban migrants, and begin the process of moving from Indian to *mestizo* status.

THE SPEECH OF THE ANCESTORS

How is this exclusivity of exogenous knowledge interpreted within the Indian communities themselves? The case of religious knowledge is particularly striking. There is a clear classificatory principle that distinguishes the upper from the lower world, marking off contrasted deities, sources of knowledge and their attendant practices. The lower, or inner, world is the domain of the pre-Christian ancestors, the deities of the earth and mountains, beings known generically as *saxra* – a term which is often glossed by the Spanish word for devil. By contrast the upper celestial world is often known as *tyusa parti* (God's part), associated with the rites of the Catholic Church and saints, and presided over by the sun and moon gods.

Many ethnographers have mentioned ways in which the two domains are treated as utterly distinct. For example, certain rituals pertaining to the lower world are not carried out if a priest is present, since he officiates for the deities of the upper world; and there is no overlap of objects or paraphernalia in the practices and observations associated with each (Harris and Bouysse-Cassagne 1987).

These two contrasted systems of knowledge can be identified with the local/

global polarity. Knowledge of, and communication with, the inner world is locally based, bounded and secret. It is focused primarily on local mountains, who are the source of shamanic power and of fertility, who embody the remote ancestors, and are the guardians of local communities. By contrast, the priests who communicate with the deities of the upper world come from outside, speak foreign languages, and are part of a global organization and hierarchy.

This correlation is far from complete: Indians too can communicate with God and the saints, and the latter are directly grounded in the local, as patrons of particular churches or communities. Moreover, the inner world of the *saxra*s and the mountain spirits may be identified in terms of particular places, but it also contains 'universal' features. For example, the local mountains form part of an encompassing regional hierarchy at whose apex are the highest peaks of the Cordillera Real. Furthermore the only religious feasts that I have heard referred to as 'universal' (*muntu intiru*) are those of the dead and the ancestors, who form part of the inner world (Harris 1982).

Nonetheless, this identification – of the inner world with the local and the upper world with the global – does have some salience, particularly as a basis for identifying the sources of knowledge. In the Amazon region of Colombia the Macuna talk of having 'two cultures', one relating to traditional songs and dances, and the other to new forms from outside, which are performed on separate dance areas (Kaj Arhem, personal communication). Similarly, in Northern Potosi, the sources of knowledge of the inner world of the *saxra*s come from direct encounters with them, and are therefore direct, personal and local. This is less true for the upper world whose presiding deities are the universal sun and moon, and knowledge of which involves the Catholic priests.

It may be more appropriate to think in terms of a contrast between the local and the exogenous, rather than the global, and to interpret this distinction as one concerning the sources of knowledge rather than their origins (as in the 'Mendelian' model outlined above). By juxtaposing these two sources of religious knowledge Indian thought is able to sidestep the issue of the exclusive nature of Christianity. They are based on different principles, each with its proper place in the life of the community and the ordering of the cosmos, and they alternate in the cycle of rituals, and in the influence they have on human affairs.

These two systems of knowledge are also related in a temporal sequence. According to myth, the world of the pre-Christian ancestors was one of half-light, in contrast to the sun whose dawning heralded the coming of the present Christian age. It is tempting to associate this opposition with the historical process of conversion to Christianity, since the upper world is that of daylight, of the present Christian world age, whereas the world of the *saxra*s corresponds to an inner space of twilight, dominated by the pre-Christian ancestors and the mountains which are their present-day manifestations. In this way religious classification is a constitutive form of knowledge concerning the past, providing the founding periodization that coordinates such knowledge.

The kinds of knowledge about the past derived from the two domains are also contrasted. There is a class of people identified as 'those who know' (*yatiri*), who can enter into communication with the inner world of the *saxra*s. The term is used of those who have undergone an initiation into esoteric knowledge, often precipitated through being struck by lightning, and de-veloped by learning from an already established *yatiri*. This knowledge derives from two particular skills: the art of divination by reading coca leaves, and the strength to speak to the lightning and the *saxra*s.[11] The contrast between light and darkness seems to have a universal salience as a guiding metaphor. In Northern Potosi, everyday knowledge of 'this world', associated with the light and vision, is distinguished from esoteric knowledge which evolves from the darkness, and the ability to speak with the spirits of the twilight. The momentary, potentially lethal, flash of lightning that initiates the *yatiri* is a brief intense illumination in this otherwise shadowy domain.[12]

These specialists of esoteric knowledge are healers as well as diviners, and they are central to the performance of any ritual that involves the mountains, the earth and the *saxra*. The figures in the landscape that are most identified with the remote ancestors speak through them, as do the recently dead.

The knowledge of the *yatiri* is an intelligent capacity, an understanding grounded in his or her experience of the deities of the inner world.[13] In this sense it has very little to do with information. *Yatiri*s are mediums for knowledge that comes from that world, rather than being themselves the repository of knowledge. De Certeau has referred to the writing of history as a way of resuscitating the dead through discourse (1988: 46–47). For the peasants of Northern Potosi there is dialogue with the dead, carried out through the medium of 'those who know', more than discourse about them. At the same time, in ritual the dead are directly embodied in the living. Here again, the power and reproductive capacity of the dead are transmitted directly to the living, not through the medium of the written word, or even of particular narratives.

In contrast to the directness of this communication, there are other people of whom it is said '*layra timpu sum yatiw*' – 'they know well the before times'. *Yati-* refers both to propositional knowledge, to direct experience, and to having skills and ability ('knowing how'). To speak of somebody as 'knowing well the before times' is to refer to a particular skill: that of telling stories. Such people not only have a fund of stories about 'before times', but also possess the performance skills to tell them, using a range of different voices and of onomatopoeic resources which are considered essential to a good narrative. Knowledge in this context is not only a question of knowing the stories but even more one of 'knowing how', and both of these aspects of knowledge are handed down from one generation to the next. The good narrator's knowledge is authenticated by having been learnt and inherited from a close kinsperson (either female or male). The stories themselves are myths (*kwintu*, from the Spanish *cuento*) mainly concerning the 'unquiet time' before differences between humans, animals and birds were clearly established, and the pastness of them is frequently emphasized in the telling, for example by the ending 'that's how it was in before times'.

A distinction is made by Peruvian Quechua-speakers between myth of this kind (*kwintu*) and legend (*leyenda*). Legend is said to be 'true' in that it refers to a particular place, whereas myths are not legitimated in this way, and are not anchored usually in the reality of 'this world' (Howard-Malverde 1990). In Northern Potosi historical narratives concerning 'this world' are not a distinctive named genre, but they are identifiable in that they recount how people fought to defend their land, or events that occurred in particular places. The emphasis in such narratives is on the land itself, how people acquired rights to it, and how those rights were defended.

There is no particular association between shamanic knowledge and the skill of 'knowing the before times' in the sense of narrating the myths. Whether these skills are considered incompatible or merely quite different I am not clear, but I have come across only one person who was thought to have them both. The difference resides in the source of knowledge. In the case of the narrators, their source is an older kinsperson, whereas for the *yatiri*, it is direct communication with the beings of the inner world.

The central value accorded to the land and to particular places in articulating the present with the past of 'this world' is exemplified by the importance attached to written documents. In Northern Potosi, every community owns documents referred to as *layra papilanaka* (old papers), which include in some cases copies of sixteenth- and seventeenth-century legal confirmation of particular *ayllus*' possession of their lands (Platt 1992). Such papers are treated with great reverence and kept secret, protected from the gaze of outsiders and celebrated with offerings. These documents are potent as a source of knowledge, but few if any of their owners can read them. Howard-Malverde suggests that stories and arguments about rights to land, which are so central to the historical narratives of 'this world', function as 'the oral counterpart of the written document of the land title' (1990: 45, also Platt 1992, Rappaport 1990), a local oral exegesis concerning a written form of knowledge whose source and whose interpretation both derive from the exogenous world of literate Spanish-speakers. Such documents constitute a codified, objectified synthesis of particular knowledge of the past.

The Aymara language places great emphasis on direct experience as a source of knowledge, and also the importance of specifying the source of one's data (Hardman *et al.* 1974: 31, 212–226). In the case of events that occurred a long time ago, direct experience is not at issue, and therefore the source of a person's knowledge is particularly important as a means of authenticating it. In the case of the knowledge of *yatiris* it is based on direct experience, but for that reason it is not propositional knowledge about the past, but communication with ancestors in the present.[14]

There is a further means by which people are connected to the past that should be mentioned. This is the way that certain objects embody the past directly. Things such as old coins or ancient weavings may constitute a sort of 'fecund archetype' of the regenerative powers of the ancestors. They are protected from the gaze of outsiders and celebrated with offerings. These objectifications of the past are closely guarded, and their loss would be a serious threat to the wellbeing or even the survival of their owners. Old documents, especially those relating to land, have something of the same status. They too are celebrated with offerings and guarded from the eyes of those outside the immediate group to whom they belong. Thus, paradoxically, documents not only represent the crystallization of knowledge through writing, but also something far more immediate: a direct communication from the ancestors who first obtained them, and who entrusted them to their descendants.[15]

CONCLUSION

One of the most striking aspects of the way knowledge of the past is orchestrated in the Indian communities of Northern Potosi is the way it is dispersed amongst different individuals, households and kin groups. Myth-tellers are thought to 'know best the before times', but their stories are generalized ones, not attached to particular people or places. Sacred objects are usually owned by individual households or kin groups, and stories about the land, about wars or migrations, or about the founding of particular communities, are usually restricted to the individuals who have heard them from a kinsperson. When I asked people to tell me about events from the past, they would often respond in puzzlement that I must know much more than they did since I could read books. Denise Arnold has noted a similar pattern of dispersal in neighbouring Qaqachaka, particularly with reference to the different historical knowledges of women and men (1994).[16]

Many anthropologists have noted that concentrated knowledge concerning the past is a function of politico-religious power and authority (Feeley-Harnik 1978: 402; cf. also Sahlins 1985: 48–53).[17] In Northern Potosi there is some degree of concentration of knowledge, for example in the case of old documents. If they concern the lands of the whole *ayllu* they may be kept by the highest authority who functions to maintain this knowledge in a centralized form, as the person who with his wife embodies the *ayllu* as collective landholding unit. Complementing this centralization in the person of the political authority is a spatial focus on a central place, known in Aymara as *marka*.

The writing of history involves a systematization and a concentration of knowledge about the past. It strives for continuity. Furthermore, given the strength of nationalist influences in western historiography, it contributes to producing an identity for collective political subjects.[18] It is a form of emergent self-knowledge. The subject of historical narration is typically a social collectivity deriving from the romantic identification of a nation with its past. These are the historical narratives considered an essential part of the school education of children, by which they learn a particular collective identity.

Bolivian national historiography has had little place for the Indian majority of its citizens. The Katarista historians have made impressive efforts (aided by ethnohistorians and anthropologists) to rewrite history in order that they should become the subject of historical narratives. This goes hand in hand with the project of a more integrated political organization and a greater centralization of identity. How far their efforts constitute recovery of a previously existing historical vision that has been lost, and how far they constitute a form of 'invention' is at this stage a matter for speculation. Children in the communities of Northern Potosi learn the basics of Bolivian history in school, but unless their schooling lasts for more than a few years they do not internalize it in such a way that they retell it as their own. They may in addition be taught the stories of collective resistance that the Kataristas have promoted as their own. This is not to say that the Indians do not consider themselves to be Bolivians, or indeed Indians. But the fashioning of collective identity does not seem to be the main purpose of the historical narratives they tell in their own communities.

'The local' is often assumed to have an intrinsic unity based on the natural singularity of place. But the degree of dispersal of historical knowledge in the *ayllu*s gives pause for thought. Insofar as people tell narratives about the events of previous centuries, or at least of a time before they were in a position to witness them themselves, they do not just tell their own private histories, or those of their immediate forebears. Nonetheless, what they tell is partial and does not attempt to give a rounded history of a place. The dispersal of knowledge concerning the past has the effect that different, potentially conflicting narratives coexist with no attempt to create a unified or continuous version.

The clash of knowledges in anthropological debate has usually been discussed in terms of rationality (for example Tambiah 1990). Historiography has its own versions of dichotomy between supposedly alien and incompatible modes of thought. The most familiar is that between myth and history. Western historiography proposes that society is the product of causes which approximate to general laws that can be arrived at through the pursuit of objective knowledge and the systematic use of archival sources as instruments to this end. For professional historians, ideally the past is 'other'. They are detached, working through archives rather than *doxa*, while myth scarcely counts as knowledge at all. A second dichotomy is that between people who 'have history' and those who 'lack' it. The latter, so it is often claimed, thereby lack a sense of their own identity. While this concept of identity, grounded in a continuous narrative from a point of origin, has become very compelling it cannot be treated as the only one.

Knowledge of the past is not usually phrased in terms of mixing or creolization. However, in the new histories emerging from the peoples of the

Fourth World, the exclusivity of western historiographical methods is some-times refused in favour of a self-consciously hybrid approach. In the writings of Katarista historians, myths about snake children and enchanted lakes are juxtaposed with citations from legal documents (Mamani 1989; THOA 1992). In this way they are trying to overcome the tensions and contradictions between the 'global' knowledge of western historiography with its concerns for factuality and continuity, and the plural knowledges of the past from their own rural communities, which emphasize discontinuity and an immediacy of contact with that past.

NOTES

1 An *ayllu* is a large landholding group with a distinctive identity and hierarchy of indigenous authorities.
2 For discussions of similar refrains, see Price (1983), Barth (1987), Strathern (1992: 97–98).
3 *Anthropology Today* (February 1992), cited by John Knight (1993).
4 As Lass, writing of early Czech nationalism has observed, for old documents to be 'discovered' they first had to be lost: 'History (like memory) depends on the cultural production of absence. . . . That which is presented to us in historical terms must first be absent' (1988: 467–468).
5 After Tupaj Katari, the insurgent who laid seige to La Paz in 1781 and presented the Spanish government with one of its greatest threats (Albo 1987).
6 Only recently have these 'people without history' been reclaimed by anthropo-logists, oral historians and others as knowers of a particular form of the past, more alive and more esoteric precisely because it is handed down from speaker to audience rather than via written documents.
7 I would take issue with Hannerz's claim that creolization is taking place with 'unique intensity' in the twentieth century. The case of sixteenth-century highland Latin America was arguably every bit as intense. As Eduardo Archetti has pointed out, some of the issues which now preoccupy all anthropologists have long been at the heart of the anthropology of Latin America, for example the questions of different knowledge systems, and of mixing and syncretism as long-term phenomena (personal communication).
8 Waman Puma, an Andean nobleman writing in the early seventeenth century, expresses an equally virulent opposition to any kind of racial mixing, equating it to miscegenation between animal species (Waman Puma 1980).
9 A related point, *à propos* of musical creolization, has been made by Steven Feld: the contemporary phenomenon of fluid intermixing of musical styles characterized as 'world beat' requires as a condition of its own existence that the distinctive traditions of 'world music' be maintained at the same time (Feld forthcoming).
10 Today there are still many priests and Protestant pastors working in rural areas who make it their business to try and root out surviving pagan practices. However, there are also sections of the Catholic Church that adopt a more relativist position these days, and assert the need for Christian *numina* to adopt a radically localized form.
11 In this context, Tomas Huanca's translation of *saxra* as 'the unknown' (*lo desconocido*) indicates how esoteric this knowledge is (1989: 103).
12 In some regions these spirit mediums are known in Aymara as *ch'amakani*, 'imbued with darkness'. In Southern Peru, the formative experiences for acquiring

the skill to communicate with the deities of below involve entering into caves, or travelling to the lowland *montaña* (Sarah Skar, personal communication).

13 Pascal Boyer's valuable discussion of the bases of esoteric knowledge emphasizes that it is inductive, not based on general principles (1990).

14 Literate people like me, or the children in secondary school, gain knowledge from books. We are said to be *sum layraniw*, with good eyes, well-endowed with sight. This specifies the source of knowledge as being the eyes, rather than direct experience, or communication from another person. Those who 'have good eyes' can read books, and the Indians of Northern Potosi know that in books, as in old documents, is stored vast quantities of information about the past, but it does not have the immediacy of authentication that orally transmitted knowledge does. Mamani discusses the significance of the homonym *layra*, used to denote both the past and the eye (1989: 57–58).

15 These objects, closely guarded by their owners, are in marked contrast to other objects from the past that turn up in all the pre-Columbian archaeological sites. The Indian communities feel no sense of ownership over these, and their loss does not affect them directly. It was I, not they, who became indignant over cases of treasure seekers, including some rural schoolteachers, who plundered local sites and removed every artefact they encountered.

16 Price's outstanding study of the Surinamese Saramaka describes the extreme dispersal of historical knowledge and the problem it raises for anthropologists (1983).

17 Rappaport makes a similar point about the Colombian Paez in explaining why certain people became historians: 'in cases in which a broad-based organization is needed, a universal history will begin to surface' (1990: 22).

18 This is not to deny that some strands of western historical thought have aimed for a universal scope. For Lord Acton the story of individual nations was subsidiary to 'the common fortunes of mankind' (Carr 1964: 150), while others have projected the vision of a universal history in a more focused way around a particular abstract subject, from Hegel to Braudel to Fukuyama.

REFERENCES

Albo, X. (1987) 'From MNRistas to Kataristas to Katari', in S. Stern (ed.) *Resistance, Rebellion and Consciousness in the Andean Peasant World*, Madison: University of Wisconsin Press.
Arnold, D. (1994) 'Adam and Eve and the red-trousered ant', *Travesía* 2(1): 49–83.
Barth, F. (1987) *Cosmologies in the Making*, Cambridge: Cambridge University Press.
Biersack, A. (1991) 'Introduction', in A. Biersack (ed.) *Clio in Oceania*, Washington, D.C.: Smithsonian Institution Press.
Bouysse-Cassagne, T. (1994) 'Incertitudes identitaires métisses: l'éloge de la bâtardise', *Caravelle* 62: 111–134.
Boyer, P. (1990) *Tradition as Truth and as Communication*, Cambridge: Cambridge University Press.
Carr, E.H. (1964) *What is History?*, Harmondsworth: Penguin.
Carrier, J. (1987) 'History and self-conception in Ponam society', *Man* (N.S.) 22(1): 111–131.
de Certeau, M. (1988) *The Writing of History*, New York: Columbia University Press.
Demelas, M-D. (1981) 'Darwinismo a la criolla: el darwinismo social en Bolivia 1809–1910', *Historia Boliviana* 1/2: 55–82.
Feeley-Harnik, G. (1978) 'Divine kingship and the meaning of history among the Sakalava of Madagascar', *Man* (N.S.) 13(3): 402–417.
Feld, S. (forthcoming) 'From schizophonia to schismogenesis: on the discourses and

commodification practices of "world music" and "world beat"', in C. Reid and S. Feld (eds) *Music Grooves*, Chicago: University of Chicago Press.

Garcilaso de la Vega, 'El Inca' (1960) [1609] *Comentarios reales de los incas*, in Fr Carmelo Saenz de Sta María (ed.) Biblioteca de Autores Españoles, Vols 133–135, Madrid.

Handler, R. (1988) *Nationalism and the Politics of Culture in Quebec*, Madison: University of Wisconsin Press.

Hannerz, U. (1987) 'The world in creolization', *Africa* 57(4): 546–559.

Hardman-de-Bautista, M., Vasquez, J. and Yapita Moya, J. (1974) *Outline of Aymara Phonological and Grammatical Structure*, Vol. 3, Ann Arbor: University Microfilms.

Harris, O. (1982) 'The dead and the devils among the Bolivian Laymi', in M. Bloch and J. Parry (eds) *Death and the Regeneration of Life*, Cambridge: Cambridge University Press.

—— (1995a) 'Ethnic identity and market relations: Indians and *mestizos* in the Andes', in B. Larson, O. Harris, and E. Tandeter (eds) *Ethnicity, Markets and Migration in the Andes*, Durham, North Carolina: Duke University Press.

—— (1995b) 'The temporalities of tradition', in V. Hubinger (ed.) *Grasping the Changing World*, London: Routledge.

Harris, O. and Bouysse-Cassagne, T. (1987) 'Pacha: en torno al pensamiento aymara', in X. Albo (ed.) *Raíces de América: el mundo aymara*, Madrid: Alianza Editorial with UNESCO.

Herskovits, M. (1967) 'Introduction', in S. Tax (ed.) *Acculturation in the Americas*, New York: Cooper Square Publishers Incorporated.

Howard-Malverde, R. (1990) *The Speaking of History: 'Willapaakushayki' or Quechua Ways of Telling the Past*, University of London: Institute of Latin American Studies Research Papers 21.

Huanca, T. (1989) *El yatiri en la comunidad aymara*, La Paz: Ediciones CADA.

Knight, J. (1993) 'On public ignorance', *Anthropology Today* 9(2): 1–2.

Lass, A. (1988) 'Romantic documents and political monuments: the meaning-fulfilment of history in nineteenth century Czech nationalism', *American Ethnologist* 15(3): 456–471.

Linnekin, J. and Poyer, L. (eds) (1990) *Cultural Identity and Ethnicity in the Pacific*, Honolulu: University of Hawaii Press.

Mamani, C. (1989) 'History and prehistory in Bolivia: what about the Indians?', in R. Layton (ed.) *Conflict in the Archaeology of Living Traditions*, London: Unwin Hyman.

Mignolo, W. (1992a) 'On the colonization of Amerindian languages and memories', *Comparative Studies of Society and History* 34: 301–330.

—— (1992b) 'Misunderstanding and colonization: the reconfiguration of memory and space'. Paper presented to *Le nouveau monde – mondes nouveaux: l'expérience américaine*, Conference of CERMACA, Ecole des Hautes Etudes en Sciences Sociales, Paris.

Platt, T. (1992) 'Writing, shamanism and Latin American identity: voices from Abya-yala', *History Workshop Journal* 34: 132–147.

Price, R. (1983) *First-Time. The Historical Vision of an Afro-American People*, Baltimore: Johns Hopkins University Press.

Rappaport, J. (1990) *The Politics of Memory. Native Historical Interpretation in the Colombian Andes*, Cambridge: Cambridge University Press.

Robertson, R. (1990) 'After nostalgia: wilful nostalgia and modernity', in B. Turner (ed.) *Theories of Modernity and Postmodernity*, London: Sage.

Sahlins, M. (1985) *Islands of History*, Chicago: University of Chicago Press.

Sallman, J-M., Gruzinski, S., Molinie-Fioravanti, A. and Salazar, C. (1992) *Visions indiennes, visions baroques: les métissages de l'inconscient*, Paris: PUF.

Salomon, F. (1982) 'Chronicles of the impossible: notes on three Peruvian indigenous historians', in R. Adorno (ed.) *From Oral to Written Expression*, Latin American Series no.4, Syracuse: Maxwell School of Citizenship and Public Affairs.

Strathern, M. (1992) *After Nature*, Cambridge: Cambridge University Press.

Tambiah, S. (1990) *Magic, Science, Religion and the Scope of Rationality*, Cambridge: Cambridge University Press.

Tedlock, D. (1983) *The Spoken Word and the Work of Interpretation*, Philadelphia: University of Pennsylvania Press.

THOA (1992) 'The Indian Santos Marka T'ula', *History Workshop Journal* 34: 101–118.

Waman Puma, F. (1980) [1615] *Nueva coronica y buen gobierno* [1615], ed. J.V. Murra and R. Adorno, Mexico: Siglo XXI.

6 It takes one to know one
Collective resentment and mutual recognition among Greeks in local and global contexts[1]

Michael Herzfeld

MIND AND BODY: FORMAL DUALISM IN EVERYDAY LIFE

This paper takes a commonplace ethnographic dilemma, and treats it as an analytical issue. At a time when anthropologists are no longer willing to accept 'the village' as the focus of exclusive attention, and where even the most localized studies must account for the co-presence of ever larger encompassments, body and person exert a centripetal counter-argument. The tension is all the more inescapable because so many of the larger entities, notably the nation-state, paradoxically ground their respective claims to a wide and inclusive reach in the embodied person – generically reconceptualized, or metonymically 'imagined' (Anderson 1983), as an ideal-typical average citizen.

My quest here is for a pragmatic understanding of how such claims actually work – and what they do – in everyday life. How do people, reduced by an encompassing national discourse to the bare outlines of an ideal type, in turn expand their own practical bodily and local knowledge to meet the challenges of their place as members of a national entity in the wider global context? People who were once thought to belong to a local community alone, and who were in most cases never so isolated as observers condescendingly thought them to be, now demonstrably travel, meet tourists, and hear international media discussing 'them'. What is the basis on which they react to these 'new' contexts? What is the collective self from which their knowledge of others proceeds?

The various, mostly unpleasant reifications that we lump together as 'nationalism' are the arenas where this tension between the near and the far, the immediate and the abstract, is most readily – because most tangibly – explored. There are media and academic texts, public demonstrations, conversations at many levels of privacy, and the symbolism of postage stamps and paid advertising. Whatever the specific historical reasons, the prima facie evidence of rampant nationalism at the very end of the twentieth century, just when everyone 'logically' thought its time was past, suggests that nationalism is indeed the place to explore the question of how people – those embodiments of local interests – find their way around in a world still felt to be too large to call home. And the encounters that ordinary people have, not only with tourists and other foreigners, but above all with each other, are the most accessible site for an ethnographic investigation of such matters.

I emphasize the significance of the ways in which people know each other at home because, without that information, we shall be at a loss to decipher the kinds of sense they make of (to them) exotic others. This is one area in which anthropology can, through its local ethnographic focus, help to explain why nationalism and prejudice seem to exercise such an effective grip on people's imaginations and emotions. In the present paper, I shall be less concerned with the way that Greeks 'read' Danish or French tourists, or the Germans and others among whom they have sojourned as migrant workers, than with the much more opaque processes through which they construct and reproduce the images of a collective self. While these two processes are far from unrelated to each other, it is the production of a local selfhood on which nationalism then contrastively builds images of bizarre and un-wholesome others; and it is therefore the interaction between nation-level self-stereotyping and the immediate forms of social interaction at home that must primarily concern us here. What is it that Greeks 'know' about each other, and that they equally 'know' foreigners not to possess? How do they acquire this form of knowledge?

To a degree that can only embarrass a field as committed as is social anthropology to the rejection of essentialism in all its forms, the members of many a national entity claim the ability, often invested with mystical force, to 'sense' others of their kind: 'I always know a *Landsmann*'. Without subscribing to such ideas, we nonetheless cannot afford to ignore them, for they represent the views of local social actors about the embodiment of identity, and clearly afford a sort of certainty – however spurious – in an uncertain world. They may sound old-fashioned, even racist; they may even be demonstrably unreliable; but they appear in modern, transnational settings as a common currency of solidarity among people who might otherwise never be able to meet or communicate – the stranger in the airport, the sports fan at the game. They are the equipment with which ordinary people try to find a toehold on modernity's glassy face; and they are, quite clearly, continually worked over at home.

Thus, we should aim for a balance between rightly refusing to generalize about 'the Greeks' – to take the example with which I shall be primarily concerned here – and acknowledging that Greeks themselves do this all the time. What is the basis for the latter phenomenon, and how does it generate that sense that any Greek can recognize another Greek anywhere? In a society with strongly localist tendencies as well as equally strident nationalism, what makes this recognition both possible and – since it *is* something of an embarrassment to our cherished creeds – anthropologically interesting?

CULTURAL INTIMACY?

There are some obvious elements: language, religion, even physical appearance. But to some extent these facile answers merely imitate nationalistic
discourse, which is hardly a site of intimacy in any sense. Indeed, nationalistic discourse in Greece actually *rejects* the more intimate dimensions of
Greek social and cultural life as being 'foreign' to its externally constituted
form (Herzfeld 1982, 1987). In contrast to the official ideology, according to
which localism simply refracts national virtue (and sometimes also corrupts
it), I suggest that there is a great deal of Greekness that the official ideology
would rather not know about, including a high degree of localism and
factionalism, but that it is precisely these features – embodied in social
attitudes and physical movement (see also Cowan 1990) but rarely articulated
in speech as a positive virtue – that constitute the basis of this confident
mutual recognition among Greeks. In Greece, the body has usually been
viewed as the contested and all too violable space of an individual's social
worth, whether assessed sexually or in other terms (Campbell 1964: 335;
Hirschon 1978). It is thus peculiarly appropriate that embodied knowledge
should in turn constitute the site of a self-knowledge not to be vouchsafed to
the inquisitive eye of the domineering official or the powerful foreigner.

Much current anthropological literature inveighs, rightly, against the
arbitrary separation of mind and body. This critical tradition originates at
least in part in Vico's (1744) twin observations that, while all truth is
constructed mentally, the mind's images are rooted in sensory experience –
an insight that has multiply ironic implications in an era when nationalisms
of various sorts claim the collective body as their ground.[2] But this move,
necessary and important though it is, entails a major risk. If it leads us
indiscriminately to deny the existence of all forms of dualism, it may
discourage the analysis of those several local discourses in which dualistic
formulations are significant elements for local actors themselves – and where
these formulations may also serve as the observable traces left by the
penetration of local discourses by larger and more intrusive ones (see
Herzfeld 1987: 115–116; Seremetakis 1991: 221–222). There is also a substantial danger of actually reproducing dualism at the very moment of denial,
as, for example, when local conflations of the mind–body opposition with
gender polarity seem to suggest that embodied experience is exclusively and
literally female; such a monolithic reading would trivialize the conditions of
state control under which gender becomes a metaphor for other kinds of
inequality (see Ferguson 1984).

The risk is that of confusing a flawed methodological representation (those
generalizing binary oppositions that are especially characteristic of certain
strains of structuralism) with actual ethnographic data about representation.
Even granted that methodological binarism is indeed reductive and fails to
respect local ways of conceptualizing social reality, we should not confuse
methodology with its object any more than we should mistake an intrusive

official binarism for the local symbols that it may have co-opted. The analysis of polarities is only deterministic when it mistakes them for the determining agents in their own right, rather than viewing them as symbolic capital which is at once the object, the instrument, and the expression of contest.

The inhabitants of the Cretan town of Rethemnos – and many other Greeks besides – make a strong categorical opposition between the work of the hands and the work of the mind. That is, they themselves articulate a distinction that anthropology has come to distrust. To a recognizable degree, the opposition they posit is an expression of class differences (Bourdieu 1984; Willis 1977). One key informant, a theoretically minded left-wing political and cultural activist of working-class background, told me that this distinction is clearly of Marxist inspiration. Such historically informed understandings are far from rare in the field situation with which I am concerned here, and should warn us against the temptation of reifying class and thus also of accepting its self-essentializing properties. The rhetoric of mind versus hands is not simply the objective mark of a class identity. On the contrary, it is part of a complex vocabulary of interaction that entails the use of irony (Chock 1987) and tactics (de Certeau 1984). It both reproduces the dominant ideology and attempts, with varying degrees and possibilities of success, to subvert the intentions that underlie it. Just as I was finishing up the last draft of this paper, I asked a close friend in Rethemnos why she insisted on keeping her watch set at the 'old time' (i.e., summer time). '[Because] I'm backward', she replied, effectively putting me in my embarrassed place. Such claims to a working-class and 'oriental' version of Greek identity are, I submit, the elements that sometimes serve to create a sense of 'national' solidarity in patently global settings (such as the airport again). They are the experiential basis of that recognition out of which cultural intimacy is built. They are also the bricks of the wall that is sometimes used to keep others out.

ETHNOGRAPHIC SETTING: INTERESTS IN FLUX

The ethnographic site of this discussion is Rethemnos,[3] a town with about 6,000 inhabitants living in a walled Renaissance zone and some 14,000 others inhabiting a slightly phantasmagoric and rapidly expanding seaside resort of high-rise buildings and dusty outlets to the main Chania–Iraklio highway. I first did some very simplistic field research here in 1970 and returned for a year's research on historic conservation and its problems in 1986–1987 and for a summer's initial probe into apprenticeship in 1992, following up with a year's field research in 1993–1994. Rethemnos is also the capital of the region of the village where I conducted research on agonistic masculinity between 1974 and 1981. Although the comments that follow are necessarily somewhat preliminary and programmatic, they are thus at least grounded in an intense acquaintance with the place itself.

Politically, like much of the rest of Crete, Rethemnos is the site of a fairly balanced contest between the socialist movement (PASOK), now the national ruling party, and the New Democracy (conservative) party, which currently holds the local mayoralty and controls the town council; an alliance of communist groups comes a poor third in most municipal elections, and the two major parties now usually split the prefecture's two seats between them in national elections. The Rethemnos economy is largely dependent on tourism, the earlier local industries – especially soap manufacture – having long since lost out to industrialized competition. While there has always been a class structure, with the most prominent distinction being made between the 'aristocracy' (actually an educated merchant and professional class) and the working class, both groups have traditionally drawn on the rural hinterland for replenishment and many family names are found at both extreme ends of this polarized spectrum. To the extent that an aristocracy exists, it is an aristocracy of wealth; but today the influx of non-local entrepreneurs, largely attracted by the commercial possibilities offered by the tourist industry, has cramped the style of the 'old families', most of whose representatives have left for Athens and overseas.

These local differences pale in the face of the massive contrasts introduced by the tourist presence. The tourists – and, through them, all foreigners – are the object of grandiose pontification about national character. Some nations (e.g., the Finns) are lauded for being straightforward and easy customers, while on the other hand the Germans are excoriated for their insistence on bargaining (which most Rethemniots interpret as relegating them to the role of picturesque orientals) and the British for their rowdiness. In general terms, the highly visible docility of package tour groups evokes derisive comments about 'little sheep' who are easily cowed, in contrast to the wily and unruly Greeks: whether the Greeks prefer to view themselves as revolutionaries (the socialists and communists) or as entrepreneurs (the New Democracy conservatives), they have inverted the ideological stereotype of the true European as an individualist and present it as the key virtue – or vice – of self-regard, the attitude that prevents them from meekly accepting subjugation to foreign powers but also from achieving unity, efficiency, and access to real power.

This knowledge of other nations, however stereotypical, means that transcendence of the boundaries of place is not confined to the wealthy, as it largely was in the past. New educational opportunities for study in Italy and elsewhere have also allowed the children of recent rural migrants to ascend the social ladder. But it is not only the new intensity of contact with the outside world that has loosened the never very rigid lines of class identity. While some of the older 'aristocratic' families were identifiable by surnames of Venetian origin, for example, several village families that have recently migrated to the town similarly bear such names and have learned enough of the official historiography to make comparable claims to ancestral distinction. Class lines in Rethemnos are highly negotiable.

Nor do they correspond to political divisions. Some of the wealthiest and best-educated professionals (for example, at least two pharmacists) are active members of the left-wing parties, while small traders and artisans of village origin often seek to consolidate their economic gains by making common cause with the conservatives. Such dualities as do surface in this arena are palpably rhetorical. A highly conservative trade unionist, for example, who today runs a tourist souvenir shop while also serving as the local agent for several major food manufacturers, spoke of the 'anti-democratic' actions of the socialists – until his son-in-law, a socialist, was beaten up by some of the conservative youth movement's toughs. Another conservative unionist – who lost his power base to communist rivals – accuses the government of pandering to Turkish demands by preserving the Ottoman remains in the Old Town; meanwhile, a communist house-painter, outraged by the government's imposition of strict restoration procedures on the houses of the Old Town, rails about the unconstitutionality of this violation – as he portrays it – of property rights (Herzfeld 1991: 192); now that he has become a small businessman, moreover, he also insists on the necessity of creating business competition. In an age when the socialists have rediscovered the neo-Classical virtues and claimed them for themselves, and when conservative propagandists play the rhetoric of local self-government back at the political left, it is important to recall that institutional political parties do not have a monopoly on any given rhetoric; on the contrary, rhetorical strategies are themselves the object of contest. Methodologically, there is a parallel in what this implies with the shift away from analysing moral values such as 'honour and shame' as systems and towards examining the pragmatic negotiation of such values in observed social action. It also suggests that the mutually contrasted images of foreign tourists and Greeks are not as fixed as they may seem, and that they, too, may provide a surprisingly flexible set of ideas for negotiating one's way into an initially unfamiliar global universe.

Much of what I am saying here may be rather obvious. It is nonetheless difficult to keep it in focus when one listens to the passionate reifications offered by local actors, and especially to the characteristically binary rhetoric of identity. Sometimes a common frame such as kinship or political allegiance may bring out the contrasts more sharply. Thus, for example, two brothers, both communists and the sons of a deeply respected local artisan, had strikingly different perspectives on the constitution of real knowledge. One brother returned from years at sea (and with a fine command of English acquired during his travels) to marriage and the grinding necessity of supporting a family by returning to his now deceased father's craft; it is he, of the two brothers, who particularly emphasizes the significance of manual labour. The younger brother, who has so far shown no inclination to marry, lives off rents collected on properties he inherited from his father, plays a highly visible role in local cultural activities, and readily admits that he detests the kind of labour to which his brother is more or less condemned. It is not too deterministic to suggest that the respective rhetorics of these two men are finely calibrated to their actual situations, which are in turn the product of a combination of circumstances beyond their control and choices that each has made about the kind of life he wants to live. But when one does not have access to such knowledge of individual circumstances, the rigid binarisms of mind and body, and of elite and working class, occlude the complex and situationally uncertain conditions that have usually given them their salience for particular actors at particular moments.

Such conditions are constantly in flux. Thus, some have made professional transitions that would not have been possible in the era before tourism became the economic mainstay of the town. Thus, for example, the left-wing house-painter now directs a tourism agency (still officially called a 'union') through which he manages the many small guest-house operators; his own impassioned rhetoric of co-operation and democracy which marked the foundation of this operation (his closest partners were a leather-goods merchant and a pharmacist) did not avert eventual fragmentation or his assumption of effective control of the entire operation; on the contrary, they were instrumental in his achieving those goals while leaving his erstwhile partners looking like the self-interested operators that he clearly also was himself – as, presumably, everyone understood.

Does this mean that people are willing dupes of a rhetoric whose self-serving implications are obvious to all? I think this is too simplistic a dismissal of the complex negotiations involved. Rather, I suggest, people recognize a reservoir of extenuating formulae, whose very conventionality – perhaps in part through intimations of great antiquity[4] – makes it possible to accept socially what one may not in fact believe. Thus, as I have argued elsewhere (Herzfeld 1991: 92–96), Rethemniots who feel humiliated by some bureaucratic embarrassment are always willing to accuse generic neighbours of having betrayed them to the authorities; as with evil eye accusations, which are never person-specific, such devices allow one to seek a face-saving explanation in the generalized evil said to lurk in the community without having to risk social rupture by charging some specific individual with the offence. In the same way, the generic charge that Rethemniots are incapable of working together is often cited in Rethemnos as the reason for the collapse of the many attempts to create local industrial co-operatives. Such conveniently stereotypical attributions, which (like the 'image of limited good') have frequently surfaced in ethnographic writings as evidence of 'endemic' problems, are part of what we might call the political economy of rhetoric, and serve the divide-and-conquer strategies that maintain class division and economic exploitation at the local level. They also provide the basis for a sense of cultural solidarity that excludes outsiders precisely because it must deny the latter any access to such potentially damaging insight. Thus, the very set of concepts that appears to pit Greek against Greek, and Rethemniot against Rethemniot, is at the same time the affective disposition that binds them together. That disposition is rarely talked about, both because elaborate, abstract speech is itself often treated as extrinsic to working-class values, and because to talk about it would be to make a public spectacle of something grounded in secrecy and intimacy. How, then, is it generated? How is it reproduced? In order to suggest some possible means of access to these necessarily opaque phenomena, I shall turn shortly to two sites where attitudes towards power are clearly and demonstrably inculcated: the bureaucrat–client interaction, and the master–apprentice relationship.

BUREAUCRATS AS THIEVES

On the bureaucrats, since I have already published much of the relevant ethnographic material elsewhere (Herzfeld 1992), I shall be brief and schematic here. The major point is that accusations against bureaucrats for being 'thieves' must be seen in a context where the term has at least the following sources of cultural resonance:

1 The guerrillas of the War of Independence (1821–1833) were, as noted above, known as 'thieves'. While subsequent 'political philology' (I borrow the term from Wace and Thompson (1913: 9); see also Politis (1972:xii–xviii)) has tried to separate the term from its semantic referent, this has not proved effective in precisely those areas – notably the highland villages of west-central Crete – where endemic livestock theft continues to play a significant role in daily social life.
2 Indeed, although condemned for their actions by the authorities and by urban public opinion, especially outside Crete, the present-day sheep-thieves of the mountainous Milopotamos region of west-central Crete (Herzfeld 1985) know enough about the nationalist historiography to represent themselves as the legitimate heirs of the national revolutionary tradition, their opponents in the government as latter-day 'Turks'.
3 Local stereotypes of the Greeks, some of them quite self-congratulatory, represent the ability to steal, especially from the wealthy, as a national capacity. Something akin to Robin Hood and the ideal-type 'social bandit' (Hobsbawm 1969) is very much a part of the modern Greek social imagination.
4 Like their colleagues as far away as Japan (for example, Kondo 1990: 238; Singleton 1989), artisanal apprentices are expected to 'steal' their masters' ideas and techniques, and are even trained to do so. These expectations acquire a peculiar resonance among Greeks because, one may suspect, of an association among theft, masculinity, and Greekness that derives – at least in part – from the circumstances outlined in the previous three points.

In all these cases, the act of theft defines a boundary between insiders and outsiders, but it is a convertible boundary. The national hero who robs the rich to feed the poor exemplifies the virtues of the proud Greek freedom-fighter, as, in a rather back-handed way, does the stereotypical 'fixer', so that what starts as an act of alienation becomes instead a mark of inclusive identity. The sheep-thief who 'steals to make friends' expects, in other words, to convert rivalry into alliance through the mutual recognition of tough men.

And the apprentices, to whom we shall return shortly, develop skills at the expense of artisans who will eventually want, if these cunning youngsters develop such skills well enough, to turn them into business partners rather than letting them turn into potentially dangerous rivals. Thus, while the term 'thief' is negative in its implications, it always also encapsulates the possibility of conversion into a more positive categorical identification. And in all cases, too, it suggests the possibility of an alliance that, while serving the convenience of both partners, inevitably disadvantages someone else. The example of the sheep-thief is especially revealing in this last regard, since the alliances of tough men entail both the denigration of women (all the objects of contest from playing-cards and animals to brides are symbolically feminized in the men's discursive practices) and the exclusion of weaker men.

This puts the common dismissal of bureaucrats as 'thieves' in a new light. Complaints about the 'thefts' committed by bureaucrats constitute a collective, cultural alibi, much like that of the traitorous neighbourhood: all the world is in collusion against the victim, who thus becomes the ideal-typical representative of the whole oppressed society.

At the same time, there is some sneaking admiration for the cunning whereby a skilled bureaucrat can operate the rules for personal gain. Those same citizens who complain bitterly about official venality all want their children to get the sort of education that will assure them, in turn, similar opportunities of rapid enrichment. Theft is not necessarily evil, although its positive aspect must always appear in the context of representing oneself as the victim of oppression forced into theft as a defence of last resort. That argument has some unexpected ramifications. Thus, 'stealing' languages – that is, picking up a smattering while working abroad – is an act of admirable skill, like stealing animals (Herzfeld 1985: 50), because the Greek – most characteristically the *Gastarbeiter* in Germany – can thereby penetrate the host population's monopoly of access to economic and political resources, and, moreover, does so in a way that (according to my present argument) is itself felt to be characteristically Greek. (The corollary is Greek unease about foreigners from powerful countries who learn the Greek language too well, thereby gaining an additional and unfair advantage.) Theft redresses a violated moral reciprocity under conditions of unequal power. Thus, in the animal-thieves' discourse, raiding rich monasteries and lowland villages (or Muslim communities in Turkish times) is morally justifiable because, so the cant goes, these entities could only have grown rich at the expense of the poor. Wealth, in Protestant ideologies a sign of divine favour (Weber 1976), here signifies moral corruption, the evil corollary of political ascendancy. From here to the idea of national heroes as thieves, *kleftes*, is a relatively small and easy step in the popular imagination.

In an outsider, theft is reprehensible, as indeed it is in someone who steals from a fellow insider. The one kind of theft that is acceptable consists of acts of raiding outsiders to benefit insiders. Thus, the bureaucrat whose venality appears to be purely self-interested cannot expect much sympathy if caught.

But this does not prevent local residents from trying to enmesh various categories of civil servant – tax officials, members of the local historic conservation bureaucracy, social security agents – in a web of constructed relationships, notably those ties of spiritual kinship (*koumbaria, sindeknia*[5]) that animal-thieves also use horizontally with pastoral allies and vertically with political patrons. Favours done for those with whom the bureaucrats are linked in relationships of categorical and mutual obligation are never reprehensible: they are simply victories over 'the system'. The distinction between local knowledge and official practice, like that between folk and ecclesiastical religion, is itself a facet of rhetorical practice. While the law is framed as a disinterested code, moreover, all those concerned are fully aware that it is this very aspect of seeming neutrality that makes it especially effective as a tool of social exclusion. When bureaucrats want to deny favours, they need only evoke the rhetoric of impartiality. Of course, the reduction of all official interactions to strategy means that no ploy is ever guaranteed success. Even the most disinterested official's insistence on the letter of the law is always represented as a power play. Whether their detractors literally believe this of them is irrelevant. What matters, in a society where reputation is based on public performance, is their failure to enter into local canons of reciprocity.

APPRENTICES: STEALING AS VIRTUE

In this context, the idea that apprentices 'steal' ideas from their masters takes on interesting implications. It is far from clear that the charge is negatively construed, especially in a context where 'theft' is a metaphor for legitimate subversion. This is less a matter of some protected abstraction called 'local knowledge', as of the delicate symbiosis between local and official values.

Rethemnos is the site of many small craft industries as well as of new service industries fuelled by the tourist economy. In addition to the usual range of carpenters, construction workers, and small-scale craft artisans (goldsmiths, leather-workers, etc.), there are also new professions like those of motor-bike mechanics and waiters. Most of the young men and women who enter these professions do not do so through the channels of formal technical schooling. There are virtually no suitable facilities for this in Rethemnos itself; travel away from home for the purposes of education rarely affects purely vocational goals, but tends to be restricted to those who study at universities in Greece and abroad. For this reason, the absence of technical schools materially accentuates the sharp differentiation between the educated and those who work with their hands. An official of the Technical High School told me that the craft class there was intended to overcome elitist attitudes towards manual labour, but the students seemed to treat that class as a source of fun rather than as a serious component of their curriculum; the effect of including it may thus be quite the opposite of what was intended.

Working-class Rethemniots (or, to be more consistent with my own argument, Rethemniots adopting a working-class identity in any given situation) often express great contempt for formal schooling and for those whose education (and contacts) may have secured them a 'chair' – a place of indolence but also of power[6] – in the civil service. They complain that such people, who are often of the same local origins as the speakers, have put on airs and that they refuse to treat their fellow citizens with respect. Like the charge of universal betrayal mentioned above, such generic charges provide an ethical alibi for the speakers' failures in their dealings with officialdom, as well as a moral defence of their own virtues as contrasted with the corruption of officialdom. (It also conveniently occludes their own attempts to achieve similar 'chairs' for their children.) Apprenticeship, which is largely illegal since it often entails employing under-age children with inadequate or non-existent insurance coverage, at least provides a vocational training for those who will not make it to the end of a formal school career. In the process, however, it reinforces attitudes and values which, precisely because they provide a 'transcript' (Scott 1985) of resistance against official norms, also furnish the means of practical discrimination whereby a working-class counter-culture is maintained and intensified – a circumstance that means that what passes for resistance is perhaps often more realistically viewed as resentment.

It would be very tempting, with such writers as Bourdieu (1977), Giddens (1984), and Willis (1977), to see this primarily as a reproductive process. That aspect is certainly present. But it also fits the logic of a society that collectively sees itself as oppressed by the outside world; a person who is 'working class' is also, *ipso facto*, 'more Greek', and can justify subversive or illegal actions both as expressions of resistance or desperation at the class level and as testament to the Greeks' self-stereotype as unruly individualists at the national level. Even as they grumble that Greeks will never make any progress unless they learn to be good Europeans, they sneer at the submissiveness of the (West) Europeans they see in the tour groups and exalt their rebellious and divisive qualities as the essence of true Greekness – independent, proud and entrepreneurial, or unruly, egotistical and greedy, depending on the speaker's politics and the context of the argument.

The contrast between 'Europeans' and 'Greeks' reproduces, in many respects, the stereotypical contrast between the local elite and the working class. Consider the bureaucrats, a group whose social status and idiom of knowledge are radically contrasted with those of artisans. The popular denial of bureaucrats' humanity (and, by extension, of their membership in a shared culture and society) is a common convention in European and many other cultures; it also closely resembles the Greek stereotype of the 'cold northerner'. It thus acquires particular force in Greece, where it becomes the focus of a battle between an allegedly 'European' and an allegedly 'Oriental' order, pitting rationalism against humanity and efficiency against social obligation.

Pragmatically as opposed to symbolically, these are not incompatible visions. Just as Stewart (1991) and Hirschon (1989) have demonstrated so well for religion, one must also realize that the relationship between official and apparently subversive discourses of identity in Greece is a highly symbiotic one. This is the logic of a national self-stereotype that hovers between two readings, of which one extols the Greeks' allegedly European 'individualism' while the other takes them to task for their supposedly un-European 'atomism'. Or, to put it more concretely, this is the logic of identity in a nation-state whose political, scholarly and legal establishment recasts as national heroes the self-styled 'thieves' (*kleftes*) who once attacked the wealthy and the landed regardless of their own or their enemies' religious, linguistic or other identity at the time.

Here another dualism enters the discussion: that of moral good and evil, or, more generally, of positive and negative valuations of human experience. It is important not to view the lability of the moral concepts discussed here as evidence of inconsistency or hypocrisy. Greek is full of evaluative concepts that English-speakers have difficulty translating precisely because they challenge assumptions about where the positive–negative line should be drawn. Thus, for example, terms denoting powerful emotions do not fit on one side of this division with the ease that we encounter in their closest English equivalents. *Lakhtara* is both sexual longing and the feeling that one might experience when sitting in a plane that seems about to crash. *Kaimos*, the intense grief one expresses at a funeral, is also the passion of the monomaniac – a stamp or butterfly collector, for example, might have *kaimos* to find rare specimens. Even representing these glosses as the extremes of semantic continua may be misleading, since it is not at all clear that they are experienced as such.

Sometimes, however, such polarization appears in the ethnographic record. These instances seem to represent a fairly explicit reaction to norms felt to have originated outside the local community. Thus, the anthropologically ubiquitous *eghoismos* (see, e.g., Campbell 1964) doubles both as a positive virtue (as competitive behaviour in a capitalist world) and as a negative fault (as destructive self-regard). While ideas like *kaimos* and *lakhtara* are more determinedly bound to personal emotion, moreover, *eghoismos* is a term of social evaluation and, as such, lends itself more easily to invasion by capitalist and occidentalist (Carrier 1992) thinking.

This penetration occurs even in locations where the denial of state authority is at its most dramatic. Milopotamos villagers, for example, say that there is a 'good *eghoismos*' and a 'bad *eghoismos*' (Herzfeld 1985: 102). The good kind makes people open more coffee-houses and send their children to university: it is, above all, economically productive. The bad kind is what leads to blood-feuds and animal-theft, and consistently conflicts with the law. This pairing might at first seem reminiscent of the classical Greeks' categorical discrimination between good and bad *eris* (Walcot 1970: 87–92), a superficially parallel doublet. The 'good' variety, however, is explicitly linked to capitalist concepts of 'good' competition in a village heavily penetrated, through the social institutions of animal-theft and patronage, by the conservative ideology, and by party allegiances to the New Democracy party. It would thus seem more probable that intrusive political values pulled into polarized precision an understanding of *eghoismos* that had hitherto looked much more like a continuum, and one with many ambiguities at that.

Theft, like *eghoismos*, is a double-edged sword. In the same way as *eghoismos*, it may appear as an act of social virtue: as an act of redistributive justice, it expresses resistance against the power of the bureaucratic, capitalist state. Let me briefly sketch the historical transformation of the 'klefts' in schematic terms. In 1821, resistance against the state came from below, from the poor mountain pastoralists in particular, and the lower clergy were warmly in favour of it; the upper hierarchy, fearing for their lives at the hands of the Turks (justifiably, as things turned out), joined forces with the wealthier landowners in supporting the Turkish authorities. It was only *after* the establishment of a nominally autonomous Greek state authority that some Greeks began to shift the opprobrium of 'symbolic Turkishness' from the landowners (Dakin 1973: 60) to the government itself, notably to its more conservative incarnations (Herzfeld 1985: 19), while at the same time the canonization of the 'klefts' as national heroes did not save some of the most popular heroes of the War of Independence – notably Theodhoros Koloko-tronis – from becoming the objects of official persecution.

Transposing this argument now from the historical plane to the more restricted one of local ethnography, we can say that the metaphor of 'theft' creates a sense of both opposition between classes and solidarity before outsiders. It is a bitter charge to hurl against a bureaucrat, that representative of an unfeeling state and elite. It is a badge of pride when one is oneself the thief, charging full tilt against the wealthy Turks or their symbolic successors, the rich lowland farmers and their political protectors, or when one is fooling the representatives of the state (for which one particularly telling metonym is to offer hospitality to a police patrol hunting down animal-thieves and then to inform its members that they have just eaten the evidence!). Justification can always be found in reciprocity: since they steal from us, what can we do but steal from them? This is why many Greeks are happy to boast of a collective, national prowess at tax evasion, never for a moment seeing this as an unpatriotic act. In short, to be a 'thief' is both an accusation and a boast, depending on context. Certainly, therefore, for many poorer Greeks, the idea of being a *kleftis* is not as clearly deprecatory as that of being a 'thief' would be in English.

It is in this light, I believe, that we must interpret the notion that apprentices 'steal' from the artisans who train them. It seems that the artisans actually encourage such actions, which would seem on the surface to undermine the artisans' authority.[7] There is a strong preference for avoiding the hiring of (especially agnatic) kin as apprentices, however, and it is also conventionally understood that kin make bad partners; the bonds of kinship are too easily exploited. Apprentices may demonstrate their suitability as potential future partners by showing how good they are at acquiring this level of deviousness.

In this way, their 'thefts' – just like those of the animal-thieves with whom many of them are still connected by ties of kinship and village origin, though to the best of my knowledge the parallel is never recognized – move, under direct provocation from their 'victims', from acts of external attrition to relations of alliance. At the same time, again as in the case of the animal-thieves, a relationship of inequality is recast as one of virtual parity. 'Stealing' from one's own kin, and especially from agnates, is – yet again as in animal-theft – an undesirable idiom of social interaction, akin to incest, because it confounds the all-important distinction between insiders and outsiders. It is precisely because of the strong injunction against hiring kin that an apprentice can 'legitimately' steal from an employer, until the employer shows sufficient respect to raise the apprentice's hopes of eventual partnership – a partnership that will rest on the older artisan's confidence in the younger man's deviousness in the often viciously competitive (*eghoistiko*) world of local trade. I have often seen artisans contemptuously mock their apprentices' knowledge and ability while at the same time refusing to teach them anything. This constant provocation, I suggest, would be difficult with close kin, for it would violate expectations of amity. With non-kin, however, it serves to goad the youths into showing their mettle.

Now clearly artisans cannot actually tell their apprentices to steal from them. Indeed, artisans deny that they encourage their apprentices' sneaky acquisition of knowledge. This, I suggest, is a clear case of 'misrecognition' (Bourdieu 1977: 5–6). It is further supported by an ideology according to which a good craftsperson does not speak in order to teach an apprentice; it is the apprentice's eyes and sense of sound and touch that guide the acquisition of technical knowledge. The literature on apprenticeship is replete with rich illustrations of non-verbal instruction.[8] Videotaping of artisan–apprentice interactions has shown that, in Rethemnos, the pattern is quite clear: there is minimal verbal intervention, and most of the talking that does occur takes the form of banter, teasing or rough insult. This is close to my own single not-quite-experience of apprenticeship in animal-theft: invited to go on a raid I replied with words of great enthusiasm, only to be told later that I had forfeited my chance by *speaking* when the thief had simply made a *noima* (non-verbal gesture, but literally 'meaning'; cf. English 'meaningful glance') to me.

It would probably be too fanciful to argue that artisans and apprentices consciously evoke the social code of animal-thieves when negotiating their professional conduct, still less that they are thinking of the heroes of the 1821 Greek War of Independence (which in any case did not bring autonomy or *enosis* to Crete; the island had to wait until 1898 for the former, 1913 for the latter). In fact, I do not think it is necessary to argue that such conscious connections exist; that argument itself presumes an intellectualist self-consciousness that would conflict with the very ideology I have just described as it appears in actual practice.

Rather, I suggest, there is a more generalized sense in which Greeks conceive of their cultural intimacy as marked by a measure of deviousness necessary to their survival under any and all conditions of repression. The oppression of apprentices by their masters, which certainly used to be a good deal rougher than it is today, reproduces larger inequalities; and, like some at least of the latter, it can be reduced and eventually negated through acts of 'theft'. Under these conditions, the educated use of speech, writing and measurement – all of which are themselves the instruments of inequality – become the objects of subversive embodiment. The tactics of resentment ensure that this stance therefore remains obdurately non-intellectual – a somatic denial of specificity. Greeks who describe foreigners as 'law-abiding' (*nomotayis*) do not usually do so with admiration. On the contrary, they view this condition as a consequence of too much book-learning, just as, to Cretans and Cypriots, all mainland Greeks are 'pen-pushers'. Being a 'thief' is not so much a literal state of dishonesty as an embodiment of this anti-intellectual stance, one that rejects formal codes and legal devices in favour of devious ingenuity – things one cannot talk about, but that one can recognize in a fellow-creature from afar, and that Rethemniots certainly recognize as emergent in the stance of those wary young apprentices as much as they do in themselves. Indeed, it truly takes one to know one.

KNOWING ONESELF, KNOWING OTHERS

Working-class Rethemniots maintain a consistent attitude of contempt for authority through their bearing at the work-place; it does not necessarily even matter to them whether the bosses see or understand. The point is less that they resist the elite – a dubious proposition – than that they experience a degree of solidarity among themselves because they recognize the self-reproducing lineaments of their common, embodied experience. This is how they acquire a sense of a collective, embodied self. Given the resentful rhetoric that Greek nationalism shares with working-class ideology, especially through the latter's equation of elite with 'European' culture, I suggest that the resulting sense of solidarity is directly analogous to the image of Greekness through which Greeks abroad recognize each other – as warm-blooded and amiable villains, lost in a coldly bureaucratic land.

I have argued elsewhere (Herzfeld 1987: 137) that the use of gesture is often regarded, in the orientalist discourse about Greek identity, as a sign of incurable otherness within the European or 'western' context. In the same way, the denial of verbality marks the elite's condescension toward 'simple people' (*apli anthropi*). But it is also, as we have seen, the workers' way of defining their own enclosed world, just as certain kinds of gesture and attitude mark Greeks for each other and reaffirm their sense of cultural intimacy and solidarity.

The body is the site of personal intimacy. Thus, through metaphors of sexuality, it becomes a bridge between gender symbolism and the discourse of national identity. 'Knowing' a person is, in Greek, rendering that person an insider, *dhikos mas* as opposed to *ksenos*. Conversely, the *ksenos* is the person from whom one 'steals', as we have seen, in order to render him or her a *dhikos mas*. Thus theft, which begins as an act of violence against another's intimacy, becomes instead a claim on that intimacy, an intimacy that is too intense for words (and far too sociable to admit of the austerity of saintliness either – being a *Khristianos* is a mark of social identity, not of virtue). It may not be a stable way to make friends and allies, and indeed is the germ of the lingering mutual suspicion powerful outsiders have the means to exploit; but, while it lasts, the relationship it creates *is* intimate and familiar – and it is a way of keeping those powerful outsiders outside. The distinction between *kseni* and *dhiki mas*, which demarcates all the boundaries of intimacy from the person to the nation (and the even larger confessional community), provides the framework for moving from one level to the other and back again.

Such is both the affective and the conceptual framework of nationalism in small, badly battered nations in an unfriendly world. It is no coincidence that Greek foreign relations are marked by what observers often unsympathetically see as a mixture of hyper-defensiveness and arrogant expansionism. This is not the place to explore such matters, but I would argue that the Greeks' repeated failures to gauge international reactions to their foreign policy often entail hiding those aspects of the national culture – elements of Turkish influence, the existence of significant minorities (still officially denied), the wide reach of patronage – that conflict with the idealization of a unified, rational, and above all gloriously verbal Hellas. In other words, they entail hiding what everyone on the inside 'knows'. To the extent that the economic powers of the western world continue to press constrictively against that enclosing defensive wall, rather than acknowledging their own part in its construction, such knowledge remains jealously guarded, an object of mixed affection and embarrassment.

Cretans often remark to me that, however much they may despise people from other parts of their shared island, even a chance encounter in Athens brings immediate solidarity. That they consciously recognize this form of segmentation, and represent it as quintessentially Cretan, fits within the larger Greek pattern, although perhaps with the added intensity of a localist cultural ideology that is not so strongly present elsewhere in the country. This localism is at once a source of pride and embarrassment, and it is justified in terms of the supposedly shared need that all Cretans in Athens – or all Greeks abroad – face in relation to their oppressive foreign surroundings: the need to help each other even – or especially – when this entails violation of the official code of law. The ability to get things fixed is greatly treasured, not only for its practical benefits, but also, and perhaps above all, for the sense it imparts of a comfortable intimacy. Again: it takes one to know one.

And Greeks meeting other Greeks at airports are unlikely, in the immediate future, to lose that determined – overdetermined? – ability to recognize each other from afar. It is their one solace in a world which, they know full well (for they are necessarily as responsive to such global matters as they are to each other's presence), does not intend to grant them licence to infect the larger order and so dilute their sense of their own historical and cultural specificity. Their global knowledge is an embittered practical epistemology, reproduced internally in multiple refractions through the internal divisions of class, politics, gender and work. It may overtly take the form of some nationalistic expression of solidarity, but it is unlikely that this is the first impulse that initiates a conversation between those chance airport acquaintances. Such impulses rest on more experiential grounds. This paper – which does not claim to be anything other than programmatic and suggestive – is intended as an exhortation to our discipline to pay greater attention to the ways in which people claim to know each other. In that way, we may be able to grasp more convincingly how they come to know the world.

NOTES

1 I am enormously grateful to Richard Fardon for providing the incentive to write this paper, which, as will become apparent, affords me the opportunity of bringing together what have hitherto been largely (and artificially) separate strands in my work in Greece. For support in that work, I would especially like to record my indebtedness to the National Endowment for the Humanities for a fellowship in 1986–1987 and the Spencer Foundation for a small grant in 1992. My present research has been supported by the American Philosophical Society and the National Science Foundation. None of these foundations should be held responsible in any way for the contents of this paper. For a brief anticipation of the findings, now seriously out of date, see Herzfeld 1991: 108–109.
2 In some recent anthropological writings on the subject (Bourdieu 1977; Cowan 1990; Feld 1982; Howes 1991; Jackson 1989; Stoller 1989), this has resulted in a critique of excessive reliance on language in ethnographic interpretation. Some new and important ethnographies (Desjarlais 1992; Pandolfi 1991; Seremetakis 1991) take advantage of the same epistemological shift.
3 The official form of the town's name is Rethymno(n) or Rethimno(n). I have preferred, as elsewhere, to follow local usage.
4 This is the concept that I have elsewhere (1992) presented as an etymology of images. In parallel, much of what I address in the present paper may be conceptualized as an etymology of sensory experience. Like verbal etymology, as Vico understood, it can be used to subvert the very certainties that it appears to legitimate.
5 On Crete, *sindeknia* (literally '[owning] a child together') is baptismal co-godparenthood, and is considered a more binding and holier tie than that of marriage sponsorship (*koumbaria*). Elsewhere in Greece, the latter term covers both relationships.
6 'Sitting' is an expression of possession in Greek, which is why those who enter a coffee-house almost invariably greet before they are greeted by the already seated. Indeed, the question of why the newcomers must greet first is often answered by the curt phrase, 'Because they [those already present] are sitting!'
7 Even when a male artisan-employer is kindly in his approach to an apprentice, the expression of contempt for the apprentice's abilities – a goad to better performance – is never far away. Some employers still hardly address a word to their apprentices. Relations among women artisans and apprentices appear to be

warmer and more direct; this provides a converse demonstration of the thesis that, in a social world where male values are especially agonistic and women are expected to bond on a neighbourhood basis, apprenticeship serves to train youths in social as well as technical skills.

8 See, Coy 1989; Lancy 1979; Lanoue 1991; Lave 1977, 1982; Lave and Wenger 1991; Rogoff and Lave 1984; Scoditti 1982.

REFERENCES

Anderson, B. (1983) *Imagined Communities: Reflections on the Origin and Spread of Nationalism*, London: Verso.

Bourdieu, P. (1977) *Outline of a Theory of Practice*, Cambridge: Cambridge University Press.

—— (1984) *Distinction: A Social Critique of the Judgement of Taste*, Cambridge: Cambridge University Press.

Campbell, J.K. (1964) *Honour, Family, and Patronage: A Study of Institutions and Moral Values in a Greek Mountain Community*, Oxford: Clarendon Press.

Carrier, J. (1992) 'Occidentalism: the world turned upside down', *American Ethnologist* 19: 195–212.

Chock, P.P. (1987) 'The irony of stereotypes: toward an anthropology of ethnicity', *Cultural Anthropology* 2: 347–368.

Cowan, J.K. (1990) *Dance and the Body Politic in Northern Greece*, Princeton: Princeton University Press.

Coy, M.W. (1989) 'From theory', in M.W. Coy (ed.) *Apprenticeship*, Albany: SUNY Press.

Dakin, D. (1973) *The Greek Struggle for Independence, 1821–1833*, London: Batsford.

de Certeau, M. (1984) *The Practice of Everyday Life*, Berkeley: University of California Press.

Desjarlais, R. (1992) *Body and Emotion: The Aesthetics of Illness and Healing in the Nepal Himalayas*, Philadelphia: University of Pennsylvania Press.

Feld, S. (1982) *Sound and Sentiment: Birds, Weeping, Poetics and Song in Kalali Expression*, Philadelphia: University of Pennsylvania Press.

Ferguson, K.E. (1984) *The Feminist Case Against Bureaucracy*, Philadelphia: Temple University Press.

Giddens, A. (1984) *The Constitution of Society: Introduction to the Theory of Structuration*, Berkeley: University of California Press.

Herzfeld, M. (1982) *Ours Once More: Folklore, Ideology, and the Making of Modern Greece*, Austin: University of Texas Press.

—— (1985) *The Poetics of Manhood: Contest and Identity in a Cretan Mountain Village*, Princeton: Princeton University Press.

—— (1987) *Anthropology through the Looking-Glass: Critical Ethnography in the Margins of Europe*, Cambridge: Cambridge University Press.

—— (1991) *A Place in History: Social and Monumental Time in a Cretan Town*, Princeton: Princeton University Press.

—— (1992) *The Social Production of Indifference: Exploring the Social Roots of Western Bureaucracy*, Oxford: Berg.

Hirschon, R. (1978) 'Open body/closed space: the transformation of female sexuality', in S. Ardener (ed.) *Defining Females*, London: Croom Helm.

—— (1989) *Heirs of the Greek Catastrophe: The Social Life of Asia Minor Refugees in Piraeus*, Oxford: Clarendon Press.

Hobsbawm, E.J. (1969) *Bandits*, London: Weidenfeld & Nicholson.

Howes, D. (ed.) (1991) *The Varieties of Sensory Experiences: A Sourcebook in the*

Anthropology of the Senses, Toronto: University of Toronto Press.

Jackson, M. (1989) *Paths toward a Clearing: Essays in Radical Empiricism*, Bloomington: Indiana University Press.

Kondo, D.K. (1990) *Crafting Selves: Power, Gender, and Discourses of Identity in a Japanese Workplace*, Chicago: Chicago University Press.

Lancy, D. (1979) 'Becoming a blacksmith in Gbarngasuakwelle', *Anthropology and Education Quarterly* 11: 266–274.

Lanoue, G. (1991) '"Life as a Guaglio": distancing in intimate relationships in central and southern Italy', *Ethnologia Europaea* 21: 47–58.

Lave, J. (1977) 'Cognitive consequences of traditional apprenticeship training in West Africa', *Anthropology and Education Quarterly* 8: 177–180.

—— (1982) 'A comparative approach to educational forms and learning processes', *Anthropology and Education Quarterly* 13: 181–188.

Lave, J. and E. Wenger (1991) *Situated Learning: Legitimate Peripheral Participation*, Cambridge: Cambridge University Press.

Pandolfi, M. (1991) *Itinerari delle emozioni: corpo e identità femminile nel Sannio campano*, Milan: F.Angeli.

Politis, A. (1972) *Kleftika traghoudhia*, Athens: Ermis.

Rogoff, B. and J. Lave (eds) (1984) *Everyday Cognition: Its Development in Social Context*, Cambridge, Mass.: Harvard University Press.

Scoditti, G.M.G. (1982) 'Aesthetics: the significance of apprenticeship on Kitawa', *Man* (N.S.) 17: 74–91.

Scott, J.C. (1985) *Weapons of the Weak: Everyday Forms of Peasant Resistance*, New Haven: Yale University Press.

Seremetakis, C.N. (1991) *The Last Word: Women, Death, and Divination in Inner Mani*, Chicago: University of Chicago Press.

Singleton, J. (1989) 'Japanese folkcraft pottery apprenticeship: cultural patterns of an educational institution', in M.W. Coy (ed.) *Apprenticeship*, Albany: SUNY Press.

Stewart, C. (1991) *Demons and the Devil: Aspects of the Moral Imagination in Modern Greek Culture*, Princeton: Princeton University Press.

Stoller, P. (1989) *The Taste of Ethnographic Things: The Senses in Anthropology*, Philadelphia: University of Pennsylvania Press.

Vico, G. (1744) *Principij di Scienza Nuova*, third edition, Naples: Stamperia Muziana.

Wace, A.J.B. and M. Thompson (1913) *Nomads of the Balkans*, London: Methuen.

Walcot, P. (1970) *Greek Peasants, Ancient and Modern: A Comparison of Social and Moral Values*, New York: Barnes & Noble.

Weber, M. (1976) *The Protestant Ethic and the Spirit of Capitalism*, trans. Talcott Parsons, London: George Allen & Unwin.

Willis, P. (1977) *Learning to Labour: How Working-Class Kids Get Working-Class Jobs*, Westmead: Saxonhouse.

7 Latticed knowledge
Eradication and dispersal of the unpalatable in Islam, medicine and anthropological theory

David Parkin

COGNITION AND SYSTEMS

With the decline of support in the late 1980s for those many different enquiry procedures that, for some commentators, have gone under the name of postmodernism, the resultant vacuum has in recent years encouraged a scramble for new theoretical territory. Combatants include Bhaskar's (1989) difficult concept of transcendental scientific realism, Ulin's suggestion (1991) of a mix between political-economy and Habermas's communicative theory which nevertheless draws on the reflexive approach to ethnographic writing, and what can only be called appeals for a return to positivism, expressed by numerous writers. Such a reaction was to be expected, given the rejection of a firm, overarching theoretical position by our postmodernist predecessors. Theoretical reactions and counter-reactions nevertheless always leave traces of each other and, as may be suggested by a reading of Macintyre (1985), it is difficult to take the notion of a coherent tradition as any more than a shorthand and provisional way of describing a tendency.

Of all the social sciences, anthropology is surely the most likely, through its fieldwork and ethnographic enquiries, continually to subvert the fiction of discrete intellectual traditions. That is to say, our fine-grained ethnographic discoveries never quite fit the grand theory. This makes regional comparison the subject's strongest contribution to knowledge, for it is plausible only in terms of local transformations of geographically contiguous practices and ideas. By contrast, many attempts at global comparison become forced, either too theoretically abstract or generalized to the point of banality. So-called middle-range theory remains our *forte*.

What, therefore, are the possible implications for anthropology of a return to universal theorizing, in which the starting-point for analysis is, ultimately, an assumed general feature of human and therefore global society? In fact, anthropologists generally are regionalists and do not start their analyses with global generalizations, yet have in the past variously embraced the universalisms of, successively, structural-functionalism, structuralism and Marxism, often only to alter them beyond recognition when confronted with the nuances of the individual societies they study. Isn't this misfit precisely one of the concerns of postmodernism, however often clumsily expressed?

Indeed, just as Habermas (1983) insisted that there was unfinished business to be concluded within modernist thinking before the postmodernist band-wagon gathered speed, so we may ask now whether there is not something to be learned from the admitted excesses of the latter which has already, and will continue to, influence the way we perceive and construct our ethno-graphic object. For instance, I find it inconceivable that the presence of anthropologists in the society they are studying and the ways in which their fieldnotes are turned into publications can be dismissed as irrelevancies or of minimal significance, or that the continual vigilance required in our imposi-tion of concepts on field data is not a central rather than incidental element of any future theorizing. I see no contradiction between these concerns and our traditional commitment to linguistically informed, fieldwork-based ethnography.

What postmodernism might most usefully have stressed is the misleading nature of the dichotomy of the universal and the particular, which can be glossed also as that of the global and the local, and which is variously put forward as an opposition, as a difference of scale, as a hierarchy of influence, or as part of an evolutionary process towards homogenization. For once we allocate our material to either element of the dichotomy, we presuppose an allocation of the rest to the other, eliding the fine nuances that are the very fruits of ethnography as carried out by anthropologists. While this is by now a familiar problem, I see it as merely perpetuated by any appeal to the idea of discrete traditions of knowledge, whether they are presented as univers-alizable theories of social science or as culturally bounded beliefs and practices of the peoples we study. After all, one discrete tradition pre-supposes another and so on, with the result that the separate rather than overlapping features of knowledge are given priority. Our starting-points in anthropology are better regarded as those of ethnographic ambiguity and initial untranslatability, as we seek to transcend existing comparative frame-works and assumptions. This renunciation of theorizing from uncontex-tualized hypotheses removes initial security, but offers greater if more frustrating challenges.

The concept of counterwork, understood as the rebounding effects of knowledge in its diversity, conveys something of this image of uncentred-ness. It must surely also pertain to our own views of our subject as well as to the ideas of peoples we study. We do, after all, purvey knowledges from interested but shifting positions of strength and weakness. Trying to account for our positions might well invoke Gellner's accusation of 'indulgent hermeneutic-subjectivist excess' (1992a: 7), except that it alludes more to the awkwardly self-sealed, classical problem of a subject questioning its premises through its own discovery procedures than to the traduced sense of personal ethnographic reflection that Gellner identifies and attacks. I concur with his denunciation of approaches which subordinate, rather than incorporate, the study of a people to the ethnographer's own meditations on the self and on the destiny of the ethnographic work. Yet, Gellner's critique itself plays a prominent role in an anthropological moment which cannot pass without some questioning of the conditions of its production.

The occasion is the launch of *Social Anthropology*, the journal of the European Association of Social Anthropologists, founded in 1989, the year of European reunification and a date whose importance for Europe Gellner places on a par with both the Reformation and French Revolution, bold parallels indeed. Gellner's article, drawing in part from his opening address to the Association's first conference in Portugal in 1990, is a resounding and entertaining dismissal of 'the "post-modernist" outburst of subjectivism in the humanities and social sciences', delivered indeed with what appears to be passionate tongue in cheek, if the caricature of the object of his attack is anything to go by. In fact, the postmodernist horse he depicts and spends much energy gleefully flogging probably had very few punters, a point to which I return.

The mode of delivery falls into what Kuper, in an article in the same issue (1992), calls a strong formulation of a thesis – which he characterizes as likely to be interesting but wrong – as against a weak form which is rather obvious and uninteresting but right. Kuper is also concerned here to attack what he calls postmodernism which, quite unlike Gellner's somewhat lugubrious caricature, is minimally defined and relies almost entirely on seven lines from the last article Leach wrote before his death in which he claimed that ethnographers necessarily impose their own personalities on the peoples they write about. In disagreeing with this, Kuper juxtaposes an account of his personal involvement in Kalahari studies with a description of the course of intellectual development in this field, concluding that theory and methodology evolved from set social facts and therefore independently of his and other personal dispositions and that this justifies and indeed heralds a return to neo-positivism.

The journal's editorial by Jean-Claude Galey, the English version of which was prepared with the help of Kuper, the principle founder of the new European association, summarizes usefully the distinctiveness of what are and might become the problems of a European tradition of anthropology. In doing so, it anxiously raises the question of whether 'we' (Europeans) must 'retreat to the redoubts of post-modernism in order to assert that the rules of interpretation – like all the rules of construction – must, themselves, be interpreted?'. There is no evidence that these authors met together to decide a common policy, yet, read together with the articles by Gellner (who talks disparagingly of the 'Californization of the West') and Kuper (who makes a firm distinction between American and European anthropology), the context of the journal's birth as a European journal (and its title, which clearly privileges the 'social' above the 'cultural') make it quite unambiguously a vehicle for the creation of a new European anthropological identity, one of whose tasks for the two authors will be to cleanse the subject of North American postmodernist influences.

As we all do to some extent, the authors engage in rhetoric, whose particular features include: the use of caricature and minimal definition to designate something called 'postmodernism'; the personalization of parts of the argument (Kuper) and use of witty phraseology, for example, 'Love rather than theoretical universality inspired them' (Gellner); a hinted stylistic evaluation of strong, interesting but invalid formulations above weak but correct ones (Kuper); unacknowledged metaphorical shifts (thus, Kuper refers to Leach's statement as supporting postmodernism and, later, as a surrender to relativism, an equation that raises too many questions to be left unanswered and would not be acceptable to many, anyway; in much the same way, Gellner equates hermeneutics with postmodernism); and a play of contrasts between so-called versions of American and British-European anthropology.

As if to add to the sense of play, the author of this paper is at the time of writing Chairman of the Commonwealth Association of Social Anthropologists which some (quite wrongly) have regarded as in competition with and threatened by the new European association. Indeed, one concurs entirely with Gellner and Kuper in the major significance of the new association and shares in their hopes. But that is not what this paper is about. It wishes rather to raise questions regarding knowledge construction among ourselves as well as others in a world allegedly made more inter-communicative, and in which the forums we ourselves create are ineluctably part of that which we study.

To return to the two critiques, perhaps their most striking feature is their assumption of an uncontestable definition of postmodernism. Indeed, one of the major criticisms (and for some, its main feature) that might be made of the 'movement' is precisely the different and often contradictory positions of those deemed by others to be 'postmodernists'. Poole argues that the label, 'postmodernist' has become a catch-all epithet to denounce a range of highly varying views which he would argue are really instances of 'high modernism' (1991). Thus, for Poole, Marcus is not a postmodernist while for Ulin (1991) he is a major exemplar. Despite their different conclusions, Poole and Ulin each make their arguments from carefully defined, and quite contrary, positions and can hardly be accused of glib judgements. What is made clear by such contrast is the non-referential quality of the label 'postmodernist', which is indeed why it appears to preclude set political positions and prompts Gellner to accuse it of treating all ideologies as equivalent and thence dissolving them in an 'anything goes' view of the world. Nor would it help to identify all that is opposed to positivism as 'postmodernism', for that would surely widen the definition beyond what the critics themselves want.

There is no one thing we can call postmodernism, but in fact a number of intellectual stances which probably have in common an opposition to high theory or so-called meta-narrative. According to Rabinow (1986), authors should declare their political and ideological stances, the *distinctiveness* of which as approaches to knowledge depends on who identifies them as distinct and so invokes the contestation that prevents settlement into any one theory. Here interpretation is at the heart of an epistemology (why this interpretation and not another) and not just a means towards verifying knowledge claims. This is not of course an easy or tidy view of the world, although, despite the current relative lack of either ideologics or theoretical 'isms', it does not seem to have stopped people having strong and decisive opinions about, say, global calamities. If they are sometimes *apparently* inconsistent from one situation to another, this is also a matter of interpretation, and it is, anyway, questionable whether the gap between claim and practice narrows significantly as a result of card-carrying ideological membership (for, after all, it is precisely because of the proliferating inner factionalism that ideological proponents compete to impose their own versions).

The attempt to essentialize postmodernism is like falling into the older essentialist traps set by such concepts as descent, kinship and incest. There is in fact no valid distinction to be drawn between the essentialization of concepts that constitute the objects of a supposed tradition of knowledge and of the tradition of knowledge itself. Neither Gellner nor Kuper would presumably fall into the first trap, and so we may assume do not wish to fall into the second. It follows that our interpretations of the conditions under which their articles were written and produced are very much a part of their content: what Gellner has to say on the superior world form of cognition which he calls science and which Kuper also calls (neo-)positivism and science, is informed by the essentialized postmodernism to which their own positions are opposed and which results in these positions also becoming essentialized.

Let me take an assertion by Gellner to illustrate the mutually verifying tendency of this kind of approach. Gellner argues that this superior form of (originally western) knowledge is *the* central fact of the world, for better or for worse. Its dominance is characterized by, among other attributes, a superior technology which has been transplanted ever more successfully to a number of rapidly industrialized and now economically ascendant non-western countries (for example, presumably Japan and the Pacific Rim). Gellner then goes on to claim that 'it transcends any one culture, and is liable to undermine the favoured beliefs of all of them', which would otherwise be left weak and deprived if they did not adopt the superior technology wholeheartedly.

Although he does not mention them, this assertion takes Gellner right into the heart of discussions concerning the alleged globalization of culture which are commonly phrased in terms of creolization and cultural ecumene as against western acculturation and homogenization, and so on. For what he is saying is that this superior (originally western) technological knowledge destroys regional or local cultures and puts itself as the new culture in their place; that western technology is applied science and carries with it 'western' culture; and that this western technological knowledge is superseding other knowledges. Gellner is, in other words, equating western technology with culture, a Tylorian equation that others have also made, and which I have had occasion to criticize (Parkin 1993: 95), arguing that the commoditization and machine-like replaceability of modern technology, unlike the personalized and semantically embedded craft techniques to which Tylor might refer, makes possible its impersonalized and culture-free transfer to other peoples.

Thus, while it is true that there is a limited number of uses to which this technology can be put and that it is to that extent a globally homogenizing influence, it does not follow that all else of a society's beliefs and practices are displaced by this technological knowledge. Indeed, as we well know, it is precisely against the power and seeming inevitability of technological homogenization that many so-called counter-cultures arise or existing cultural practices and beliefs are re-accentuated. They not only work *against* each other, as peoples set up such distinctive categories as 'western', 'Islamic' and 'indigenous', but also *within* each other, as the same people constantly relocate the origins of beliefs and behaviour, so engaging in the equivalent of a kind of phonemic dispersal by which sound contrasts between languages may be recontextualized as occurring within a self-recognized language and vice versa.

Moreover, the isomorphy of technology with culture – either as reflections of each other, or as substitutable – once again engages in an essentialism which the recent work by, for example, Hannerz (1992) on creolization has sought to dissolve. The question now is: how do we account for the undoubted spread throughout much of the world of the same or similar technology and its coexistence with a comparable spread of ideologies and religions whose provenance may be western but which, as in the case of Islam, may not be? Do we think of each of these as competing, conflicting or mutually reinforcing 'systems' or do we try to express their latticed interaction in other, less familiar terms? I think that an answer to this surely draws from and in turn affects the positions we adopt in creating our own anthropological knowledge. I would expect Gellner and Kuper to talk in terms of 'systems' or the like, and indeed Gellner does refer to unequally efficacious traditions of knowledge as separable 'belief systems' (1992a: 7), with Kuper also arguing for the boundedness of what he identifies as a distinctive, and self-determining theoretical or scientific 'framework'. Conversely, I would expect many of those they would criticize to talk in other ways, undoubtedly often inconsistently. What might these other ways be?

Rather than take the familiar case of western scientific knowledge conjoined with capitalist consumerism as constituting the basis of the present 'world system', I take the more focused examples of medical technology and of Islam as two critically significant areas of knowledge which blend so-called western with non-western provenances and which are regarded as global phenomena on a scale of crucial significance.

To take medicine first, it has commonly been argued that, despite the scholarly and western consumer interest in alternative medicine, western bio-medicine has in fact for some years increasingly dominated the countries of Asia and Africa to the detriment of their own indigenous modes of therapy, a development that seems to accord with Gellner's claim for the superiority of 'modern' science. Thus, nearly twenty years ago, Bhardwaj (1976) reported a preference in Punjab for western medicine over Ayurvedic and Unani, especially with regard to the treatment of acute stages of sickness, and Bhatia *et al.* (1975) also noted that increasing numbers of Indian healers were losing patients to western-medicine practitioners and so had to incorporate bio-medical styles and techniques. Ahern (1976) also saw western medicine as gradually superseding Chinese medicine in Taiwan, while Last speculated on the possibility of bio-medical hegemony in Nigeria (1980). Central government and pharmaceutical interests are likely to be involved, however, and Topley (1976) described for Hong Kong the difficulties faced by Chinese healers, whose work is illegal unless carried out by a doctor trained in bio-medicine, yet who are tacitly tolerated in view of the burdens on government medical provision.

Is, then, this apparent dominance of western bio-medicine really the result of its greater efficacy with regard to health care? It would be churlish to deny the increased longevity that derives from the more extensive nutrition and health care, including vaccination, provided on the basis of bio-medical assumptions. But bio-medicine is more effective in some areas than others. The continued vitality of spirit possession cults in Africa, of shamanism in areas of the Far East, and of the use of amulets and Koranic-based prescriptions throughout the Islamic world, to take only a few examples, indicate that people do not find their need for emotional stability and cognitive reassurance well served by bio-medicine. And lest this be seen as a division of labour on the part of bio-medicine and alternative medicine between physical and mental health, it should be remarked also that most ailments are reportedly self-remedying and are often of a conjoined psychological and physiological nature with both areas of medical knowledge commonly deployed to the apparent satisfaction of clients. What we appear to be witnessing throughout the world, then, is not a wholesale demonstration of technological superiority by bio-medicine but rather a reorganization of partially overlapping areas of competence as between it and pre-existing therapies.

Islam shares with other Semitic religions prescriptive procedures for better and longer lives, and for those after this world. To that extent health care and therapeutic advice are inscribed in its pronouncements and expectations. But local-level versions of Islam commonly also provide for much more specific therapy, whether through marabouts or their equivalents, as Gellner has himself described (1984), or through practitioners who are regarded as medically adept and not necessarily saintly but necessarily law-abiding Muslims. Here, then, we have a joining together of medical practices and assumptions and of religious necessity. Add to this the impingement of assumptions from bio-medicine and we have an encapsulation of one of the most prevalent forms of interaction between global and local knowledges.

In what sense, within this apparent mêlée, can we refer to either Islam, or bio-medicine, or the indigenous alternative medicines and religions as bounded systems competing or synthesizing? As outside analysts we can of course debate among ourselves the evolutionary course of each so-called tradition or system: where it came from and how it arrived where it now is. This is valuable, if necessarily contestable, history. But it is a quite different exercise from the analysis of the users' own views of the therapies and religions they see before them. We generally act consistently within situations but not necessarily between them. In other words, of course all peoples think 'systematically' in the sense of speaking and acting in ways regarded by others around them as consistent within a given situation. But that doesn't mean that all their different situations themselves have to be consistent with each other as if governed by some overall system, to use the term in its substantive sense. The contestability here is whether and to what extent each of us as analyst imposes a view of system or of non-system on the indigenous users. Whether we are theoretically oriented to seeing systems in the world or instead grapple tortuously with new combinations of words to describe the contradictions, inconsistencies and flux of reality, does make a difference to the ethnographic description and explanation which eventuates in printed form.

In a pioneering article published in 1980 and significantly entitled 'The importance of knowing about not knowing', Murray Last questioned the assumption that so-called medical systems were in fact necessarily bounded by a common practice and set of assumptions held together by a single logic. In the area of Hausaland, in northern Nigeria, in which he worked, he could concede that western and Islamic medicine might each be *spoken* of locally as constituting a system, but this distinction was less clear in practice, and so-called traditional medicine, although increasingly used, was recognized to consist of fragmented and newly invented methods, claims and medicines. He speculated that in due course western bio-medicine might assume the nominal position of *the* system, since it was heavily backed by government finance and initiative.

Part of this fragmentary aspect of the whole medical culture, as Last calls the totality of medical services available, is the tendency on the part of patients rarely to complete their prescribed therapy: medicines remain uncollected or undigested and advice is only half-followed; patients filter through different, reported kinds of expertise, not in the manner of code-switching but in the spirit of polite or, one might add, desperate trying. Basic to this fragmentary appropriation of medical resources is the simple fact that, on the whole, people are not concerned to know what the boundaries of any putative medical systems are, nor to know what lies behind diagnosis, therapy or the canons of any supposed system. People are much too concerned with the voluminous and exacting practical demands of everyday life to focus intellectually on the rules of medicine that we, as analysts, might uncover. Surprisingly, perhaps, Last argues that medical practitioners, likewise, are more concerned with getting on with the job, so to speak, than seeking answers to intellectual questions in the theory of their practice.

TWO ETHNOGRAPHIC SUGGESTIONS: MALADIC ELIMINATION AND DISPERSAL

Given this situation of symptomatic, diagnostic and curative flux, I turn to my own ethnography and draw from it two broad metaphors for describing the way ailments are dealt with, namely *elimination* or *dispersal*. Sontag (1977) urges us to resist thinking of illness metaphorically (for example, tuberculosis was once viewed as constitutive of feverish, passionate romanticism) and so to 'purify' our understanding of illness. But there is also a heuristic use of metaphor. I suggest that describing disease as dispersable but never eliminable helps us question the extent to which we can talk of an overarching western medical system and of alternative Islamic and traditional ones, and at the same time enables us analytically to refashion the medical and religious tendencies being observed. To refer back to the preceding discussion, the distinction between elimination as dependent on boundaries (beyond which ailments can be pushed forever) and dispersal as the absence of such boundaries (so that ailments cannot vanish beyond them), reproduces that between the systems-and-boundaries thinking of positivism and the contrasting image of reality as constant counterwork.

I begin with a brief reference to the work of bio-medically trained doctors and health workers operating along the Swahili-speaking coast of Kenya, where I have carried out fieldwork. Whether they are expatriate medical staff on aid programmes or Kenya citizens, they take the view that their medical treatment aims to eliminate disease either by prevention through vaccination and health campaigns or by curative procedures. Their understanding is that it is possible, through the correct preventive, curative and post-curative methods, to ensure that disease does not recur, at least not within a particular phase of a person's lifetime. If there is recurrence, then this constitutes failure on the part of the therapy or the patient, who omitted to take post-curative precautions. Alternatively, recurrence can mean that the disease is fatal and so beyond cure. They also practice quite different methods of childbirth delivery from local, indigenous ones, insisting that the expectant mother be confined to a bed and ward and be limited to a few visitors at set hours.

All this is perfectly familiar to western observers and duplicates, though in perhaps rather more regimental form, similar practices in, say, Europe and America. There is much more that one can say on this adaptation of bio-medical assumptions to an African context, but for the moment I wish to draw attention to what I perceive to be a stress placed by the bio-medical clinical and hospital staff on the twin concepts of confinement and elimination with regard to disease and what they regard as bodily disorder. Most of these

medics, especially the physicians, are perfectly aware in outline at least
of bio-medical technological developments in Europe and America: organ
transplants, laser surgery, genetic engineering and new reproductive methods.
Physicians meet other physicians and some travel overseas or are themselves
from abroad. In this way their notion of the need to confine victims and
eliminate their diseases is reinforced by further directions along which this
kind of thinking can travel. Increasingly nowadays bio-medical thinking
admits to a despairing realization that curing one epidemic may seem to open
the gates for another, but this theoretical qualification of the possibilities of
eliminating disease really has not worked its way into mainstream methods
and assumptions. Confinement and elimination remain key metaphors.

We get a composite picture which, building upon Foucault's history of the
clinic (1973), sees western medicine passing from one idea to a second within
a root metaphor. The first comprises 'confinement', as in Martin's (1987)
description of women in labour defined as patients; 'isolation' (for instance,
of wards or of vulnerable groups and individuals); and 'containment', for
example, of the invasion of viruses. The second idea is that of focused
elimination of the injurious or life-threatening diseased organ or virus.

The first notion, that of containment, isolation and confinement, suggests
the determined resistance of siege warfare, with the enemy at the gates and
held at bay but not eliminable. The second idea, that of focused elimination,
as in the modern use of laser surgery, suggests a much more assertive march
upon the enemy, which must be routed and literally forced out of existence.
This shift in metaphor parallels radical alterations in the ideas and techniques
of modern surgery, in which an ideal is to reach a stage where the body need
never be opened by incision but internally reached instead by non-material
forces remotely controlled and visualized in their effects on an external
screen. The spectacle of internal bodily expurgation becomes amenable to an
audience whose intrusion into the patient's body is through minimal and even
distant bodily contact. This retains Foucault's 'clinical gaze' but stays the
surgeon's knife.

It is no disrespect to the practitioners of such modern tele-surgery for us
to express horror that the supposed cleanness and neatness of their operations
should have been incorporated in recent military vocabulary, as in the well-
known use of the term 'surgical warfare' in the Gulf War of 1990 to describe
an early strike in the attack upon an Iraqi intelligence building. This
expression, and the glee with which it was used by western commentators,
was well known and much resented by many of the Muslim Swahili-Arab
population of coastal Kenya, whose support for the Iraqi leader, Saddam
Hussein, was thereby reinforced. The implication that this clean surgery now
made war acceptable and on a level with video games watched on television
in comfort around the world, appears to have seduced many viewers, but was
later shown to be nothing more than the sensationalist rhetoric of certain
media purveyors and military apologists. The example does, however, reveal

the power of this kind of final solution to problems within and outside medicine, and, in its benign sense of disease eradication, clearly has increasing appeal as an ideal to which medical technology and practice will attach itself.

At root, here, is a theory of the possibility of eliminating existences. King Lear may have protested to the Fool that 'nothing can be made out of nothing', but he never reversed the thought by raising the possibility of a vanishing point into which problems could permanently disappear, a kind of black-hole solution.

Alongside this western-derived view, there is expressed what I perceive is a quite contrary way of thinking about medical problems on the Kenya coast. It is that medical problems are not fundamentally eliminable but can only be dispersed or even passed on and away in different forms. It is a theory of maladic dispersal. Moreover, it is not in fact evident just from the practices of the Muslim healers whom I observed. It stems rather from ideas held by Muslims and non-Muslims alike about how to purify a contaminated person or place. Indeed, it is possibly non-Muslim in origin and raises the question of how much is really Islamic about the medical practices of Muslim healers.

Let me first give some idea of what I understand by this medical theory of dispersal without elimination. There is an interpenetration of ideas and practices among Muslims and non-Muslims on the East African coast. Just as one can begin a study of Islamic medicine there by excavating non-Muslim ideas, so one can engage in the reverse process. The 'medical culture' of the coast offers an infinite number of such entry points.

For instance, the non-Muslim Giriama of Kenya cope with the life-threatening contaminations of a bad death (that is, the death of someone who has died from homicide, a road accident, a falling coconut, lightning, or who has drowned) by displacing the contaminating effects onto a non-residential area away from the homestead and, ideally, by causing, say, the widow of the dead man to have sex with a total stranger who will then carry the contamination with him to a far and foreign place.

Illnesses caused by spirits are dealt with according to the same paradigm. Spirits are themselves wandering, ubiquitous entities who, through appeasement, may be sent away and dispersed or who, if they permanently site themselves in the possessed person, must continue to be placated periodically. Like the effects of a bad death which can be visited unto subsequent generations, spirits can never be eliminated. The consequences of witchcraft, too, can only be reversed, and the cycle of witchcraft 'eradication' movements, each followed by failure and eventually by a new movement, testifies to this ineradicability of witchcraft as a force in human affairs. Thus, people looking back into the past may claim that witchcraft was less common and could then be eliminated, but that 'nowadays' (that is, a recurring present time) all they can do is reverse it, once the promises and hopes of witchcraft eradicators are shown to have been misplaced. Such examples are familiar to students of African society and underline the dominant theme not just of cleansing, purification and expurgation, but also of fragmentation and dispersal, as the means by which the grip of maladies and misfortunes may be loosened.

I also became aware of this sense of fragmentation and dispersal in the work of Muslim practitioners, seeing it from two perspectives. First, there is constant referral to other Muslim healers who are linked to each other in complex chains of master–tutor and tutor–tutor relationships. That is to say, while there is an acknowledged hierarchy of tutelage, the areas of specialization overlap, and for various reasons a patient's problem may be referred up or down the hierarchy. A standard reason is that the other healer is more expert in treating the problem diagnosed. But this is in many cases rhetorical since the problem has not been satisfactorily diagnosed in the first place. Other acknowledged reasons for referral are, for instance, that the healer may be too busy, that he is unhappy with his own diagnosis or therapy in the particular case, or that he may express a kind of filial, patrial or sibling loyalty to another practitioner by transferring a patient to him in this way. The healer may also suggest that a patient visit a hospital if s/he has not already done so. There is no predictable pattern in these referrals, for in apparently identical cases one patient may be referred and another retained. Referral is practised largely without regard to rules or principles but as an aspect of medical presence. The practitioner's referrals are the counterpart to the patient's different choices as to which kind of healer to seek. Again, there is no predictable pattern. People visit government hospitals, private clinics staffed by western-trained physicians and nurses, non-Muslim diviners and herbalists, as well as Muslim doctors, doing so in a variety of orders and with different degrees of intensity, sometimes simultaneously.

As elsewhere in the world, patients tend to distinguish between 'European' practices – good for the treatment of acute problems for which a dose of penicillin may provide quick relief (so reinforcing the bio-medical view of disease as eliminable) – and Islamic medicine, which they seek for what are perceived to be longer-term, chronic ailments, the more rounded treatment of which includes divining who, as well as what, is the causative agent of the apparently ineliminable affliction. But, in addition to this complementary distinction, people perceive overlapping areas of competence and medicines; and there is certainly no sense of either form of therapy being superior in all instances to the other. Instead, it is the skills of individual doctors that are ranked.

A second perspective on this dispersal is the extraordinary variety of public roles played by the Muslim healers, who are well aware of this diversity. At one day-long session which I witnessed, the Muslim doctor, a Sharif called Khitamy, prescribed medicines, married a couple, negotiated a land dispute by phone, provided social counselling both to a woman and, later, her husband, whose marriage was under stress, and finished his short day in the clinic by rushing off to help some Somali refugees who had recently arrived in Mombasa. He and other Muslim healers in his network of masters and tutors also hold time-consuming public positions in party political branches, professional medical associations and Muslim welfare and education societies.

Just as one can enter the coastal medical culture at any one of a number of points, say through ideas of bad death or the art of bone-setting, so one can grasp any one of these many roles held by an individual as, for that moment in time, being his most significant activity. At most, a Muslim healer is only ever part-time. But sometimes, during the long periods when he is involved in another duty or interest, he is not practising medicine at all. In this respect he is like many non-Muslim traditional healers and diviners who have reputations of greater or lesser worth and scale but who all, at some point, fit themselves into an array of other personas.

How, then, do potential patients regard Islamic medicine and its practitioners? The patients themselves do not appear over-concerned with defining a distinctively Islamic medical category. They are, however, concerned with the reputation of any particular practitioner who is recommended to them, along with a variety of others of different persuasions, as the malady proceeds. The network of recommenders and recommended not surprisingly consists almost entirely of coastal Muslims and comprises Arabs, Swahili, other African Muslims and some non-Muslims, including among these latter a few from up-country. It is through such a network that Muslim patients seek Muslim healers and that certain putative aspects of Islam reinforce the settings in which they meet.

A typical clinic is urban, has a waiting room or external space which is separate from the clinic, and may in some cases have a pharmacy with pharmacist attached. The inner room or clinic may contain a stethoscope and will probably include shelves of books in Arabic and English on Arab-Islamic medicine. These are referred to in certain cases, especially in relating astrological determinants to the diagnosis of an illness. More prominently displayed than the statutory picture of the Kenya president, are posters carrying verses from the Koran written in Arabic. My impression was of a spatial form and arrangement which blended a 'western' bio-medical doctor's general practice with indications of Islamic legitimacy.

Sharif Khitamy, as a Sharif (*saayid*), is greeted with a bow and kiss on the hand. His pupils, although themselves often quite old men, refuse such advances and are greeted by the Swahili *shikamoo* rather than the Muslim Arabic *wa'asalaam alekum* as is Khitamy. While he is referred to as Sharif, they may be called *maalim*.

The terms Sharif and *maalim* indicate the intertwining of what we may separately, and provisionally, call the medical and the religious. The medical draws on an assumed Islamic ritual and religious attitude, while more explicitly religious activities – such as mosque and private prayer, saint veneration, and the various celebrations of *maulidi* and of religious days – inevitably involve expectations of health, prosperity and good fortune. The intertwining of the medical and religious is also evident in the parallel and partially overlapping genealogies of tutelage. While practitioners can trace their intellectual pedigree through a recitation of earlier teachers and pupils, *maalims* can do the same, more explicitly by pointing to ancestral mentors' grave sites as well as by naming them. In both cases, teachers and pupils are likely to be related biologically but, while remarked on, this is definitely a secondary aspect of the continuity created through religious and medical instruction. Moreover, it is not uncommon for a *maalim* to focus almost exlusively on religious activity centred on his own mosque for some of his career and later to become increasingly concerned with his medical practice. The elaboration of a religious emphasis into a medical one, rather than the other way round of medical into religious expertise, may be explained by the financial profitability of medical success compared with mosque stewardship.

People are, however, aware of an inherent tension between overlapping medical and religious practices, which occasionally comes out in their denunciation of a mosque *maalim* for being negligent of his religious duties. If he spends too much time in his medical role, and thereby earns good money, a *maalim* may be regarded to have strayed from a spiritual–therapeutic constellation of inherited or acquired *baraka* in order to become a medical professional – hawking desired but more mundane, non-miraculous skills. By the same token, it is difficult to imagine a failed medical *maalim* reverting to mosque leadership; for, if he could not succeed in the mundane world, how could he then acquire *baraka*?

This continuum of 'doctors' having greater or lesser amounts of *baraka* is what I am translating as the intertwining of the religious and the medical. People do distinguish categories that seem at first to come close to those of medicine and religion. They do so through the use of terms and of spatial and temporal divisions. Thus, *utabibu* is not *ulama* or *dini*, although a good *mtabibu* may be either a good scholar or pious worshipper, or both. However, there are elements within both categories which are commonly legitimated by exclusive reference to the Koran and Hadithi and, in principle, medicine should never move far from the light of Islam, otherwise it may be regarded as *shirk* or *ushirikina*, polytheistic practices. Such penumbral distinctions make up what we may call the religious and the medical, which, taken together, seem to contain revolving aims and claims. In his medical role a *maalim*, *mtabibu* or Sharif seeks to disperse ills inflicted on humankind while, in his role as mosque leader, he tries to prevent their occurrence by exhorting a congregation to desist from improper human conduct leading to such ills. In either role, action may be prophylactic, as in the use of medicines and Koranic amulets, or curative, through the use of white jinns and exorcism as well as medicines and bodily manipulation.

As I have described elsewhere (1985), mosque pronouncments are authoritarian and threaten sinners with annihilation by God, while those of the clinic, as explained in this paper, are for the most part advisory and are accompanied by attempts to push back the effects of sickness and misfortune. Rather than talk in terms of separate medical and religious domains, it is these two tendencies, of maladic dispersal on the one hand and of a drive to explain through absolute and essentialist principles of containment and elimination on the other, which best describe the complex of ideas and practices centred on human wellbeing or 'health'.

AN ISLAMIC GLOSS?

Let me clarify my position so far. Mosque authoritarianism is like bio-medicine, and therefore applied science and technology, in its faith in written, fundamental truths than can be drawn upon to eliminate sin or sickness. This is the ultimate form of thinking in terms of systems and boundaries. By contrast, although Muslim healers may first make a bow in this direction of textual certainties, they then treat each patient not necessarily as curable but as likely to gain different measures of relief from suffering and misfortune through successive layers of explanation which disperse rather than eliminate the malady. They set up textual limits to their knowledge (thereby gaining clerical approval) but best help their patients by ignoring such limits.

I see a notion of maladic dispersal without elimination as evident in a range of practices which are carried over from non-Muslim into Muslim medicine, for example, treatments of bad deaths, spirit possession and witchcraft. However, except for the use of so-called white or good jinns (*rohani*), Muslim clerics condemn even responding to such beliefs, in much the same way as Christian clergy would regard them as at best ignorant 'superstition' and at worst as the work of Satan. Despite this, divination, spirit fumigation, the use of locally available herbal medicines and of protective magical amulets, and the sacrifice of chickens of appropriate colours, as among non-Muslim practitioners, account for much of the work of the Muslim practitioners, alongside prescribed medicines pharmaceutically prepared allegedly according to textual instruction and made up of imported materials bought in Indian shops.

What appears to give a medical practice its Islamic gloss is its doctor's involvement in the other Islamic roles I have mentioned, the facts that, at the appropriate times of the day, he will stop for prayer either in his surgery or another room, and that from time to time he will use specific books, usually written in Arabic.

A kind of legitimation of this Islamic gloss is provided by the claims made for the distinctiveness of Islamic medicine by one or two sages along the Kenya and East African coast. But they only make these claims if you question them: the general principles of medicine to which such claims appeal are not part of everyday diagnosis and cure, and they are known at best only in outline by most Muslim practitioners, who indeed do not need to know them.

Nevertheless, it is right that we ask what is the outer limit, so to speak, of Islamic legitimation. Throughout Kenya, the same small number of sages are identified as knowing the theory of Islamic medicine, and, though few, they are indeed impressive. One, called Harith Swaleh, is acknowledged as a famous authority on all aspects of Islam, including its medicine. In conversation with me over some days, he spoke of the conflict between Wahabi reformism and local traditional approaches to religious expression and juxtaposed this absurdity, as he called it, to the cross-fertilization and harmony between viewpoints embraced by the thinkers at the Greek–Arabic or Galenic origins of modern Islamic medicine. This tradition he traced via the medieval philosopher Arvi Sena (his Latin name) or Ibn Sena and his volume, *Al-Khanoun* (the canons or principles of medicine), through Abubakr Al Rhasi, whose repudiation of alchemy and insistence on experimentation he claimed to have influenced Roger and Francis Bacon, down to more recent Arab natural philosophers, and thence to those of the East African coast.

Harith Swaleh classified types of medicine, selecting *utabibu* as the main, direct heir to Galenic medicine, but he also specified a range of therapy specializations – including bone- and joint-setting, blood-letting, herbalism, geomancy, astronomy, exorcism, white and black magic, and even witchcraft (as a kind of implied medical inversion) – each identified by its specific Swahili name, of which all except the Arabic-derived *utabibu* were etymologically Bantu.

Harith Swaleh's focus was on *utabibu*, the class of medicine in which Muslim practitioners see themselves as specialists. Although incorporating principles of Greek–Arabic origin, the medical complex and texts covered by the term *utabibu* are attributed initially to God's inspiration, which has been relayed through Islamic teaching. Other branches of medicine either come under the general heading of *utabibu* or are regarded as supplements to it. *Utabibu* is indeed comprehensive; its procedures include first listening to the patient's own story of what is wrong or has happened, taking his or her pulse, touching any aching parts of the body, asking what meals the patient has taken or how he or she feels when swallowing food, and then relating such information to whether the illness is 'hot' or 'cold' and to the season of the year. Hot illnesses include high blood pressure, heart problems, malaria and various types of flu and cold, and are especially bad during the hot season of the year. Paralysis, pneumonia, diarrhoea, and vomiting are cold illnesses and, therefore, more acute during the cold season. While hot illnesses need cooling medicines and foods, cold illnesses require treatment by warming, including oil embrocations.

Now, what is interesting is that, the more Harith Swaleh talks, the more flexible he becomes in his classifications. For example, having located *utabibu* firmly within the texts and principles of Islam, he then goes on to talk of what he calls *utabibu wa wenyeji* or '*utabibu* of the local people', with the implication that this type of medicine is not specifically Islamic. He then calls this kind of qualified *utabibu* by the Bantu Swahili name of *uuguzi* and its practitioner *muuguzi*, which translated means simply a healer who uses local roots, herbs, leaves and bark that he saturates, boils or grinds for use as medicines to cure the same range of illnesses, from high blood pressure, to ulcers, anaemia, rheumatism and so on, similarly classified into hot or cold. Yet, like Sharif Khitamy discussed earlier, Harith Swaleh insists that he himself is a *mtabibu* and not a *muuguzi* or *mganga*, whom he regards as concerned with *ushirikina* or 'superstition' (derived from *shirk* or poly-theism). Harith Swaleh then concedes, without prompting on my part, that even a *muuguzi* is not always guided by what he calls 'superstitition' and actually identifies some such to me. The various specialists known to him (specialists in herbalism and in bone- and joint-setting and blood-letting, and those who use the amulets and charms known by the Swahili Bantu terms of *hirizi* and *kombe*, and who divine through the *rohani* jinns) are in all cases Muslim, sometimes with important religious positions. He comes, then, to describe what in practice the Muslim practitioners observed by me, including Sharif Khitamy, actually do.

This shift from a firm distinction between Islamic and non-Islamic prin-ciples and practices to a more fluid definition of differences, is probably familiar to many throughout the Muslim world and elsewhere. It appears in this case to turn on the distinction between textually governed principles and a kind of practical improvisation on these principles. The overarching appeal to textually based principles and methods, the presence of such books on shelves in the clinic, their occasional use as reference sources by the *mtabibu* concerned, his reading knowledge of at least some Arabic, and his use of written verses from the Koran to make *kombe* charms and protection, all give force to the idea that such principles rest in some central source, ultimately in the wisdom of the early natural philosophers.

This idea of a Galenic or pre-Islamic central source is, however, superseded in the minds of most if not all practitioners, by the centrality attributed the Koran, not only for having provided the inspirational wisdom but also for having predicted all subsequent medical and technological developments. In other words, even the appeal to central, textually based principles contains within itself the potential for a division of opinion whether the force of cure is religious or non-religious in origin. The one or two Muslim sages prepared to address this matter contain this split by insisting that even the earlier wisdom was only made possible through God's good grace and was revealed as such by the divinely inspired interventions of the Prophet Mohammed.

Improvisation itself consists in making use of all the different methods available in the coastal medical culture but constantly giving them an Islamic guise by appeal to the clinic as itself a kind of text to be read by patients as they sit waiting to be seen and surrounded by Arabic inscriptions and books, Islamic salutations, prayers, consultations and counselling. Fumigation at Sharif Khitamy's surgery is a good example of this. The patient sits in a chair facing either north or west. A cloth is placed over his or her head. The Koran is moved three times over his head in a clockwise direction. Incense is burned in an earthenware pot under the cloth and the malevolent spirits are urged to leave the patient. This then clears the way for more extensive therapy involving the use of medicines to be swallowed or rubbed on the body. At the same and other practices I have seen a chicken of a specified colour used instead of the Koran, with no evident suggestion that this might be inconsistent let alone sacrilegious or 'superstitious'. Sharif Khitamy once told me it was done to reassure patients that everything possible was being done to help them, so that the medicine of lotions and pills would work. But he did not distinguish the pills and oils as in some sense the 'real' medicine and the fumigation as illusory, but rather saw the fumigation and prescriptions together as necessary. Each patient therefore evokes a distinctive response on the part of the practitioner who combines and recombines aspects of a very large repertoire of possible responses.

This combinatorial approach to cure means that there is no sense that the pills and oils, or the herbal medicines, alone are able to eliminate illness. Dispersal, especially through fumigation, is also often necessary and acts as a kind of check on the idea that maladies can simply be eliminated and cease to exist. Pills, powders and oils are not accorded the priority in cure they enjoy in western bio-medicine. The improvisation that defies the claims of textual authority has constantly to find new ways of pushing the symptoms and effects of maladies out of sight, hence the predilection for dispersal which in turn reinforces hesitancy in the faith that symptoms and effects can be eliminated totally through the use of medicines alone.

Elimination or eradication is not therefore the dominant assumption in Islamic medical practice. To find this we have to turn to the emphasis given by local Muslim clerics to the need for people to eradicate their own evil sinfulness. This is exhorted in sermons in mosques or at religious events such as *maulidi*. The possibility of repeated confession in Catholicism perhaps presupposes sin's inevitable recurrence among most people. We would therefore expect that canonization in Catholicism would be difficult, for how many mortals can achieve the state of sinlessness? Kenya coastal Muslims do not permit confession but expect instead that people prevent the sin at source and anticipate that, according to the sermons I have heard, it is indeed possible to eliminate sin. By this token it should be easier to become a saint or the equivalent in local Islam, and indeed this is the case, for every small community has its graveyard of illustriously remembered religious worthies who by their lifetime's end did transcend sinfulness, as did the Prophet himself (cf. Eickelman 1981: 225).

Muslim clerics are therefore systems-thinkers when it comes to sin: it can be eliminated through correct, textually prescribed observances, which take the form of a self-sealed, self-determining, religious–legal amalgam of the five pillars and *sharia*, pre-empted by God as the one and only path and divine law (as Gellner observes 1992b: 7) and with little room for acknowledged human revision.

As healers, however, they stay in business not on the basis of self-verifying faith but through results which individual clients compare with each other and with those of other healers. It is healers' reputations which count, whatever we may regard as their empirical justification, and these require performative subtleties and novelties that defy the rigours of systems-thinking.

Ordinarily, of course, we would not make the scandalous suggestion that the positions of Gellner and Kuper outlined at the beginning of this paper are caricatured by the systems-thinking of the Muslim clerics I have described. Gellner has made clear in his recent work (1992b) that, while enlightenment rationalism may have emerged from religious fundamentalism, it has long since left it behind. Yet, and it is here that we return to the conditions of a *particular* work's production, the extra and perhaps underlying aim, as I see it, of his and Kuper's two articles in *Social Anthropology* – the concern to cleanse the 'new' European anthropology of 'American' postmodernist influences – does indeed place them on a par with the clerics. For they have allowed this discourse of elimination to limit, govern and so systematize their interpretations of the postmodernism they attack in the way that I have earlier suggested.

Nor would I regard the Muslim healers' attempts to disperse maladies rather than eliminate them as comparable to the postmodernist distrust of master narratives or final-solution arch-theories. Rather, I see the healers as empiricists to the extent that they take note of apparent curative successes and of the means by which they arrived at them. But I see them as also having to provide an expanding variety of performative as well as textual explanations able to satisfy clients' expectations: the premise of maladic dispersal presupposes endless reasons for suffering and misfortune which patients seek from the healer.

If, for experimental purposes, we abandon the opposition between, for instance, positivism and hermeneutics, universalism and relativism, and the macro and micro, and recast our observations in terms of a different, ethnographically extracted dichotomy such as that of elimination and dispersal, however provisional its status, we perhaps loosen the hold of essentialized concepts and draw analytical observation closer to practice. Let me suggest an ethnographic conclusion resulting from this approach.

CONCLUSION

So-called western bio-medicine has increasingly moved towards the assumption that disease can and should be eradicated and not simply repulsed or passed on. Perhaps at the same time, there has developed a view, also associated with western world liberalism (but also found, for instance, in African ideas of witchcraft (see Middleton 1960)), of evil as fragmentary and an inevitable aspect of human personality which can be dispersed only by creating moral and social conditions under which it may be domesticated. Among the Muslims I have studied, it is an idea of bodily and mental disorder and affliction, rather than evil, which seems most likely to be part of a policy of infinite referral or dispersal, a view they share with neighbouring non-

Muslims. What is distinctive about these Muslims is that evil, in the humanly responsible form of 'sin' (*dhambi* or *makosa makubwa*), can be eliminated if you try, but not illness (*ugonjwa* or *maradhi*), which can only be passed on or is expected to recur, especially after 'sinful' behaviour.

The very term, 'to be cured/to cure' (*ku-pona/ku-poza*) derives from the root term, 'to cool' (*ku-poa*). There is here the implication that what is cool is an intermediary condition between becoming too cold or inflamed, and that people and their bodies are therefore constantly subject to alternating states of hot and cold, either of which is represented as sickness. Thus, there are hot and cold sicknesses requiring, as antidotes, cold and hot herbal medicines and foods, and a person is constituted by this complex of alternations which s/he can try to control but never eliminate.

The intertwining of the religious and the medical among these Muslims is also that of the eliminability of evil existence as sin and of its ineliminable dispersal as illness. If we were to view this spiritual–medical complex in terms of systems, we might well distinguish the medical from the religious, and the bio-medical from Islamic and non-Islamic medicine. And, if we were to do this, we might well conclude that increasing foreign aid and the expanding numbers of modern hospitals, clinics and western-trained doctors had made bio-medicine the dominant system, especially since many of the visual and spatial idioms of the modern clinic have been incorporated in Muslim medical practices. But, by looking at diagnosis, cure and human wellbeing ('health' and 'Islam'), as premised on such ideas as eradication and dispersal which cross-cut in a series of loops and feedbacks what we otherwise define as religion and medicine, we see a different kind of proliferation: of spirit beliefs and ideas of cosmic marginalization jostling with monotheism; and of newly combined ways of treating ailments which are as much misfortunes as they are psychological and physiological symptoms and which draw on a pool of images and practices, but which compete with the bio-medical view that personal disorder is principally a matter of bodily malfunctioning.

We then see that the crucial struggle is between tendencies towards cognitive absolutism and increasing cognitive variation: between, on the one hand, the bio-medical body as the site of disorder and sin as a codified and eradicable personal responsibility, both textually defined, and, on the other hand, an overlapping, anaphoric and combinatorial approach to treating the mind–spirit–body. This not only dissolves the systems we may have started with, namely of medicine and religion, and of 'western', Islamic, and 'traditional' medicine, it also obviates the possibility of talking consistently in terms of a superior technology or science. At the same time, it is not nihilistic, for it suggests different cognitive tendencies, in this case in the direction of forms of knowing premised respectively on ideas of eradication and dispersal, neither of which can be privileged nor exhaust other possible tendencies.

ACKNOWLEDGEMENT

I would like to thank Aidan Southall for provocative and stimulating comments on this paper.

REFERENCES

Ahern, E. (1976) 'Chinese-style and western-style doctors in Northern Taiwan', in A. Kleinman, P. Kunstadter, E.R. Alexander and J.L. Gale (eds) *Medicine in Chinese Cultures: Comparative Studies of Health Care in Chinese and Other Societies*, Washington, D.C.: Department of Health, Education and Welfare.

Bhardwaj, S. (1976) 'Attitudes toward different systems of medicine in a survey of four villages in the Punjab of India', *Social Science and Medicine* 9: 603–612.

Bhaskar, R. (1989) *Redefining Reality*, London: Verso Books.

Bhatia, J.C., Dharam Vir, A. Timmappaya and C.C. Chuttani (1975) 'Traditional healers and modern medicine', *Social Science and Medicine* 9: 15–22.

Eickelman, D. (1981) *The Middle East: An Anthropological Approach*, Englewood Cliffs, New Jersey: Prentice Hall.

Foucault, M. (1973) *The Birth of the Clinic*, London: Tavistock.

Gellner, E. (1984) 'Doctor and saint', in A.S.Ahmed and D.M.Hart (eds) *Islam in Tribal Societies*, London: Routledge & Kegan Paul.

—— (1992a) 'Anthropology and Europe', *Social Anthropology* 1(1A): 1–7.

—— (1992b) *Postmodernism, Reason and Religion*, London: Routledge.

Habermas, J. (1983) 'Modernity – an incomplete project', in H.Foster (ed.) *Postmodern Culture*, London and Sydney: Pluto Press.

Hannerz, U. (1992) *Cultural Complexity: Studies in the Social Organization of Meaning*, New York: Columbia University Press.

Kuper, A. (1992) 'Post-modernism, Cambridge and the Great Kalahari Debate', *Social Anthropology* 1(1A): 57–71.

Last, M. (1980) 'The importance of knowing about not knowing', *Social Science and Medicine* 15B: 387–392.

Macintyre, A. (1985) *After Virtue: A Study in Moral Theory*, London: Duckworth.

Martin, E. (1987) *The Woman in the Body: A Cultural Analysis of Reproduction*, Boston: Beacon Press.

Middleton, J. (1960) *Lugbara Religion*, London: Oxford University Press.

Parkin, D. (1985) 'Being and selfhood among intermediary Swahili', in J. Maw and D.Parkin (eds) *Swahili Language and Society*, Vienna: Institut für Afrikanistik und Ägyptologie der Universität Wien.

—— (1993) 'Nemi in the modern world: return of the exotic?', *Man* 28: 79–99.

Poole, R. (1991) 'Postmodern ethnography?', *Critique of Anthropology* 11 (4): 309–332.

Rabinow, P. (1986) 'Representations are social facts: modernity and post-modernity in anthropology', in J.Clifford and G.Marcus (eds) *Writing Culture: The Poetics and Politics of Ethnography*, Berkeley: University of California Press.

Sontag, S. (1977) *Illness as Metaphor*, Harmondsworth: Penguin.

Topley, M. (1976) 'Chinese and western medicine in Hong Kong: some cultural determinants of variations, interaction and change', in A.Kleinman, P. Kunstadter, E.R. Alexander and J.L. Gale (eds) *Medicine in Chinese Cultures: Comparative Studies of Health Care in Chinese and Other Societies*, Washington, D.C.: Department of Health, Education and Welfare.

Ulin, R.C. (1991) 'Critical anthropology twenty years later', *Critique of Anthropology* 11(1): 63–89.

8 Whose knowledge and whose power?

A new perspective on cultural diffusion

Signe Howell

TWO EXEMPLARS

I

Boas loved to depict the indifference of this man from Vancouver Island toward Manhattan skyscrapers ('we build houses next to one another, and you stack them on top of each other'), toward the Aquarium ('we throw such fish back in the lake') or towards the motion pictures which seemed tedious and senseless. On the other hand, the stranger stood for hours spellbound in Times Square freak shows with their giants and dwarfs, bearded ladies and fox-tailed girls, or in the Automats where drinks and sandwiches appear miraculously and where he felt transformed into the universe of Kwakiutl fairy-tales.

(Roman Jacobson's recollection, quoted in Clifford 1988: 239)

II

In the 1930s, an American psychologist named Kilton Stewart accompanied a British anthropologist, Pat Noone, into the tropical rainforest of the Malay Peninsula to meet those whom he subsequently and idyllically described as the 'dream people' – the Senoi aboriginals. On the basis of what he saw there and was told by Noone, Stewart returned to the USA and started to practise 'Senoi dream therapy' – a technique through which, it is claimed, individuals work out their frustrations and re-establish amicable relations. It became popular and spread rapidly through the USA and Northern Europe. Today one may encounter therapy groups legitimizing their philosophy by reference to the Senoi anywhere from California to Oslo. Anthropologists (including myself) who have worked more recently among different Senoi groups have found no manifestation of the beliefs and practices as they are reported in the writings of Stewart and his followers. Senoi groups certainly practice various forms of trancing and shamanistic rituals, and they do adhere to egalitarian and peaceful ideologies, but there is no evidence that they think about or use dreaming in the way that Stewart portrays. He, however, felt conveyed into the universe of Freudian fairy-tales.

My purpose in telling these stories is to juxtapose two occasions when members of cultural groups with radically different views of reality confronted one other for the first time. Or rather, they confronted some manifestations of local knowledge and in both cases, to those in the know, got hold of the wrong end of the stick. Both the western intellectual faced with a 'primitive' culture, and the North American Indian faced with 'modern western' culture, carry with them their own significant cultural categories and rapidly make sense of the alien ones in terms of their own. These exemplars strike at the core of inter-cultural communication and raise questions concerning the ways that distinct groups of humanity (however defined) imagine, describe, and comprehend each other: what kinds of expectations do they have from their interaction and what kinds of knowledge result?[1]

I wish to link my discussion critically to the ongoing debate about the 'globalization of culture' and to suggest that, contrary to most commentators (discussed below) who perceive this process as a unidirectional flow of knowledge from the First to the Third Worlds, the flow also goes the other way – from less powerful, non-western societies to powerful, western ones. For present purposes I use the concept of knowledge very loosely, to cover cultural products of all kinds: artefacts, art, concepts, ideas, beliefs, values, practices. Knowledge in this sense can never be the privileged possession of any one group; curiosity about others, imagination and creativity are universal human qualities, and mental trafficking across cultural boundaries is part of the human condition. My argument will be that when they are confronted with some form of alien knowledge which, for whatever reason, provokes a resonance – that is activates a cultural latency or lacuna[2] – insiders may appropriate it and use it according to local perceptions. This means that, in some cases, we witness structural continuities and, in others, radical changes.

The thrust of my argument is that the borrowing of alien knowledge, and its adaptation to local needs, is going on constantly, and that such processes of indigenization of alien knowledge occur just as much 'here' as 'there'. Rather than such processes resulting in impoverishment, I wish to suggest the very opposite: that cultural diversity rather than cultural uniformity often results. But for such a view to gain acceptance, we would need to forego a current tendency towards moralistic preoccupation with authenticity and single origins – especially because such moralizing is most noticeable in considerations of non-western forms of life. Confrontation with new knowledge does indeed lead to profound effects on perceptions and practices – both others' and our own – but these effects are unpredictable. In order to redress the prevailing trend I noted above (in which the significant flow of knowledge is perceived as going from the First to the Third World), in this paper I shall concentrate on instances when knowledge from the Third World has affected the First World. I argue that such influences need not be superficial, but may strike at profound experiential levels by opening cultural lacunae which dramatically shift the parameters of previous understanding.

As examples I choose western use – and abuse – of 'primitive art' and of non-Christian religions; both domains in which an explosion of importation to the West has occurred over the past couple of decades.[3] Other important domains which have been equally influential but, for reason of space, cannot be discussed here, include music – especially pop music – dance, food and healing.

I conclude the paper by briefly discussing some examples of the effect of influences from the First World upon ideas and practices in the Third World. Although 'primitivism' has been a significant influence on western art practice, and many of the 'New Age' religious movements draw on various non-Christian mystical traditions, such examples are not often discussed in the same breath as the more familiar cases in which western practices have resonated in non-western parts of the world. But surely these should be considered together if the notion of cultural globalization is to be interpreted other than in its most common sense: as an encroachment of western products and values upon the rest of the world.

It is interesting to note in this context how many educated, thoughtful members of the middle-classes in both the First and Third Worlds, entertain fundamental paradoxes in their attitude to the importation of alien knowledge. Broadly speaking, on the part of western thinkers one senses an uneasy combination of guilt over exploitation of the Third World and existential insecurity about the western world itself. Many individuals are conscious of their part in a colonial past which has resulted in 'orientalist', 'primitivist' and other patronizing representations, and the continuing lopsided power relationship (to which I return below). Much western interest in Third World knowledge and cultural products is a kind of spiritual quest – a searching for a deeper meaning to life or art which somehow got lost during the industrialization of western societies. The attempts to resolve this ambivalent mixture of guilt, insecurity and quest tend to result in the insertion of a romanticized, exotic other as a term within a psychic and cognitive universalism.

By contrast, much of the interest amongst people of the Third World (and these days Second World as well) in the knowledge and cultural products of the West is directed towards gaining access to the material manifestations derived from western technology. People in other parts of the world may combine this desire for western prosperity, and all that it entails, with deep resentment of what they perceive as neo-colonialism made manifest in attempts at imposing western values such as democracy, individual human rights, feminism or sexual liberation. For many intellectuals of the ex-colonized nations, the spiritual or moral gains to be made from interaction with western cultures are perceived to be few – indeed, influences in these respects are often to be avoided. Given these complex and different motivations, just how we describe the mutual influences of First and Third Worlds cannot but become highly charged.

PRIMITIVE(?) ART AND ARTEFACTS IN
CIVILIZED(?) PLACES

During a recent visit to London, I was alerted to questions concerning cultural globalization, but from the perspective of influences coming *to* London, not going out from it. On a Saturday morning I went to Camden Lock (a popular North London market of stall-holders) and in the afternoon I attended the exhibition *The Jean Pigozzi Contemporary African Art Collection at the Saatchi Collection.* At Camden market, I was overwhelmed by the explosive increase in British (western?) desire for all kinds of objects from 'exotic' places. At the Saatchi Collection – one of the most prestigious venues for contemporary art in London – I was again overwhelmed, this time by western art connoisseurs' decontextualization of 'exotic art' and their celebration of a postulated primitive wisdom and creative urge coupled with an implicit, but unexamined, liberal claim for a universal aesthetic sense which somehow made the objects on display 'art'. At Camden market many of the salesmen provided background information on the cultures from which the items originated. Whenever possible, they tended to emphasize the exotic and mystical aspects of their wares, thus supporting my thesis that many western customers want more than just the object, they want it exotically packaged.

In itself there is nothing new in the appeal to urban westerners of culturally disembodied objects and artefacts from Asia, Africa and the indigenous Americas, and there is a large anthropological literature on some of the interpretative implications of the phenomenon. But whereas earlier this taste was primarily restricted to small groups of the intellectual middle classes and artists it has now reached mass proportions.

The Saatchi exhibition showed the work of eleven African artists, from seven countries, who appeared to have nothing in common – apart from having their origins in the African sub-continent. According to the catalogue they were 'carefully chosen for their consistent approach to their work, their originality and inventiveness in dealing with their cultural environment, and their perseverance and technical skills' (Magnin 1991: 1). Moreover, 'Academic painters who produce standard work without ever challenging its aesthetic principles have been deliberately excluded' (Magnin 1991: 1). Magnin, who collected the items on behalf of the Swiss collector Jean Pigozzi, shares with Pigozzi an ambition to 'create a great Third World contemporary collection' (Pigozzi 1991: 13). My question is 'why?'

After a closer reading of the catalogues, I was struck by the lack of information about the artists and their work – or rather by ambiguities and contradictions in the texts. For instance, after having walked through the exhibition and read the catalogues, one does not know to what extent the various artists are primitives in a Douanier Rousseau sense, or to what extent they are individuals fulfilling specific needs of their community, or to what extent they are sophisticated participants in contemporary western art discourse. Nor is one told whether the objects are made for use in traditional local rituals or for display and sale as 'art'. I was left with an impression that the collectors and curators were consciously or unconsciously blurring the issues, and that the overriding concern was to maintain notions of primitiveness, of the exotic, and of the mystical. Above all, it appeared important to stress non-intellectual forces in the work. This was explicit when the original exhibition was shown at the Pompidou Centre in Paris and entitled *Magiciens de la Terre*. In the words of Pigozzi, 'The most important lesson we have learnt from putting together this collection is that artists, if they have power, imagination, energy and vision, don't have to go to art school or to visit the Louvre or the Whitney. If they have the internal fire of creation, it will come out in the work' (Pigozzi 1991: 14). And yet, the work of several, if not most, of the artists on display makes it difficult to believe that they have not looked at picture books from – if not the Louvre – at least the Tate Gallery, the New York Museum of Modern Art or other museums and galleries of contemporary art. The interesting point here is not whether they have or have not, but why the issue is blurred by the western art experts. I suggest this is because the organizers want both to assert the presence of some primeval force in the African artists as well as to confirm them as 'artists'. To judge from the popularity of the show (and similar ones) one can only assume that the public shares these expectations. The more inquiring spectators, however, are at a loss regarding both the status of their own cultural values, and those of the African artists. Where do the Africans position themselves *vis-à-vis* their own local beliefs and practices and aesthetic traditions? How do they position themselves *vis-à-vis* western aesthetic traditions? What do they take from them, what do they reject, what do they transform – and why? There is neither any indication in the texts whether local connoisseurs were consulted nor whether the chosen artists were given the opportunity to meet and discuss their work. From the point of view of European audiences – both experts and the general public – one may legitimately ask what their needs and expectations are of creative manifestations emanating from non-western cultural and aesthetic practices.

Despite lively critique of primitivism in art, it is still western experts who define and, in a sense, make art, or meaningful objects, from non-western cultures. And it is western artists who lament the effects of the piecemeal influence of western art on art being made in Africa and Asia, while simultaneously appropriating and incorporating into their own work piecemeal snippets that appeal to them from whatever aesthetic products and regardless of origin. Many contemporary artists even call themselves, with impunity, shamans. Clearly, the significance of appropriation depends on who appropriates from whom.

The flow of knowledge from the 'primitive' worlds to the West, is not a recent phenomenon. The effect of African and Indian sculpture on artists working in Paris at the turn of the century is well documented (see Clifford 1981; Price 1989) as is the assumed understanding of the primitive artist's intention by many western artists. The following quote from Gottlieb typifies the attitude of some western artists,

> If we profess kinship to the art of primitive man it is because the feelings they expressed have a particular pertinence today . . . . All primitive expression reveals the constant awareness of powerful forces, the imminent presence of terror and fear, a recognition of the terror of the animal world.
>
> (Quoted by Cooke 1984: 19)

In a similar vein, Picasso described his first encounter with African sculpture, 'They [the tribal artists] were against everything – against unknown threatening spirits . . . . I too am against everything . . . . I understand what the Negroes used their sculpture for . . . all were weapons' (quoted by Foster 1985: 45). The sentiments and assumptions are not very different from those expressed in the Saatchi exhibition catalogue: a total disregard for the cultural context that produced the work and the accompanying elevation of an assumed primitive mind with which they identify at one level – only evaluatively to distance themselves at another level; *they* 'understand' the wider ramifications, the primitives do not.

These examples do not represent the first self-conscious aesthetic contact between the European art world and exotic cultures. In Paris, several decades before Picasso and others began to frequent the Musée de l'Homme, the impact of the opening of trade with Japan in 1853 had been immense. Within ten years Japanese art – hitherto unknown – became one of the principle points of departure not only for the Impressionists but also for several other groups of artists. Japanese wood-cuts inspired, amongst others, Monet, Whistler, Degas, Odilon Redon, James Tissot, Manet and Van Gogh. Following a major exhibition of art from Japan, China, India and Java at the Palais d'Industrie in 1873, *Le Japonisme* was soon felt in architecture, interior and fabric design, in music and poetry as well as the fine arts (see Brody 1987: ch 3).

QUESTIONS ABOUT GLOBALIZATION OF CULTURE

Most of the debate concerning the existence and/or spreading of a global culture tends to perceive this in terms of the slow encroachment of western cultural values, technologies and consumer goods on the rest of the world (e.g. Hall 1991; Robertson 1990, 1992). Many view the nation-state as integral to this development, although they place different analytic emphasis on its significance (Wallerstein 1990; Hannerz 1990, 1991; Featherstone 1990). Despite the qualification of some of the cultural studies writers (e.g. Featherstone 1990) – that specifically western developments are themselves the result of particular socio-political and historical circumstances – the underlying assumption is of an inevitable development towards the 'making of the world-as-a-whole' and that 'there is a general autonomy and "logic" to the globalization process – which operates in *relative* independence of strictly societal and other more conventionally studied sociocultural processes' (Robertson 1990: 27, original emphasis). Appadurai (1990) seeks to modify such rather stark perceptions by identifying five dimensions of global cultural flow which he suggests move along non-isomorphic paths. While Appadurai is sensitive to the more common anthropological stance (e.g. Howell 1991; Hannerz 1990; Barber 1987; Clifford 1988) that an indigenization of western, capitalist values and products is frequently going on, his schema is nevertheless one that concentrates on uni-directional flow: from the more powerful to the less powerful of the world – whether this be a generalized Americanization or a more particular Japanization of Korea, Vietnamization of Cambodia, etc. (Appadurai 1990: 295). He does not consider the possibility of reverse flows.

The situation is clearly complex. The question of relative power enters, but this may be less clear-cut than most writers tend to assume – depending on the definition of power. The legacy of colonial authority, coupled with the world economic system, perhaps enables members of the First World to define and, more importantly, elevate (or dismiss) alien domains of significance in ways very different from the use made of First World ideas and artefacts in the Third World. Criteria for inclusion and exclusion, in the West, are largely premised upon western aesthetic values and western needs which are then presented as if they were global. However, this does not mean either that in many instances members of Third World societies do not also choose their influences and equally use and abuse them, or that the foreign influences upon the First World are occurring at superficial levels only.

The experiences from Camden market and the Saatchi Collection both demonstrate something of this complexity. Depending upon your political standpoint, the two examples may appear to demonstrate a flow of values from the ex-colonial parts of the world to the ex-colonial powers – or precisely the opposite. The presence of exotic objects in a London market points to the activating force of fashion-creating First World taste in the Third World. The objects singled out for import are those desired by westerners. By no means all products from other countries are bought. By the same token, African artists on show are chosen by western art critics employing western aesthetic and cultural values as guiding principles. Similarly, as I shall argue below, the explosion in the numbers of western followers of various Eastern and primitive mystical religious practices could arguably be construed as an arrogant western appropriation to suit their needs. But one could argue for the reverse: that foreign objects, creativity, and deeper understanding provoke resonances that challenge those of the West so profoundly as to dislocate existing values.

What I want to suggest is that current western desire for what is perceived as exotic, primitive, uncontaminated, pure, wise and natural, is in part a manifestation of experienced lacunae in western knowledge which perhaps is analogous – but by no means identical – to the desire for what is perceived as modern, and exciting, in the 'peripheral' parts of the world. I return to this below. Camden market and the exhibition at Saatchi, as well as the numerous

New Age religious movements are indices of something very profound. What is at issue, I suggest, is both an orientalism and a primitivism of knowledge and taste in the two domains I have focused upon: art and religion. This particular process goes from the perceived periphery to the perceived centre, and on terms largely defined by the centre. But much of western knowledge which flows outwards is also received on terms largely defined by the recipients. Members of any group that has been the source of an influence (concept, item) may not recognize its adoption by members of another group. This may occur equally in western groups as in eastern, African or indigenous American ones.

As an aside, I wish to suggest that there is a general human tendency to dichotomize, to construct differences and essentialize 'the other' which, in many parts of the world, has led to various forms of 'americanism' or 'white manism'. These have not yet been properly studied, but from the evidence so far they display many features analogous to those of 'orientalism' and 'primitivism' in the West.[4]

WHOSE KNOWLEDGE AND WHOSE POWER?

In this context, I am less concerned with the consumption of the exotic (whether in London or in Bombay) than with local reactions to and per-ceptions of alien objects, modes of thought and modes of life wherever they occur. What motivates people to seek knowledge outside their own cultural traditions? Clearly there can be no definitive answer to such a question, given variations in motivation from region to region and between social groups within any society or culture. Nonetheless, we need to address such motiva-tion in any specific study and in doing so would do well to avoid two pitfalls and, perhaps, to entertain a third, positive, suggestion I offer below.

Overestimation of First World supremacy

Current writers on the theme of globalization overestimate the extent of westernization and, correlatively, underestimate the degree to which societies are affected by it only superficially. Much current anthropological writing seems to dismiss not only the existence of small-scale, bounded societies, whose members' own epistemologies are firmly embedded within, and informed by, their institutions and cosmologies, but also points a suspicious finger at anthropologists who claim to have worked in such societies. I wish to state unequivocally that, much as we flatter ourselves that an inevitable destruction follows in the wake of western ideas, products, and practices, many African, Asian, and Oceanic small-scale societies are alive, well and kicking in most parts of the world, taking or rejecting western influences as they deem appropriate. They are different from what they were fifty or a hundred years ago, but so are European societies.

Hannerz exaggerates the current situation when he says,

> When culture . . . was altogether a matter of meaning in face-to-face
> relationships between people who do not move around much, it could be
> a simple enough matter to think of cultures in the plural as entities located
> in territories . . . . With the globalization of culture . . . where we are now
> . . . it all becomes more complicated.
>
> (Hannerz 1991: 117)

It may be more complicated to live (anywhere) today, but this does not mean
that people no longer create meaning through face-to-face interaction or that
they do not maintain notions of localities as cultural entities – whether they
live in the hills of eastern Indonesia or in the suburbs of London. In all cases,
meaning is created within a constitutive and re-contextualizing frame of
reference. I am not convinced that recent technological inventions actually
render this void. As Hannerz has pointed out elsewhere (1990), we must neither
mistake all kinds of travel for cosmopolitanism nor confuse global distribution
of certain artefacts with globalization of knowledge or meaning. The vast
majority of those who travel to foreign parts – as tourists, migrant workers,
exiles, multinational executives – carry with them 'home' and just put a highly
selective gloss on the experience. This of course applies equally to Japanese,
Indians, Ugandans, Frenchmen, North Americans, Filipinos or whoever.

Underestimation of general diffusion

The flow of knowledge between societies goes in more than one or even two
directions. It also goes – and has done so for some considerable time – both
from non-western parts of the globe to the West, and between non-western
societies. Hannerz, however, insists that, 'Much as we feel called upon to
make note of any examples of counterflow, it is difficult to avoid the
conclusion that at least as things stand now, the relationship is lopsided'
(1991: 107). At least as regards my chosen foci – art and religion – I would
argue that this is not the case. No more is it the case for the current pop scene,
or for contemporary dance or theatre, or for the mushrooming interest in
alternative healing practices. I am thus reiterating the reality of the diffusion
of knowledge and know-how, but from an epistemological position different
from that of nineteenth-century diffusionists.

Cultural latencies

Following from the preceding point, I argue that the diffusion of cultural
constructs often serves to provoke a latency or make manifest lacunae (as
defined in note 2) in any one cultural domain. The confrontation with
something unknown – be this of a philosophical, ritual, technological,
political, economic, emotional or aesthetic kind – may or may not strike a
cultural resonance. If something which presents itself finds a resonance
among a sufficient number of people in a community, then it may be

borrowed, transformed to fit local perceptions (re-contextualized), and become part of the local discourse – in short, conventionalized (Eidheim 1992). Thus foreign artefacts, words, practices, ideas are absorbed selectively and for different reasons, making for continuous inter-societal flows of knowledge. Lacunae, in this sense, are potentially present in all systems of knowledge. Anthropologists have repeatedly warned against drawing evaluative conclusions from the comparison of cultures, but rather to interpret the contexts in which change occurs. Lacunae, as I am defining them, are absences or openings that may only become apparent, or more diffusely felt, when a conjuncture of circumstances arises. I am not suggesting such lacunae pre-exist such circumstances in some positivistic sense.

EASTERN MYSTICISM AND THE 'HOMELESS HEART'

Having discussed how exposure to 'oriental' and 'primitive' art led to a vitalization of western aesthetic consciousness, I now turn to a discussion of some of the effects of First World meetings with oriental and primitive religions. 'New Age' religions have become part of the western cultural landscape over the past twenty to thirty years because, it has been argued, they fill a moral and spiritual need. A large number of these religious movements have a strong reference point either in eastern mysticism or in some primitive religious practices. Many are led or initiated by Eastern teachers. Just as new inspirations were received in the fine arts from the Far East, Oceania, Africa and the indigenous Americas during the second half of the nineteenth century, so influences in spheres of religion and mysticism also came to Europe and North America during the same period, but the results of the impact took longer to become manifest.[5]

Swami Vivikananda (1863–1902), who was Ramakrishna's leading disciple, visited Chicago in 1893. He is generally credited with introducing Indian philosophy to the West. Krishnamurti of Madras was 'discovered' by the Englishwoman Annie Bessant, the head of the Theosophical Society whose collaborator, Leadbeater, was instrumental in reviving Buddhism in Sri Lanka at the turn of the century. Bessant set up many schools in India (which are still running) in which she tried to merge what she considered to be the best of the English and Indian traditions of knowledge. Paramahansa Yogananda was the first Indian mystic to live and teach for a long time in the West. He came to California from India after the Second World War where he established an ashram. Among the better-known religious leaders of recent years, are the Indian gurus: Maharishi, made famous by his association with the Beatles, and Bhagwan, renowned for his huge number of young American followers, his style of conspicuous consumption and his buying up large tracts of Oregon. In the 1960s, the Javanese Muslim, Bapak, attracted a large following of intellectuals in New York, London, Paris, Athens, Colombo, Jakarta, etc. in the movement called Subud. The yellow robes and cheerful drumming and chanting of members of the Harekrishna movement can be encountered in most European and North American cities. The young followers of another famous (or infamous) religious leader from the east, the Korean Moon, had to turn their backs upon family and friends in order to take on what is apparently an intellectual and spiritual straitjacket.

All these recent eastern-inspired religious movements can be said to be part of the pop-culture of the 1960s exemplified by the hippies and brought to the masses by the Beatles. Numerous westerners have sought wisdom in India, Nepal, the Middle East, on Indian Reservations in North America and elsewhere. The reverberation of their enlightenment has been felt by individuals and groups in towns and villages from Scandinavia to California. On the anthropological fringes, Castaneda's descriptions of his conversations with Don Juan sold in the millions. Today there are numerous organized systematic new approaches to religion that have attracted large numbers of adherents, and much of the approach has filtered through into business communities; of which *est* is one of the more influential. More than ten million people in the USA have taken the training programme that was developed by Werner Erhard. According to Rhinehart, *est* 'may be seen as in many ways the culmination to date of the "Easternization of America", a process that first became notable in the late fifties and early sixties' (1977: 197). Erhard himself states that in order to create *est* he immersed himself over a ten year period in 'many of the consciousness-expanding disciplines available – scientology, Mind Dynamics, Subud, gestalt therapy, Zen, Hinduism' (quoted by Rhinehart 1977: 198).

TOURISTS OF ALIEN MIND SETS

Shamanism has also been adopted recently as a religious practice in the West. The anthropologist Harner has used his knowledge of Jivaro shamanic practices (e.g. Harner 1982) to start a school. I have already noted that many contemporary western artists also call themselves shamans. Several self-appointed European and North American shamans are teaching their craft and writing books about it. Gaup, the most famous Sami shaman, states openly that he draws on the literature describing North American Indian beliefs and practices (Odner 1994). Scanning this literature (e.g. Doore 1988; Meadows 1991), I am struck by the concentration on semi-scientific exposition of techniques at the expense of contextualized meaning more familiar to anthropologists. Shamanistic trancing, it is claimed, is something everyone may learn. Trancing represents, like the assumed creative impulses of primitives, a deeper level of our humanity – a level disregarded by the civilizing process but which may be rekindled when approached correctly and by employing the wisdom of past and living shamanic cultures.

The religious heritage from the North American Indians is, according to reports in the *Guardian* (24 November 1992), being nurtured among large groups of 'hobby Indians' in Germany and Poland.[6] An estimated 85,000 Teutonic Indians dress in authentic Indian garments, dance, live in tipi and perform rituals and pow-wow. Some even insist that their dress is more 'authentic' than that of today's North American Indians, that they and not the biological descendants of the Americans are the 'real' Indians. The Iroquois of Potsdam are fighting for their landrights against a planned supermarket.

The literature on various esoteric ideas and practices from non-western cultures and traditions intended for the western public is huge. Specialist bookshops have mushroomed. The largest of these is the Yes Bookshop in Washington, established in 1972. The following remarks by the founder are instructive, 'While in College in the late 1960s and early 1970s I became a vegetarian, meditated and did yoga, studied astrology, and took a number of courses in Eastern philosophy' (Popenoe 1979: 6). The number of publications dealing with non-Christian religions available at the bookshop has increased enormously: a 1979 annotated guide, written in English and entitled *Inner Development*, offered the prospective purchaser guidance on 11,000 selected books held in stock. Yes Bookshop published a similar guide to books on alternative medicine entitled *Wellness*. At the risk of being superficial, I would suggest that the emphases placed on unworldliness, on spiritual power and spiritual development, and on beliefs deliberately presented as irrational, all filled an existential vacuum in the post-war European and American pursuit of material development. To resort to the exotic, the primitive, the intuitive and emotional was not so much a rebellion of a younger generation against their parents, as a counterweight to an overall trend perceived in terms of materialism, rationality, economic development and the failure of all these to produce individual and social 'happiness'. Again, the literature on this is huge. What I want to highlight in the present context is the attitudes of the westerners towards the alien knowledges. A monumental decontextualization not to mention simplification has taken place in the translation of Eastern and other non-Christian religions to the western market. The vast majority of the converters to, and consumers of, Eastern mysticism could be described as tourists of alien mind sets. Ideas and practices are, appropriately, 'packaged' for their needs.

The mishmash of Buddhist, Hindu, Sufi, Kwakiutl, Sami, Malaysian aboriginal and so forth tenets and practices represent in many cases a transformation of the original to fit the local needs – just as cricket was transformed to fit the Trobriand needs. The employment of such socially and culturally disembodied ideas and practices may be just as offensive to the cultural expert as Trobriand cricket is to members of the Marylebone Cricket Club in the pavilion of Lord's Cricket Ground (the 'home' of cricket). But a question remains about the extent to which members of the non-western groups take offence in the same way that the western 'experts' do. Whatever the process, the new religious movements appear to meet unfulfilled needs of the western 'homeless heart', to paraphrase Berger. If we can distance ourselves sufficiently from a purist (puritanical?) stance in these cases, we might be able to accept these novel categories on their own terms, not as dreadful hybrids.

Closely related to the influence of exotic religions in the West is the influence of exotic medical systems. In a western world where medical knowledge and practice, and religious knowledge and practice, are allocated distinct and separate discourses, it is intriguing to observe an increasing interest in a merging of the two domains in ways familiar to non-Christian traditions. With the introduction of Buddhist and Hindu ideas came ideas of vegetarianism as a means to obtain a healthy mind in a healthy body, and other distinct medical practices from the East ranging from divination practices through Ayurvedic medicine to acupuncture. While many practices remain on the fringes of western social institutions, acupuncture at least is rapidly becoming respectable as a method within the official medical world.

WESTERNIZATION OF THE THIRD WORLD?

My point is that, just as we in the industrialized West take what we want from other cultural practices and make them compatible with our own, so in many cases do members of other cultures take what they want from western traditions and inventions. In principle this need be no cause for concern. But what tends to happen in western debates is that instances of non-western influences on western ideas or products are hailed as good and revitalizing, whereas the opposite flow, resulting in transformations of local knowledge elsewhere, is condemned. An implicit assumption is that while 'we' are able to incorporate alien ideas into our existing discourses without destroying these, 'they' are less able to do so.

While I do not deny that western influences are effective on a global level – through technology, media, production, education and consumption – we should nevertheless be extremely careful in the way we draw conclusions from this. We know too little about the local meanings in many cases. As anthropologists we must maintain a highly sceptical stance *vis-à-vis* sweeping generalizations. In a certain sense the world is getting smaller, but it is too simple to assert that the flow of information and understanding is uni-directional, from the West to the Rest – or even from the politically or economically powerful to those less so. I have tried to give some examples of significant flows of knowledge that go the other way.

Strong influences clearly go from the First World outwards. At a national level the whole world is linked to the capitalist monetary economy, but the degree to which this is meaningful on local levels clearly varies enormously – not only from country to country, but also between social groups and regions within each country. The effects of industrialization and technol-ogization can be felt everywhere – even deep in the rainforest of Malaysia. The question is how to interpret the manifestations: as profound transforma-tions of existing knowledge or superficial adoptions of the signifier without the accompanying signified.

The idea that the adoption of western products in itself is sufficient to change knowledge radically is arrogant in the extreme. We can all produce examples from our fieldwork in which Americanization appears to be going on but where, on closer inspection, we find that local attitudes are radically different to expected standard ones. Consider the following cases:

Coca Cola shapes the world

A Coca Cola bottle has pride of place on altars in the temples of the islanders of the South Ryukyus, Japan. An unsuspecting observer might conclude with horror that it is in some sense worshipped. However, the shape of the bottle struck the priests as a good expression of the torso of a pregnant woman. Pregnancy is a major symbol of happiness, and is always represented on altars. It used to be represented in ceramic shapes, then tin bottles of appropriate shape were used, to be replaced more recently by one easily at hand, the Coca Cola bottle (Røkkum 1992).

The invention of a primitive art tradition

In the 1960s, in the tropical rainforest of Peninsular Malaysia a group of people known as the Jah Hut began to make 'primitive art' for sale to foreigners at the suggestion of a British official at the Department of Aboriginal Affairs. Knowing that the Jah Hut had a rich pantheon of disease-causing spirits, stylized miniature effigies of which were made for healing ceremonies, he presented them with randomly collected pictures of wooden sculptures from different parts of Africa and Polynesia and suggested they made large wooden images of their own spirits. Many Jah Hut became enthusiastic woodcarvers. They showed a keen interest in similar work from elsewhere, refined their own styles, and particularly competent individuals emerged. While the new practice of depicting spirits in wood has not been incorporated into existing healing practices, it has nevertheless contributed to an elaboration of existing knowledge (Howell 1991; Couillard 1970).

The point I wish to make is that both Ryukyu Islanders and Jah Hut were able to confront the alien objects as suitable *objets trouvés*. Indigenous cultural meanings were of no interest and they made use of the objects according to their own particular needs.

Indigenous film industries

Making films is a western invention. Films from Hollywood swamp European cinemas and TV screens. But they swamp the Third World to a rapidly decreasing extent. The Indian film industry is the largest in the world, and Indian films are eagerly viewed in every village in South Asia, and in many parts of South-East Asia. Here, few American films are ever shown. In the Middle East, Egyptian, not American, films are distributed, contributing to modern Egyptian Arabic becoming the standard language throughout the region. The Japanese film industry is also huge, in addition to which, country after country in Asia is developing films for its own population. Even in the much poorer African sub-continent, locally produced films are replacing western ones. Referring to Nigeria, Barber states that while some years ago film theatres showed mainly American, Hong Kong, or Indian films these are becoming increasingly hard to find. 'Locally produced films, in the language of the area and using the personnel, style and themes of a well-established tradition of travelling popular theatre, have replaced the imports' (quoted in Hannerz 1991: 120).

In other words, western technology is used to create meaningful cultural events within local idioms *at the expense of equivalent western products*.

'CONTAMINATION' OF TRADITIONS?

When debating issues of social change on a global scale, it is important to be reflexive. Are we (anthropologists as well as lesser mortals) absolutely certain that our aim is not to reconfirm the *exotic* other so dear to the West whereby primitives have to remain unchanged, suspended in a time warp like beautiful butterflies pinned to a board? Not only unchanging but, perhaps more compellingly, retaining their assumed proximity to nature, to the real things in life. While we encourage pushing back the frontiers of knowledge in our own establishments – and allow the employment of anything from anywhere that assists in this – we have a tendency to deplore such processes elsewhere. When people of the modern, industrial (read sophisticated) First World adopt some object or concept from the Third World, questions of true understanding and appropriate employment are not seriously debated. It is certainly not assumed that the mere fact of such an adoption is inherently destructive of local knowledge. By contrast, in the case of non-westerners there is a ready assumption that the reverse is the case. Thus, one might posit that amongst commentators there is an implicit assumption that with regard to the First World, the thing (or the concept or idea) and the original context can be (and is) separated, while such a separation is not being made in the Third World. Hence the assumed susceptibility of Third World cultures.

A preoccupation with authenticity and posited contamination of traditions is found, I suggest, primarily among an elite group of western intellectuals thinking about the Third World and amongst groups anywhere concerned with creating ethnic or national boundaries or fighting for cultural survival. It is, however, a dubious preoccupation. Not only is it unlikely that traditions have single origins, it is equally unlikely that their manifestations develop along a single path devoid of outside influences. Rather, cultural products of all kinds are manifestations of human beings' creativity and ingenuity, and this very creativity is often ignited by outside influences. People have always borrowed from each other. Alien ideas, products and values may at any time find some cultural resonance elsewhere. However, this does not mean an absence of cultural continuities.

Hall is right to point out that of the multiplicity of factors that make up the English identity, many have their origin far from Britain: 'Not a single tea plantation exists within the United Kingdom. This is the symbolization of English identity – I mean, what does anybody in the world know about an English person except that they can't get through the day without a cup of tea?' (1991: 49). The drinking of tea, a plant grown in China and then in colonial territories, has been *conventionalized* into the English way of life, and the connotations of tea-drinking in England have become quite different from those in its place of origin. It is difficult to say whether the particular tea-drinking ritual amongst the English filled a lacuna or just replaced one practice of commensality with another. By what standards could one claim that afternoon tea is an authentic British custom?

While the exchange of knowledge goes on between groups of people, new knowledge is not always incorporated. It may be unheeded or rejected because it has no relevance at the time – finds no resonance. The Norwegian folk instrument, the dulcimer, is a string instrument on which the pitch of each tone is determined by the position of its frets. A well-known dulcimer musician was told by an urban musical expert that two of the tones were 'false'. He offered to 'correct' this by moving the relevant frets. The result was a classically tempered scale which was so incompatible with the musician's own conception of music that he gave up the instrument altogether (Sinding-Larsen 1988).

There is no shortage of examples of new technology being absorbed across the world. It is within this domain that one probably can find most examples of something novel first being exoticized and then, through sustained use, recontextualized and conventionalized. It seems probable that the more specific the purpose, the more likely it is that the use made of a tool is identical. However, even here the surrounding meanings may vary widely; the famous example of the introduction of steel axes to the Yir Yoront in Australia is a case in point (Sharp 1968).

To conclude, the management of diverse knowledges goes on in all human groups. The necessity to cope with one's relationship to the past and to one's neighbours ignites a process of having to cope with alternative knowledges. In so far as one may talk of global knowledge (or culture) this can only be done at a very high level of abstraction; a level largely devoid of accompanying semantics. Different cultural configurations use (and abuse) alien knowledges in ways which best support pressing needs, appeal to the imagination, or fill local lacunae. Moreover, such needs and lacunae exist in the modern West as much as in Africa or the Far East – and may be met by adoption and conventionalizing of extra-cultural knowledge. Two examples have been focused upon in this paper: the elevation of 'primitive' visual arts and religions demonstrates that the economically and politically powerful First World has borrowed extensively from Third World knowledges in domains that affect cultural categories and individuals at a deep level.

A question remains whether the effects of an increasing global availability of knowledge and the products of various knowledges is to be viewed as a homogenization process, or one of diversification. Does de-/re-contextualization and conventionalization imply regression to the mean, or does it open up for an enrichment of existing or dominant ideas and practices? If we do not allow our gaze to be clouded by superficial manifestations, and take full account of human adaptability and creativity, together with an overriding necessity for continuity (Keesing 1992), we might accept the latter claim.

NOTES

1 The following read and commented extensively on earlier versions of this paper: Desmond McNeill, Marit Melhuus, Sarah Skar, and Olaf Smedal (who also showed me the *Yes!* catalogue discussed in the text). I am grateful to all of them for finding me time in their busy schedules.
2 I do not use the word 'lacuna' to mean a missing part or gap in local knowledge, but rather in its other sense of 'opening' or 'interval'. Complete knowledge exists nowhere; all local knowledges have their 'intervals' even if these become apparent only under certain circumstances. In some situations, lacunae may become clearly perceived. For example, the Indonesian language has no neutral and general term for 'you'; when Indonesian was adopted as *lingua franca*, many solved the resultant social dilemmas by employing the English word. The lacuna, thus, emerged precisely from the historical situation of the changing usage of Indonesian.
3 My phrasing is open to an accusation of misplaced concreteness: that I make a dichotomization of 'the human continuum into we–they contrasts and essentialize the resultant "other"' (Clifford 1988: 254). Current attacks on sweeping dichotomizations are certainly valid. However, my assertion is that there is a universal human tendency to create 'we–they' dichotomies and to essentialize 'the other', and that such dichotomous essentialization has been integral to debates about globalization. As Herzfeld notes in this volume, studying essentialization seriously does not amount to endorsing it.
4 A particularly fascinating area of study would be Japanese tourism. We know next to nothing about Japanese motives in and expectations from visiting the European capitals and historical sites.
5 Obviously, I am aware that strong influences went in the other direction, and that Christianity has been construed as an imposed world religion. Similarly, western aesthetic values have influenced both creative and consumer behaviour in many parts of the world. At the risk of repetition, in this paper my concern is to emphasize that profound influences in the same domains have also come to the West – especially in recent times.
6 I am grateful to Olivia Harris for pointing out this article to me. Her scholarly discussions at the University of Oslo during the academic year 1992–1993 have helped to clarify my own thoughts.

REFERENCES

Appadurai, A. (1990) 'Disjuncture and difference in the global cultural economy', in M. Featherstone (ed.) *Global Culture: Nationalism, Globalization and Modernity*, London: Sage.
Barber, K. (1987) 'Popular arts in Africa', *African Studies Review* 30(3): 1–18.
Brody, E. (1987) *Paris: The Musical Kaleidoscope 1870–1925*, New York: Braziller.

Clifford, J. (1981) 'On ethnographic surrealism', *Comparative Studies in Society and History* 23(4): 563–564; reprinted in J. Clifford (1988) *The Predicament of Culture: Twentieth-century Ethnography, Literature, and Art*, Cambridge, Mass.: Harvard University Press.

—— (1988) 'On collecting art and culture', in J. Clifford *The Predicament of Culture: Twentieth-century Ethnography, Literature, and Art*, Cambridge, Mass.: Harvard University Press.

Cooke, L. (1984) 'Neo-primitivism: a regression to the domain of the "night-mind" or adolescent persiflage?', *Artscribe* 51: 16–24.

Couillard, M.A. (1970) *Traditions in Tensions: Carving in a Jah Hut Community*, Penang: Pererbit University Sains Malaysia.

Doore, G. (ed.) (1988) *Shaman's Path: Healing, Personal Growth and Empowerment*, Boston: Shambhala.

Eidheim, H. (1992) *Stages in the Development of Sami Selfhood*, Working Paper 7, Oslo: Department of Social Anthropology, University of Oslo.

Featherstone, M. (1990) 'Global culture: an introduction', in M. Featherstone (ed.) *Global Culture: Nationalism, Globalization and Modernity*, London: Sage.

Foster, H. (1985) 'The "primitive" unconscious of modern art', *October* 34: 45–70.

Hall, S. (1991) 'The local and the global: globalization and ethnicity', in A.D. King (ed.) *Culture, Globalization and the World System*, London: Macmillan.

Hannerz, U. (1990) 'Cosmopolitans and locals in world culture', in M. Featherstone (ed.) *Global Culture: Nationalism, Globalization and Modernity*, London: Sage.

—— (1991) 'Scenarios for peripheral cultures', in A.D. King (ed.) *Culture, Globalization and the World System*, London: Macmillan.

Harner, M. (1982) *The Way of the Shaman: A Guide to Power and Healing*, Toronto: Bantam Books.

Howell, S. (1991) 'The meaning of art', in S. Hiller (ed.) *The Myth of Primitivism*, London: Routledge.

Keesing, R. (1992) *Custom and Confrontation: The Kwaio Struggle for Cultural Autonomy*, Chicago: Chicago University Press.

Magnin, A. (n.d.; presumably 1991) *The Jean Pigozzi Contemporary African Art Collection at the Saatchi Collection*, London: Saatchi Collection.

Meadows, K. (1991) *Shamanic Experience: A Practical Guide to Contemporary Shamanism*, Shaftesbury Dorset: Element.

Odner, K. (1994) '(Nord-)samisk religion og identitet', Unpublished.

Pigozzi, J. (1991) *Africa Now: Jean Pigozzi Collection*, Groningen: Groninger Museum.

Popenoe, C. (1979) *Inner Development: The 'Yes!' Bookshop Guide*, Washington: Yes Inc. (Random House).

Price, S. (1989) *Primitive Art in Civilized Places*, Chicago: University of Chicago Press.

Rhinehart, L. (1977) *The Book of est*, London: Abacus.

Robertson, R. (1990) 'Mapping the global condition: globalization as the central concept', in M. Featherstone (ed.) *Global Culture: Nationalism, Globalization and Modernity*, London: Sage.

—— (1992) *Globalization: Social Theory and Global Culture*, London: Sage.

Røkkum, A. (1992) 'Writing and Thought', Unpublished.

Sharp, L. (1968) 'Steel axes for Stone Age Australians', reprinted in E. LeClair and H.K. Schneider (eds) *Economic Anthropology: Readings in Theory and Practice*, New York: Holt, Rhinehart & Winston.

Sinding-Larsen, H. (1988) 'Notation and music: the history of a tool of description and its domain to be described', *Cybernetics* (Winter).

Wallerstein, I. (1990) 'Culture as the ideological battleground of the modern world-system', in M.Featherstone (ed.) *Global Culture: Nationalism, Globalization and Modernity*, London: Sage.

9 From cosmology to environmentalism

Shamanism as local knowledge in a global setting

Piers Vitebsky

[My dead father] may be underground, but we can't know – we don't speak to him any more.

> (a young Sora who has converted from shamanism to Christianity)

A communist police chief threatened a Sakha (Yakut) shaman with his revolver. The shaman warned the young man, 'My son, don't do that, you'll hurt yourself!' The policeman then shot off his own thumb. Furious, he put the shaman in prison. The shaman escaped. Several times the policeman put him in ever more secure cells, but each time he escaped and came walking back in through the front door. Finally, the shaman was tried and sentenced to hard labour in the forest, cutting down trees for firewood. An inspection team visited him there in the summer and saw the axe flying magically around the clearing, felling trees and stacking the wood up in neat piles. At the beginning of winter, they went to collect it but the shaman had disappeared. So had the pieces of firewood: they had joined together again to make the living trees, which were standing just as they had been before the shaman had ever begun his work.

KNOWLEDGES AND KNOWERS

In the jungles and the tundra, shamanism is dying. An intensely local kind of knowledge is being abandoned in favour of various kinds of knowledge which are cosmopolitan and distant-led. Meanwhile, something called shamanism thrives in western magazines, sweat lodges and weekend workshops. The New Age movement, which includes this strand of neo-shamanism, is in part a rebellion against the principle of distant-led knowledge. This rebellion comes from within the very society which does the leading and looks for inspiration to the most distant societies findable or even conceivable. In the wild, shamanism is dying because local people are becoming more global in their orientation, while here it is flourishing – apparently for the same sort of reason. And yet again, in other parts of the jungle and the tundra there is a revival, supposedly of traditional shamanism.

What is local and what is global in all this? Do these phenomena affect our view of these terms? I shall try to tackle this question by asking which elements of shamanism can be transmitted to certain subcultures of contemporary society and how they are appropriated and transmuted on the way. The following exploration is only tentative, more in the form of 'Notes towards . . .' since shamanism is already a problematic term, while it is even more foolhardy to generalize about the 'New Age'. Yet what follows will at least give the lie to any smooth model of 'globalization' as a one-way current, an acculturation leading implicitly to a cultural homogenization. Rather, it compels us to regard the global process as a continual realignment of a system of epistemological and political relationships. Shamanism in turn is a form of 'indigenous knowledge'. Even if the flow of power is largely one-way, nonetheless 'indigenous knowledge' does not simply yield to cosmopolitan knowledge. Even on its own territory, the former may include commentaries, critiques and parodies of the latter. Abroad, indigenous knowledge may infiltrate and subvert the knowledge of industrial society, and in this it is aided by a loss of nerve at the centre of industrial society which leads its members to appropriate, for instance, shamanic motifs as part of their own radical self-critique. Does indigenous knowledge survive this appropriation?

The terms 'global' and 'local' between them constitute a metaphor of place. A few years ago, the problem of globalization might have been framed in terms of time, as 'modernization'. Since the evolutionary and teleological assumptions of evolutionism (and of its policy arm 'development') are now under question, space seems at first sight to offer a more neutral, pluralist dimension for the analysis of social difference. Linear time is so obviously a metaphor of domination because it moves in only one direction, so that some people will inevitably be found to be more backward than others. On the other hand, space is the foundation of maps rather than of time charts and can be read in any direction. Yet, once again, it turns out to contain dominant and subordinate positions: the global subsumes the local and supposedly homogenizes it, so that even on the map there is only one path for which anyone's visa is valid.

Is there no clean dimension, then? The ambiguity which surrounds time and space suggests that these are not here concepts from physics, but ways of talking about social context or setting. How can one compare a kind of knowledge which is local with one which is global? If the latter is also universal or absolute, it should thereby negate the former by logical necessity so that there will be nothing further to discuss. If not, this already implies a recognition that the arena of operation of 'knowledge' is not just truth, but also appropriateness and applicability. As soon as one asks, 'Knowledge for whom?', one is in the realm of multiple knowledges. The nature of any given knowledge depends on where each party to it stands, as does its power. It is through power relationships between knowledges that some of them can be turned into forms of ignorance (Vitebsky 1993b).

Using examples from my own experience of the Sora of tribal India and the Sakha of Siberia (pronounced Sakhá, formerly known by the Russian term

Yakut), I shall explore how it is that shamanic ideas can be considered knowledge in one setting and not in another, wisdom in one setting and foolishness in another – in effect true in one and false in another. How can Sora shamanism become enlightening for western psychotherapists at the very moment when it is becoming inappropriate for the youngest generation of Sora themselves? In what sense has shamanism suddenly become true again for Sakha nationalists after two generations of being false for these same people when they were Soviet communists?

Clearly, these are not just questions of the value of different epistemologies. But neither are they simply political questions; rather, they involve a relationship between these two domains which will ultimately bring us back to the complexities of any adequate concept of globality. It is no longer possible to make a watertight distinction between 'traditional' shamanistic societies (a mainstay of the old ethnographic literature and of comparative religion), and the new wave of neo-shamanist movements (still barely studied in depth). For shamanism, as with any other kind of local knowledge, the essence of globality today is that it belongs both in the past of remote tribes, and in the present of industrial subcultures. But there are further twists: the shamanic revival is now reappearing in the *present* of some of these remote tribes – only now these are neither remote nor tribal.

Thus, globalization (or modernization) may lead either to the downgrading and abandonment of indigenous knowledge, or on the contrary to its reassertion and transformation. The Sora and the Sakha demonstrate respectively a fall and a rise in the indigenous valuation of their respective forms of shamanism. Both space and time are involved: these processes are going on in various parts of the same globe, at the same time – as is the New Age movement, with which the Sakha have much in common and the Sora virtually nothing.

There is no agreed cross-cultural definition of 'shamanism' (for major statements, see Eliade 1964; de Heusch 1981; Lewis 1989). Indeed, it is characterized by a chameleon-like elusiveness. Shamanic thinking is fluid rather than doctrinal, so that it is questionable whether the practices surrounding shamans should be seen as an 'ism' at all. However, I shall not put a great weight on definitional criteria, since much of my argument will apply by extension to the much wider realm of 'indigenous knowledge' as this filters in all its diversity through to the New Age. There is, nonetheless, a certain combination of key characteristics which it is reasonable to see as distinctively shamanic. These include a layered cosmology, with the flight of the shaman's soul to other levels of this cosmos, and the power to use this journey to fight, command and control spirits which inhabit these realms and affect human destiny. Thus shamanism is both an epistemology, that is a system of contemplative thought with an implicit set of propositions, and a blueprint for action, as in the location of game animals or the retrieval of kidnapped souls. Shamanic thinking has certain implications for the appropriation of shamanism by global culture today:

- It is *local*, in that cosmic space merges experientially into the space of everyday living through the features, such as graves and sacred sites, of a specific landscape.
- At the same time, it is *holistic*, in that (even allowing for the existence of other tribes, white men, etc.) the cosmos and the local landscape between them give a total rendering of the universe.
- This holism does not imply a steady state: shamanism is also *eristic*, in that the shamanic world-view openly acknowledges the role of battle and risk. The shaman is a hero who makes a bold and necessary intervention into cosmic processes. The power to act is precarious and this human action is fraught with danger.
- Finally, shamans are often politically *dissident* or anti-centrist. In Soraland, Siberia and elsewhere, they are contrasted to non-ecstatic priests or elders who perform more sober, routine cults.

I shall later try to trace how each of these features is carried over into the New Age appropriations of shamanic motifs, where I shall focus in particular on two developments: the individualistic psychologization of religion; and environmentalist activism in the public domain.

FALLS AND RISES OF INDIGENOUS SHAMANIC IDIOMS

The decline of shamans in tribal India

The Sora are a scheduled tribe of some 450,000 who live in an area about 30 miles across on the border between Orissa and Andhra Pradesh. I lived among them for much of the late 1970s and was able to visit them briefly in 1984 and again in 1992. This last visit was not only an anthropological experience, but also a historical one. Though there were many obvious modern touches, the Sora society I had studied in the late 1970s was a jungle society organized round an elaborate and dramatic cult of the dead, who speak with the living in dialogues which pass through shamans and shamanesses in trance (Elwin 1955; Vitebsky 1993a).

But what I have witnessed over nearly twenty years is a key period of transformation. Looking back, I now have the sense of having been on the spot at the culmination of a historical process in which strains can be absorbed for a long period by a society, before it finally snaps or changes quite suddenly. In the late 1970s, laymen depended on shamans for funerals and cures, and a number of children and young adults were learning to become shamans. There were only a few Christian households or individuals here and there living in otherwise shamanist families. However, in 1992 I found that almost the entire population of this area under 25 years of age had become Baptists. This movement was already apparent in 1984 and has now encompassed even those adults who were training to become shamans when I knew them as children. The Ancestor cult is maintained by those over 30 years old, but the practising shamans have few successors, and the more large-scale rites, such as the annual festival of the dead, are being abandoned. The overwhelming impression I received was that the shamanist world-view was losing heart.

What is the essence of this world-view which younger people are renouncing? Under Sora shamanism, groups of living people hold dialogues more or less daily with the dead, who come one at a time to speak to them through the mouth of a shaman in trance. Closely related groups thus find themselves in constantly recurring contact: family conversations, jokes and quarrels continue after some of their participants have crossed the dividing line between what are called life and death. Each of these dialogues is precipitated by an illness or a death and, in holding these dialogues, living Sora attempt to understand the state of mind of the dead and how this will affect them. But at the same time, each dialogue is only a fleeting episode in an open-ended relationship which before it runs its course will have served to explore, and maybe resolve, a range of emotional ambiguities in the lives of the participants (Vitebsky 1993a).

This is a deeply local religion, closely tied to the Sora's awareness of their landscape. After death, a person's consciousness becomes a form of spirit called *sonum*. The concept *sonum*, manifested in a range of particular named *sonum*s, is a powerful causal principle in the affairs of the living. But it is also a contradictory one, nourishing its living kin through the soul-force it puts into their growing crops, but at the same time precipitating illness and death among them. Thus, in one aspect, the dead give to the living their continued sustenance and their very existence, yet in another aspect these same dead persons impinge on the living and consume them.

The Sora tackle this causal relationship through an elaborate classification of states of being dead. Different categories of *sonum* are located in different features of the landscape. As a living person moves around this landscape, he or she may encounter *sonum*s and become involved with them. This happens, not at random, but as a development of their long-term relationships with various dead persons. Though these encounters with *sonum*s may cause illness, they do not constitute a person's medical history so much as a history of his states of mind in relation to other persons. The illness in the living person is the reflection of a mood or attitude in a dead person, so that the living person's awareness of the dead is an integral part of the symptoms and of the definition of his illnesses. A person's medical history thus amounts to a social and emotional biography.

A Sora person's innermost sense of who he or she is in relation to other persons, is thus dependent on an understanding of the way in which this landscape is peopled with human consciousness. But this relationship to the landscape in general is mediated through particular plots of land, by means of the grain that grows there. Ancestors each reside in a particular plot of productive agricultural land, infusing their own soul-force into the grain crops which grow there. So with every meal that living people eat, they are ingesting something of their own parents and grandparents as a form of nourishment. Since these Ancestors cannot be conceptualized except as residing in specific plots of land, the Sora are taking part in a cycle which unites their landscape, their close relatives and their sense of their own soul or consciousness.

So long as the soul-force of the Sora people is underground, it remains firmly in the realm which the Sora share with the life-forms of the jungle. But how does the soul-force in crops circulate when it is above ground, in the harvested grain itself? Much of it, in an ever-increasing amount, leaves the area through the market, under steadily growing economic and political pressure (Vitebsky 1978, 1995). It is here that a problem arises. These grains are the very crops which contain the soul-force of the Ancestors of the people who grow them – and then sell them to be eaten by strangers. The fact that grain has human, Sora soul-force in it reflects its role as the staple of Sora diet; yet at the same time it is the most frequently alienated of all Sora crops, on by far the largest scale.

The circuits of Sora political and economic relations have included outsiders for a very long time. This is not the same as saying that the Sora are ethnically pluralist. The psychology and theology of being Sora, by contrast, maintain a sharp distinction between insiders and outsiders. The Sora have traditionally disliked and feared neighbouring peoples and in their cosmology have assigned them specific, often somewhat demonic roles (such as were-leopards). Sora soul-force does not pass in and out of the souls or bodies of Oriya Paik policemen or Telugu Komiti moneylenders, to take only two of the semi-demonic races in their world. However, it does pass explicitly in and out of animals, alcohol and grain. So while the shamanist world-view is *socially* inward-turning, based on lineages, households and their precise location on the local landscape, in *cosmic* terms it is extremely wide-ranging, involving elaborate patterns of association and soul-exchange with the landscape, plants and animals.

My preliminary interpretation of this situation (Vitebsky 1995) is that this way of relating to one's environment becomes more and more inappropriate the more that its ancestral soul-force, at the most nourishing peak of its cycle, is sold off through the market place. If the produce of the land can be sold fully to outsiders, then it belongs to anybody and nobody. The concept of crops itself is changing: rather than being a carrier of one's parents' soul, grain can become no more than just 'food'; instead of being part of a cyclical model in which production and consumption feed into and regenerate each other, the production of food moves further and further away from the goal of its consumption and becomes alienated as a mere commodity. A vital link between people and their environment is severed, and it becomes less meaningful or appropriate (Sora: *tam-*) for the environment to serve as a walkaround map of social relations, kinship groups, theological concepts, states of mind and personal emotions.

Shamanism and ethnic revival in arctic Siberia

The Sora have shamans, but are not aware of having anything called shaman*ism*. By contrast the Sakha, who have their own Republic in north-eastern Siberia, have almost no shamans but a rapidly growing ideology called shamanism. At the most, there are said to be no more than about eight 'real' shamans left among a Sakha population of 350,000 who occupy an area nearly the size of India (now increasingly dominating a guest population of 700,000 Russians and other whites).

The city of Yakutsk contains flourishing societies for the revival of shamanism, and their members are largely doctors, teachers, anthropologists, historians, vets, physicists, biologists, writers and film directors. These people explore shamanism as the ancient wisdom of their own people, from the points of view of healing, self-realization, psychotherapy, telepathy, bioenergetic fields, their own ethnic origins, oral epic tradition and modern theatre (Balzer in press).

The Soviet regime (in which the Sakha intelligentsia were themselves implicated) never managed to cope fully with the combination of religiosity and nationalism implicit in Sakha shamanic thinking. Sakha writers like Oyunsky (a pen name from the Sakha word for 'shaman') and Kulakovsky tried to reconcile shamanist and communist themes in the 1920s, but were killed off in the less compromising 1930s. From then until the mid-1980s, shamans were ridiculed or exiled, and at times (especially from the 1930s to 1950s) shot or dropped out of helicopters and challenged to fly.

Until recently, the local knowledge associated with shamanism was cordoned off, studied academically and patronized. In a typical statement, a Sakha author wrote that before the advent of Lenin and the 'beneficial influence of advanced Russian culture and social thought', 'the intellectual talents of the benighted, unlettered Yakut [i.e. Sakha] people . . . were apparent . . . in the fashioning of a many-genred folklore handed down from generation to generation' (Makarov 1983: 3).

But shamanism is not so much an institution – indeed, when it is not adopted by a revivalist movement it is hardly an 'ism' at all – as a part of a wider complex of ideas (and a somewhat variable one). The shamanic world-view was very diffuse throughout everyday life and did not depend solely on one particular kind of performer, even the shaman. Everyone still partakes of this world-view every time they toss a glass of vodka into the fire to feed the hearth spirit, or check the flight of birds to see if they will have a good day. Some practices, such as feeding the fire, are carried out constantly and unselfconsciously by most town-dwellers and even party officials. Mean-while, the rural population still lives by hunting, cattle and horse herding, and a range of corresponding elements and motifs, involving animals, ghosts and features of the landscape, have proved very resilient. So the young intellectuals of the city can turn to their own rural grandparents for authentic 'ethnic wisdom', as well as to books on anthropology and folklore, which are very popular reading matter. This wisdom is the local knowledge contained in traditional ideas about man and nature: about seasons, the weather, the behaviour of animals, medicinal herbs, health and illness. The village informants, who used to be listed at the back of ethnographies only by way of scholastic documentation, are now becoming public figures.

This assertive new ideology rides on the crest of a particular historical wave: the breakup of the USSR which offered the possibility for each of its (partly ethnically defined) constituent regions to claim a higher degree of autonomy. All the thirty-odd indigenous Siberian peoples have a strong shamanic tradition, but the Sakha are exceptionally well placed in their numbers (many of the other peoples number only a few thousands) and in the fact that they have a Republic which possesses a large share of Russia's gold and virtually all the country's diamonds.

The boosting of shamanic ideas to iconic status goes hand in hand with the sudden, vastly increased export potential of these natural resources. The ambiguities and dilemmas which this raises for the Sakha elite's approach to their land emerge in the following quotation (cf Vitebsky 1990).

Today my Republic reminds me of a huge ship, laden with treasure and boarded by assorted departmental pirates. As they shove diamonds, tin, gold, coal and mica feverishly into chests, they cast their predatory eyes yet further at the piles of timber, which like a giant float keep this ship from sinking. If they ever reach the timber, then the ship will go down once and for all.

(Tumarcha 1989)

On the one hand, the victim of the ministerial pirates from Moscow is not 'my people', but 'my Republic': the point seems to be not that the treasure should not be enjoyed, but that others are stealing it from its rightful owners. On the other hand, the remark about timber suggests that the extraction of natural resources is destructive whoever does it. The position of the Republic's regional government is that coal, gold and diamonds must be mined – but that the profits must return to Yakutia. Their agenda for action works in terms of tariffs and an enhanced degree of sovereignty within the idiom of the modern state. In ethnic terms, people who talk like this are thinking of the development and the autonomy of a region or territory, rather than of a people. The idiom is economic and statist.

The alternative view sees autonomy, not in economic terms but in terms which are ethnically exclusive. Nativist thinkers sometimes push concepts of the state into the background, or even deny them altogether. Supporters of this approach look towards Sakha ethnic wisdom to guide man's use of the local landscape. They favour the renewable animal resources of traditional Sakha culture and may reject large-scale development projects altogether. In a landmark article entitled 'Man lives by Nature' (Danilov 1989) the author writes that southern models of development do not take account of special northern conditions, so that in their concern only with their own products, the mining agencies are breaking the laws of nature. These are precisely the laws which Sakha ethnic wisdom respects. Since time immemorial, Danilov writes, the Sakha have believed that one must respect the silence of the forest, not pollute Nature and not wound the Earth. The world and man's soul are both made up of three corresponding elements. In polluting Nature, we are polluting our own flesh and blood. So we must protect the landscape like our own body and soul. This 'ethnic wisdom' is seen as amounting to a sort of essence which one has (or can rediscover in oneself) by virtue of belonging to a certain people and through partaking in that people's relationship to their land. Only the Sakha people understand this vast, wild and difficult northern environment and know how to use it properly.[1]

The urban Sakha interpretation of their shamanic tradition has shifted from the religious sensibility of the herder's and hunter's movement across a local landscape towards a more abstract sense of ethnicity. On the way, this passes through the concept of a landscape of the mind and of the Sakha person's freedom of movement over this landscape. Many of the Sakha intelligentsia interpret the shamanic landscape symbolically as the domain of a liberated consciousness, with shamans' journeys into different cosmological realms representing changes of states of mind or 'altered states of consciousness'. This move is reinforced by the wide circulation of magazine articles in Sakha and Russian which combine local ideas of this sort with themes from abroad which chime with them. It is significant that, whereas nationalist societies in the early twentieth century had titles like 'Yakut Nation', the most conspicuous new society of the late perestroika period is called *Kut-Syur*, 'Consciousness-Soul'.[2] As yet, there seems to be only one 'real' new young shaman, who lives in a remote village and avoids the hype in the city. But many circles in the capital live in a feverish state of excitement over the idea of shamanism, the icons of which reappear constantly in plays and newspaper articles and on television. Numerous hypnotists, wizards and 'extra-sensories' ply their trade and toy with how far they can get away with calling themselves shamans. As the Sakha Minister of Culture, one of Russia's most prominent theatre directors and a leading figure in the movement, put it to me, 'shamanism is a void at the heart of things: everyone circles around it and no-one knows how to get in'.

NON-INDIGENOUS SHAMANISM: FROM COSMOLOGICAL GROUND TO POLITICAL AGENDA

Locality and belief in the New Age

In each case, a change in the significance of 'shamanism' is linked to a change in the meaning of place. The Sora and the Sakha represent two contrasting ways in which a local sense of place becomes more global, though less cosmic. In one, locality comes to mean less, in the other, it means more.

Local knowledge is the basis for action by the intellect on the environment and gives to its knowers the conviction of commanding a certain area of experience. This remains 'knowledge' for as long as it continues to satisfy that conviction. Under certain circumstances, experience itself can move away from the certainty of knowledge, defy it, slip out of its grasp. An entire system of knowledge, or parts of it, become ineffectual in the face of reality. Here, the Sora present what may be called a standard old-fashioned modernization scenario. They are ceasing to practise shamanism under a complex set of conditions which are dominated by a growing sense of ethnic inferiority. It would be hard to imagine a revival of Sora shamans unless this were part of an ethnic reassertion against the state, brahminism or some other dominant outside force. But since christianization is already a way of asserting oneself against these, a revival seems doubly unlikely. So they are not abandoning their previous local knowledge because it was objectively bad knowledge: as we shall see, from the point of view of psychology and psychiatry, Sora shamanistic knowledge may be considered an exceptionally good and effective knowledge, representing a great insight about human emotion (Vitebsky 1993a: ch. 10). Rather, it is because the scope and expectations of its application have changed. In particular, as the quotation at the head of this paper showed, it has lost its narrative power to link the past, present and future.

For the Sakha, however, a rhetorical emphasis on Sakha ethnic wisdom fits in well with the pragmatic move towards a localization of political authority and of control over economic resources. Shamanic ideas are absolutely of the place. In the present move towards decentralization this local character is seen, not as a sign of provincialism, but as a sign of appropriateness and power. Shamanism offers a revitalized narrative link with the past, a sense that one's condition today can be seen as the developmental and experiential outcome of this past, a revivification of memory. This is a reversal of the old Soviet doctrine that in order to be good, one's present condition should be the outcome of severing such links with the past.

By being caught up in a modern revival at all, the Sakha share certain features with the New Age movement in the West, in particular what I would call the crisis of literal belief. They know their knowledge about shamanic ideas, not as *habitus* but as facts. When the aged mother of a friend of mine died recently, he described her as one of the last people who knew these things. Yet in another sense, he knows them too, but as an anthropology student in the city writing about her cosmology. The difference is that as a herdswoman, she also did them, and did them because for her there was no distinction between knowing and doing.

Yet even as *habitus* becomes packaged into facts, it comes with a trademark and a copyright. The landscape has a new meaning, which is primarily as 'ours' rather than anyone else's. Here, then, is narrative restored, but on a national scale. Not only the Sakha mineral ministries' but even the most radical Sakha environmentalist positions emerge also as nationalistic stances. The radical Sakha greens are effectively saying to both their own people and outsiders, 'The world is in desperate need of environmental wisdom. But our people have already got it'. This much has been said or implied by Black Elk (Neihardt 1972 [1932]) and many others elsewhere. But in Yakutia, the powerful global idiom of environment is being used during a political free-for-all to legitimate vital ethnic claims. Shamanism becomes a future-oriented claim-staker in terms of ethnic politics, dressed up in its older rhetoric as a rationale. A political vacuum has brought about a cultural, epistemological and even moral vacuum which is rare in the modern world. The shamanist-ecologists of Yakutia are positing an essence of their own ethnicity distilled in a wisdom which is at one and the same time ancient, avant-garde and – crucially for the ethnic and territorial climate of the ex-USSR – inalienable.

So the Sakha are succeeding in linking their local knowledge and their own narrative advantageously to global developments, while the Sora are failing (and probably not even aware of this possibility). When converting local knowledge into global currency, the exchange rate is more favourable for some newcomers than for others. For the Sakha just now, this is because they have diamonds on their land combined with a political vacuum which invites bold new initiatives.

But there is at least a third kind of situation in which shamanic ideas function in the modern world. The Sora and Sakha represent largely 'tribal' areas with an indigenous tradition, which is either being abandoned or revived after a recent abandonment. In the western New Age movement, however, shamanism has never been indigenous. These neo-shamanists are practising shamanism for the first time, in a cosmopolitan way but sometimes with the additional claim that it is somehow a revival of ancient wisdom. These movements are inchoate and barely studied, so that any generalization can be no more than tentative. But it seems to me that one can sketch certain prominent overall tendencies.

As in Yakutia, such movements turn to a place or time, real or imagined, which is other than here and now. This is necessary because they state or imply a radical critique of that same here and now. Unlike the Yakuts, the proponents of these movements cannot plausibly claim to be basing themselves on a recent indigenous tradition (unless one invokes druids etc., and strains the argument to extremes). So in addition, such movements are therefore generally not nationalistic but cosmopolitan and universalist in tone. They cannot be otherwise since the inspiration and legitimation of such syncretistic wisdom is provided by cultures which are avowedly foreign. This knowledge has a local flavour, but it is local elsewhere in time or space: it comes from Red Indian shamans, Tibetan lamas, ancient Egyptian priests – it might even come from the Sakha if their ideas were widely available in English. As it is adopted into a wider world, this kind of wisdom is stripped of certain specific elements (such as clan cults and ancestor worship) which are so local that they do not travel well. But this new re-localization also takes place on a global scale and with global claims. Indeed, this is what gives a millennial tone to much New Age rhetoric: it is both community-based and a new sort of world religion.

Yet, because it is largely middle class and urban, this approach raises severe problems about where people stand between degrees of literal belief and of literary conceit, as with the gods and fauns of pastoral poetry. The Sakha intelligentsia still lie further back along this continuum. Most of my friends in this class retain great faith in traditional dream interpretation, read omens, fear ghosts and are in awe of the power in shamanic objects in their own museum, going so far as to claim that these still emanate the distinctive smell which surrounds the shaman's person.

Perfecting the self and saving the planet

The New Age may be cosmopolitan; but at the same time, it moves away from cosmology by dissolving the realm of the religious. Among many others, I shall focus on two conflicting directions to this move, which drift like clouds of gas away from the exploded centre of cosmology. On the one hand, there is a tendency to annihilate the distinction between humans and cosmos by psychologizing the realm of the religious, that is, to take the cosmos into oneself and use it as a tool for therapizing the psyche; on the other hand, there is also a tendency to enlarge the disjunction between humans and cosmos, as though they relate to each other only with difficulty. This dualism between humans and their setting feeds into ideologies of the 'environment'.

Both psychotherapy and environmentalism find much to quarry in the old shamanism. They may be said to represent, respectively, a more private (individualist) and a more public (collective) approach. But this appropriation takes place in the context of a dissatisfaction with the way things are, and a yearning to make things better. This yearning is post-Edenic and sometimes apocalyptic, but must do without the explicit theological rationales which originally underpinned the ideas of Eden or the apocalypse (though one can sometimes detect more veiled themes of sin and redemption). The individualist and collective approaches to making things better emerge respectively as improving or perfecting the self, and saving the world (the 'planet'). The self is no longer a target for 'saving' since this is a deeply theological idiom which has been left behind, along with sin and Satan, outside the sweat lodge or gestalt group; 'saving' the world, however, fits into current rhetoric because this combines two powerful current dramas: the adventure story, in which heroes save humanity from a fate worse than death at the eleventh hour and in the nick of time, and the idea of the earth's vulnerability. 'Spaceship earth', photographed from outside the atmosphere and repeated endlessly on record covers and advertisements, has become a new outer membrane which circumscribes our consciousness, a new icon of finitude.

From religion to psychology

In contrast to the New Age, and even to the Sakha, the Sora abandonment of their Ancestors retains a largely religious tone. The rationale of their conversion does not lie in a denial of the theological idiom. They are denying the old beliefs only to the extent that the new one may be more powerful or appropriate ('of course *sonum*s still exist, since there's a word for them and they've all got names'). God and Jesus do not so much render the old *sonum*s unreal or part of a false knowledge, as supersede them: they are bigger and better *sonum*s. So even if the dead do really reside underground, the living no longer know how to relate to this fact. Consequently, they are losing interest in the technique of dialogue which allows them to find out what the dead have to say to them from down there. One of my closest friends in the 1970s lent me his young son to live with me as my own son. This child has now grown up and become a Christian. His father was never a Christian but nevertheless received a Christian burial instead of the lengthy sequence of funerals, with dialogues, which he had himself taken part in for others in his time. In 1992 I asked the son where his father, my old friend, was now. The young man replied that he was with Jesus, but then added, rather wistfully I thought, 'He may be underground, but we can't know – we don't speak to him any more' (*anin kînorai lungen daku pede, do ellen a'galambe – a'nolongbe*).

Thus, the Sora are abandoning their Ancestor worship in favour of an alternative model of religion. Yet the main interest of their old religion for the modern outside world lies in the extraordinary ways in which its insights parallel theories and techniques in contemporary psychotherapy but can be used to refine and develop the latter. Nobody is likely to want to believe literally in the myriad categories of Sora *sonum* or to repeat the minutiae of performing the appropriate rites. But the overall picture of human emotions and interrelationships given by traditional Sora *religion* is ripe for appropriation by our own avant-garde thinking – but only as *psychology*.

Kleinman (1986: 55–56) has identified a large-scale 'psychologizing process' which he argues has affected American culture since World War I and which forms part of a 'cultural transformation in which the self has been culturally constituted as the now dominant western ethnopsychology'. The expanded psyche fills the space left by the retreat of religion. So far has this process advanced that even transcending one's own limitations has become as much a psychic as a religious quest.

> From the perspective of the American Firewalking movement the beliefs that constitute religious systems like the Anastenaria are limiting beliefs; they are the 'programs' and 'tapes' that keep us from further spiritual growth. . . . The highest good is not obedience to the will of some supernatural being but self-expression and direct experience. It isn't Saint Constantine who protects us from the fire; it's the fact of who we are. When

we identify with who we really are, we don't get burned because who we really are can never get burned.

(Danforth 1989: 270)

The Sakha intelligentsia have likewise moved significantly from shamanism as religion (the form in which I have still seen it among old herders and hunters in the wilderness, as they apologize to bears they have killed and return the souls of elks to the Lord of the Forest for reincarnation) to a psychology. With a nationalist cultural society named 'Consciousness-Soul', they have moved from outer (cosmological) to inner (psychological) space as they embark on journeys which are avowedly journeys of the mind. Whereas I do not believe the language exists with which to explain psychology to my Sora friends, in Yakutia many of the old herders and hunters (all of whom read Russian popular magazines) are able to point out the parallels for themselves.

From cosmology to environment

New Age psychologized religion also tends to downplay the political. To quote Danforth again,

[a]ccording to the New Age ideology, because society is nothing more than a collection of individuals, social and political problems are reduced to psychological problems. Social change is therefore equated with personal growth and self-transformation.

(Danforth 1989: 284)

However, cosmology involves not only a vision of how the universe works, but also uses this as a basis for decisive action upon the world. Environmentalism, as one of its successor ideologies, takes this even further by concentrating directly on how things ought to be. As the concept of government falters, the world moves further and further into the realm of pressure groups and lobbying. Knowledge, whether indigenous or otherwise, moves out of the realm of epistemology and increasingly serves or underpins an 'agenda'. (This is another, completely non-epistemological reason why knowledge today cannot be concerned primarily with a timeless 'truth'.)

This kind of agenda does not lie at the private end of the spectrum, like many of the self-perfection techniques of the psychotherapies. Practices like apologizing to animals' souls and returning them to the Master or Mistress of the Animals, acknowledging new moons and solstices, picking only the plants you need, not using cars, recycling environmentally costly products like glass bottles and bears' souls – all these are perceived as good ways of behaving and thinking. But at the same time, most of us cannot do these things without being fey or pretentious, or feeling that we are making little impact. We want our government and our society to do these things on our behalf, since this is the only scale on which such ideas will have any substantial effect. Thus concern for the environment is necessarily tied closely to an attempt to influence public policy.

FROM COSMIC HOLISM TO GLOBAL MANAGEMENT

Shamanistic cosmologies are anthropocentric, but in a certain holistic way which makes the activity of man indispensable, even while constraining it. The world is animized and gendered on the model of human consciousness, and the shaman's operations are done by humans, for humans. But meanwhile, bears and tigers have their own realities and even their own shamans, often with humans cast in the loser's role. The visions of equilibrium and of cycles of reciprocity in the shamanic vision make man's position humble and precarious – hence the dangers in the shaman's use of power and his or her commitment to battle. Crucially, a shamanic world-view acknowledges that the processes of the world can be held only within partial human control, and at the cost of continual struggle.

The concept of 'environment' is anthropocentric in a different and more overwhelming sense, which is perhaps why the current sense of environmental failure generates a combination of public panic and ostrichism. It involves a more one-sided and total concept of control, one based on domination and regulation, rather than on shamanism's delicate and constantly renewed negotiation. And in policy, this emerges in sub-fields like natural resource management.

Environmentalism considers humanity as distinct from its 'environment' and amounts to a strategy for the management of that environment as a 'resource base'. This approach is frankly anthropocentric to the point of being utilitarian: the entire landscape is seen as a farm, a mine or a supermarket. True, there is another category, 'ecology', which seeks to soften the harsh dualism which pitches humans against their surroundings (I am talking about ecology as an ideology, not as a science). This ecological approach, by contrast, sees the human race as merely one component of a wider system. The landscape remains ultimately untamed and the practicality, and even the ethics, of man's attempts to exploit it become problematic. Though the terminology varies, a sense of this contrast persists through much modern writing in this field: between the 'imperial' and the 'arcadian' traditions in environmental history (Worster 1985); between 'technological' and 'empathetic' knowledge (Rifkin 1983); between 'technocentric' and 'ecocentric' attitudes which concentrate respectively on means and ends (O'Riordan 1976); between something presumably shallow and the 'deep ecology' of Naess (1973) or between something isolationist and the 'transpersonal ecology' of Fox (1990).[3] These pairs of terms correspond closely to the tension among the Sakha elite between the agendas of their mineral ministries and of their mystical nationalists – a measure of how far they are implicated in global patterns of rhetoric.

But even 'ecology' is ultimately utilitarian, concerned not so much with how the world works as with how we handle it. Both terms – environment and ecology – derive their current importance from a perception that the world is no longer working as it should, and that this is happening, not because the gods are angry at our impiety but because we have mismanaged the environment and must change our management strategy. In this view, the environment almost becomes one with the economy, a term which is in no way divine but which has meaning only within the context of its management by human agents.

But ecology is ultimately no more holistic than environment. Not only does it remain utilitarian but it, too, works with a weak metaphysic based on a concept of nature which is de-deified. This 'nature' lacks totality and consciousness or intentionality: it is something less than cosmos.

If we turn to environmentalism as a form of knowledge, we see that through being tied so closely as a blueprint for action, it becomes very vulnerable to the shifting weathercock of 'real-life scenarios'. Environmental knowledge is widely associated with anxiety and confusion in its knowers, who frequently change viewpoint with the latest fashion or panic or published report. As knowledge, it is strikingly un-systemic, or fragmented. The New Age movements and their environmentalist allies endorse the very elements which are irretrievably absent in their own appropriating society: in terms of social structure, they emphasize community, tribe or clan; epistemologically, they may favour animistic presuppositions about the souls of plants and animals and the spiritual forces in the land; historically, they seek a continuity of consciousness from ancient times (the land speaks to us and we know how to hear it); economically, they insist that one needs time to reflect at length and without anxiety on all this and even to engage in elaborate rituals (and to the extent that people do so, this is perhaps a partial explanation for the predominance of middle-class people with adequate salaries and flexible professional schedules). Such a quest must be unsuccessful, since the absence of these elements is a necessary condition for the existence of the movement which would aim to restore them.

The fragmentation of environmentalist knowledge can be seen on both social and epistemological planes. The social fragmentation takes place as people drift rapidly in and out of organizations and pressure groups. This leads to the formation of single-issue groupings representing interests which are ideologically poorly anchored: a group may protest about a specific motorway or nuclear station and then break up as soon as that battle is over.[4] The effect of this is to create an ideological kaleidoscope, colourful but fleeting. These movements are generally politically weak because their opponents, that is the state and the corporations, have more cohesive and enduring structures and ideologies.

Epistemologically, too, environmentalism is correspondingly badly placed to constitute a core form of knowledge for any substantial section of the public. The same argument perhaps applies by extension to the New Age movement as a whole. Contradictions between the presuppositions of one campaign and of another do not bounce off each other in the generative way of contradictions in theology. The latter may be expressed as a dualistic tension amenable to resolution by synthesis, as in the nature of the Trinity or the old Manichaean relationship between God and Satan (Forsyth 1987): here, they are not sterile contradictions but creative paradoxes. Or they may form a gradation of levels of understanding revealed through stages of initiation, as in tantrism or in many puberty rites. Either way, they are understood to express the heart of the mystery of the human condition and they presuppose a holism in knowledge of reality.

This holism, it seems to me, is the weak point in the modern appropriation of any kind of indigenous knowledge. Returning to the features of shamanistic thought outlined at the start of this paper, and focusing on our two examples of psychotherapy and environmentalism, we see that:

- Its *local* nature is co-opted, but in a transplanted form which makes it a metaphor for the rejection of the appropriators' own, more diffused sense of locality. It becomes re-localized on the spot, creating a kind of global indigenosity. Through the idiom of therapy, it is also relocated inside the self.
- Its *holistic* nature is shattered for social, political and epistemological reasons, but is retained as a cardinal value. This ideal is unattainable and is replaced by the weaker concept of globality.
- Its *eristic* nature suffers a variable fate in the new therapies (for example, some forms of crystal healing are less gutsy than shamanism because they do not accommodate anger and violence) but becomes a driving force in the heroic side of environmental campaigning.
- Its *dissident* or anti-centrist nature is likewise retained and enhanced ('alternative'), both in the private and the public form.

Yet overall, I suggest that shamanism cannot avoid sharing the fate of any other kind of indigenous knowledge in the industrial world: its full implications are too challenging even for radicals to accommodate.

At the global level of decision making, it is the impetus towards action which drags indigenous knowledge into being a commodity rather than a way of doing and ensures that it could never take deep root in a new context. Action also pulls it towards current concerns which may not be local. This is clearest when we see indigenous peoples themselves bringing their 'indigenous knowledge' to what is now called the 'marketplace'. Teachers take their students to visit traditional healers and tell them that this is the indigenous knowledge which we must 'collect' and 'preserve'; a man from the Sakha Ministry of Education gives a deadpan lecture in which he points with a stick at a diagram of the cosmos and announces which spirits reside at each level (this is not a lecture for scholars of religious history but instruction for schoolchildren, for whom 'Consciousness-Soul' is now a compulsory subject on the curriculum!).

This is not a true marketplace, but a rigged one in which your product will sell only if you pretend that it is something else, far less distinctive and valuable, but also far less trouble to come to terms with, than what it really is. Jungle herbalists fight pharmaceutical multinationals through the legal quagmire of intellectual property rights (Gray 1991), but in a debate which is already set in these companies' terms: plants amount to no more than molecule factories. Indigenous knowledge must be controlled to the point at which it cannot subvert hegemonic knowledge. Indigenous wisdom must be packaged into the format of a database: the butterfly must be killed in order to take its rightful place in the glass case.

Perhaps the most successful players in this game are some North American Arctic peoples, such as the Inuit. A combination of factors (starting to fight for their land rights early because of mineral extraction projects; living in a Protestant liberal-democratic state) have left them extremely well placed: an international organization like the Inuit Circumpolar Conference, has had observer status at the UN since the 1970s. But this privileged position has been bought at the price of an advanced commoditization of their indigenous knowledge.

Why is traditional knowledge useful?
[Over thousands of years] a collective body of knowledge . . . has been passed down through the generations . . . It represents an understanding of a dynamic ecosystem . . . . This collective knowledge forms a data base for predictive modelling, for forecasting, and for selecting harvest areas.
The goal of the Program is to help the Inuit and Cree people of Hudson Bay bring forward their knowledge in such a way that it can be integrated into the cumulative effects assessment . . . . TEK [Traditional Ecological Knowledge] has several useful features as a data base. One is that data can be independently verified by separate interviews with people who harvest in the same area . . . . It is important to seek the information and let patterns of change emerge through its collation and display.
The Hudson's Bay Program will offer a neutral forum to all interested parties to work in partnership to tackle cumulative impact assessment (Phase I), and sustainable development (Phase II), in the Hudson Bay bioregion . . . . The program will hopefully 'jump start' the political process . . .
                                                        (Northern Perspectives 1992: 15–16)

This text, which is typical of the North American Arctic, invites extensive commentary. It is perhaps enough here to suggest that indigenous knowledge would probably not have homogenized the hunters' experience by 'independently verifying' one hunter's account through another, but would have generated a different plan for each hunter in accordance with his own biography; the shaman may have played a key role in fine-tuning these differences. Through all the trappings of liberal consultation in the last paragraph, the project-ese language reveals the epistemological coercion inside the velvet glove. Indigenous knowledge, whatever this is, could filter through this process only as a thing and not as a way of doing or being. And as a thing, it is clearly the local people's strongest card in cutting political deals.

But not ace of trumps. Even when adopting a high moral tone, the shrewd indigenous negotiator knows where ultimate power lies. Inuit economies and communities have been ravaged by anti-fur campaigns among the bourgeois city-dwellers whose life-style is built around 'options'. The Inuit, who do not have these options, are sometimes reduced to adopting a tortuous special pleading. Here is an extract from the advance blurb to a book by a Greenlander.

> by devaluing indigenous cultures and depriving them of the right to use and manage natural resources, dominant European and American cultures are endangering not only the lives of native peoples, but the very natural balance urbanites seek to protect.
> To support the case in favour of native peoples' continued 'wise use' of natural resources, Lynge introduces readers to Inuit philosophy, economics, religion . . . revealing . . . their deep respect for all forms of life. Lynge argues forcefully that *the native perspective is entirely consistent with international conservation strategies and global environmental concerns.*

> (Lynge 1993, my emphasis)

With its bows to 'wise use' and a questionable 'natural balance', this text seems designed to appease the fur-forbidders out of a recognition that it is futile to oppose them. The esoteric soul theories of Inuit shamanism were really a form of rational resource management after all, only the old shamans simply failed to put it in these terms.

If the non-Russian Arctic represents one of the most advanced areas for the negotiation between indigenous knowledge and the hegemonic urban view, then it seems hard to foresee any alternative worldwide to a simple sell-out by any aspect of indigenous knowledge to a partially matching area of global epistemology. The strands which make up shamanism are complex and feed into a range of modern concerns, from rational resource management to radical psychotherapy. Where will the central features of shamanism be in each of these: the transformation of the Sora shamaness's soul into a monkey as she links her tail to her teacher and climbs down the cosmic tree to fetch her client's patrilineal ancestor; the old woman at the bottom of the sea who withholds seals from the Inuit and releases them only when the shaman goes down there and combs her hair; the austerities of Sakha initiation, in which the novice shaman is taken apart by the spirits bone by bone and then reconstituted? The answer seems to be that they will be either absent or watered down, perhaps reduced to folklore or inspiration for theatre. The shamanic sense of place, at once cosmic and local, becomes difficult to sustain but is replaced largely by a sense that each person carries the totality of space within themselves; the impetus of the eristic element of struggle moves into new arenas such as environmental agendas.

To the extent that more specific elements of shamanism are carried over, they become separated out from each other. And this is perhaps the heart of the dilemma of New Ageism: it can never authentically recapture the holistic vision which is the rationale for its own striving. It is unable to transmute mere contradiction into the powerful totalizing function of paradox. Consider a New Age workshop in shamanistic drumming, during which there may be talk about Inuit wisdom and the kind of 'natural balance' mentioned in the blurb to Lynge's book, but in which some of the clients may have diversified their ideological portfolios to include anti-fur lobbying and whale-saving. Under these circumstances, holism itself becomes just one value, rather than the ground for all other values – and so becomes no more than an option; indigenous knowledge, when transplanted and commoditized, comes to take on the fragmentary nature of the society by which it is appropriated. This is surely why indigenous or local knowledge must always remain epistemologically marginal to global knowledge. The one thing global culture cannot recapture is the holistic nature of indigenous knowledge. Even where the epistemology is admired, there is a lack of appropriate context for belief and application.

Even as astronomy sees ever further into space, the arena of human consciousness has shrunk from the cosmos to a mere globe. So ironically, the more global things become, the less holistic they are since they pertain *only* to this globe. Meanwhile, the coercive nature of interaction between the components of this globe requires, not the homogenization of the Coca-Cola model, but the perpetuation of some kinds of difference. These differences are ones of relative power and involve a sort of class structure of epistemologies in which global knowledge can rest assured of its superiority only if it can point to other, inferior knowledges. Perhaps this is the true consequence of globality: that the coercive nature of the interaction between the different components leads the weaker parties to surrender or to adopt ever more cunning disguises. In terms of purveying their local knowledge to the globe, the Inuit lead the field, with the Sakha moving up fast behind; the Sora, for the time being, are scarcely in the race.

NOTES

1 This argument is presented at different levels. Here I talk about Sakha (Yakut) deploying it against Russian; but the Sakha Republic's minority Evén (a Tungus people) advance a similar argument, based on their specialist reindeer herding, to support a higher degree of autonomy from the provincial Sakha government (see Vitebsky 1992). I am grateful to the Wenner–Gren Foundation for Anthropological Research for funding my recent research in this region.
2 I am grateful to Marjorie Balzer for discussions on this topic. The responsibility for any misunderstandings remains my own.
3 Fox explicitly based his 'transpersonal ecology' on the 'transpersonal psychology'

of Maslow and Sutich, a vision which moves beyond the separated, isolated ego, beyond the gulf which separates self from other, and so psychologizes the domain of ecology too.

4 I am grateful to my student Eeva Berglund for use of her field material on environmentalist agendas among civic action groups in Germany.

REFERENCES

Balzer, M. (in press) 'Shamanism and the politics of culture: an anthropological view of the 1992 International conference on shamanism, Yakutsk, the Sakha Republic', *Shaman* 2.

Danforth, M. (1989) *Firewalking and Religious Healing: The Anastenaria of Greece and the American Firewalking Movement*, Princeton: Princeton University Press.

Danilov, I. (1989) 'Chelovek zhivet prirodoy [Man lives by nature]', *Polyarnaya Zvezda [Polar Star]* 3: 108–109.

de Heusch, L. (1981) 'Possession and shamanism', in *Why Marry Her? Society and Symbolic Structures*, Cambridge: Cambridge University Press.

Eliade, M. (1964) *Shamanism: Archaic Techniques of Ecstasy*, New York: Pantheon.

Elwin, V. (1955) *The Religion of an Indian Tribe*, Bombay: Oxford University Press.

Forsyth, N. (1987) *The Old Enemy: Satan and the Combat Myth*, Princeton: Princeton University Press.

Fox, W. (1990) *Toward a Transpersonal Ecology: Developing New Foundations for Environmentalism*, Boston and London: Shambala.

Gray, A. (1991) *Between the Spice of Life and the Melting Pot: Biodiversity Conservation and its Impact on Indigenous Peoples*, Copenhagen: IWGIA Document No.70.

Kleinman, A. (1986) *Social Origins of Distress and Disease: Depression, Neurasthenia and Pain in Modern China*, New Haven: Yale University Press.

Lewis, I.M. (1989) *Ecstatic Religion: A Study of Shamanism and Spirit Possession*, London: Routledge.

Lynge, F. (1993) *Arctic Wars, Animal Rights, Endangered Species*, Hanover: University Press of New England.

Makarov, D.S. (1983) *Narodnaya mudrost': zaniya i predstavleniya [National Wisdom: Knowledge and Representations]*, Yakutsk.

Naess, A. (1973) 'The shallow and the deep, long-range ecology movement: a summary', *Inquiry* 16: 95–100.

Neihardt, J.G. (1972) [1932] *Black Elk Speaks: Being the Life of a Holy Man of the Oglala Sioux*, New York: Washington Square Press.

Northern Perspectives (1992) 'Traditional ecological knowledge', 20(2): 15–16.

O'Riordan, T. (1976) *Environmentalism*, London: Pion.

Rifkin, J. (1983) *Algeny: A New Word – a New World*, New York: Viking.

Tumarcha, L. (1989) 'Sprosi khozyayna [Ask the owner]', letter in *Severnyye Prostory [Northern Expanses]* 3: 2.

Vitebsky, P. (1978) 'Political relations among the Sora of India', cyclostyled, 2 papers.

—— (1990) 'Yakut', in G.Smith (ed.) *The Nationalities Question in the Soviet Union*, London: Longman.

—— (1992) 'Landscape and self-determination among the Evény: the political environment of Siberian reindeer herders today', in E. Croll and D. Parkin (eds) *Bush Base: Forest Farm – Culture, Environment and Development*, London: Routledge.

—— (1993a) *Dialogues with the Dead: The Discussion of Mortality among the Sora of Eastern India*, Cambridge: Cambridge University Press.

—— (1993b) 'Is death the same everywhere? Contexts of knowing and doubting', in M. Hobart (ed.) *An Anthropological Critique of Development: The Growth of Ignorance*, London: Routledge.
—— (1995) 'Deforestation and the changing spiritual environment of the Sora', in R. Grove (ed.) *Essays in the Environmental History of Southeast Asia*, Delhi: Oxford University Press, 2 vols.
Worster, D. (1985) *Nature's Economy: History of Ecological Ideas*, Cambridge: Cambridge University Press.

10 The production of locality

Arjun Appadurai

This paper addresses related questions that have arisen in an ongoing series of writings about global cultural flows. I begin with three such questions. What is the place of locality in schemes about global cultural flow? Does anthropology retain any special rhetorical privilege in a world where locality seems to have lost its ontological moorings? Can the mutually constitutive relationship between anthropology and locality survive in a dramatically delocalized world?

Although they broadly inform my response to these questions, my argument does not stem directly from concern with either the production of space (Lefebvre 1991) or the disciplinary anxieties of anthropology as such. Rather, it engages a continuing debate about the future of the nation-state (Appadurai 1993). My concern is with what locality might mean in a situation where the nation-state faces particular sorts of transnational destabilization.

I view locality as primarily relational and contextual rather than as scalar or spatial. I see it as a complex phenomenological quality, constituted by a series of links between the sense of social immediacy, the technologies of interactivity and the relativity of contexts. This phenomenological quality, which expresses itself in certain kinds of agency, sociality and reproducability, is the main predicate of locality as a category (or subject) that I seek to explore.

In contrast, I use the term 'neighbourhood' to refer to the actually existing social forms in which locality, as a dimension or value, is variably realized. Neighbourhoods, in this usage, are situated communities characterized by their actuality, whether spatial or virtual, and their potential for social reproduction.[1]

As part of this exploration, I address two further questions. How does *locality*, as an aspect of social life, relate to *neighbourhoods* as substantive social forms? Is the relationship of locality to neighbourhoods substantially altered by recent history, and especially by the global crisis of the nation-state? A simpler way to characterize these multiple goals is through this question: what can locality mean in a world where spatial localization, quotidian interaction and social scale are not always isomorphic?

LOCATING THE SUBJECT

It is one of the grand clichés of social theory (going back to Tönnies, Weber and Durkheim) that locality as a property or diacritic of social life comes under siege in modern societies. But locality is an inherently fragile social achievement. Even in the most intimate, spatially confined, geographically isolated situations, locality must be maintained carefully against various kinds of odds. These odds have at various times and places been conceptualized differently. In many societies, boundaries are zones of danger, requiring special ritual maintenance; in other sorts of societies, social relations are inherently fissive, creating a persistent tendency for some neighbourhoods to dissolve. In yet other situations, ecology and technology dictate that houses and inhabited spaces are forever shifting, thus contributing an endemic sense of anxiety and instability to social life.

Much of what we call the ethnographic record can be rewritten, and re-read, from this point of view. In the first instance, a great deal of what have been termed 'rites of passage' is concerned with the production of what we might call *local subjects*, actors who properly belong to a situated community of kin, neighbours, friends and enemies. Ceremonies of naming and tonsure, scarification and segregation, circumcision and deprivation, are complex social techniques for the inscription of locality onto bodies. Looked at slightly differently, they are ways to embody locality as well as to locate bodies in socially and spatially defined communities. The spatial symbolism of rites of passage has probably been paid less attention than its bodily and social symbolism. Such rites are not simply mechanical techniques for social aggregation but social techniques for the production of 'natives', a category I have discussed elsewhere (Appadurai 1988).

What is true of the production of local subjects in the ethnographic record is as true of the processes by which locality is materially produced. The building of houses, the organization of paths and passages, the making and remaking of fields and gardens, the mapping and negotiation of transhumant spaces and hunter-gatherer terrains is the incessant, often humdrum, pre-occupation of many small communities studied by anthropologists. These techniques for the *spatial* production of locality have been copiously documented. But they have not usually been viewed as instances of the production of locality, both as a general property of social life and as a particular valuation of that property. Broken down descriptively into technologies for house-building, garden cultivation, and the like, these material outcomes have been taken as ends in themselves, rather than as moments in a general technology (and teleology) of localization.

The production of locality in the societies historically studied by anthropologists (in islands and forests, agricultural villages and hunting camps) is not simply a matter of producing local subjects as well as the very neighbourhoods which contextualize these subjectivities. As some of the best work in the social logic of ritual in the last few decades so amply shows (Lewis 1986;

Munn 1986; Schieffelin 1985), space and time are themselves socialized and localized through complex and deliberate practices of performance, representation and action. We have tended to call these practices 'cosmological' or 'ritual'; terms that by distracting us from their active, intentional, and productive character create the dubious impression of mechanical reproduction.

One of the most remarkable general features of the ritual process is its highly specific way of localizing duration and extension, of giving these categories names and properties, values and meanings, symptoms and legibility. A vast amount of what we know of ritual in small-scale societies can be revisited from this point of view. The large literature on techniques for naming places, for protecting fields, animals and other reproductive spaces and resources, for marking seasonal change and agricultural rhythms, for properly situating new houses and wells, for appropriately demarcating boundaries (both domestic and communal), is substantially a literature documenting the socialization of space and time. More precisely, it is a record of the spatio-temporal production of locality. Looked at this way, van Gennep's extraordinary and vital study of rites of passage, much of Frazer's bizarre encyclopaedia, and Malinowski's monumental study of Trobriand garden magic are substantially records of the myriad ways in which small-scale societies do not and cannot take locality as given. Rather they seem to assume that locality is ephemeral unless hard and regular work is undertaken to produce and maintain its materiality. Yet this very materiality is sometimes mistaken for the terminus of such work, thus obscuring the more abstract effects of such work on the production of locality as a structure of feeling.

Much that has been considered 'local' knowledge is actually knowledge of how to produce and reproduce locality under conditions of anxiety and entropy, social wear and flux, ecological uncertainty and cosmic volatility, and the always present quirkiness of kinsmen, enemies, spirits and quarks of all sorts. The 'locality' of local knowledge is not only, or even mainly, its embeddedness in a non-negotiable here-and-now, nor its stubborn disinterest in things at large, though these are certainly crucial properties as Geertz has reminded us in much of his work (Geertz 1975, 1983). Local knowledge is substantially about producing reliably local subjects as well as about producing reliably local neighbourhoods within which such subjects can be recognized and organized. In this sense, local knowledge is what it is, not principally by contrast with other knowledges – which (from some non-local point of view) the observer might regard as less localized – but by virtue of its local teleology and ethos. We might say, adapting Marx, that local knowledge is not only local in itself, but even more importantly, for itself.

Even in the smallest of societies, with the humblest of technologies and in the most desolate of ecological contexts, the relationship between the production of local subjects and the neighbourhoods in which such subjects can be produced, named and empowered to act socially is an historical and dialectical relationship. Without reliably local subjects, the construction of a local terrain of nabitation, production and moral security would have no interests attached to it. But by the same token, without such a known, named and negotiable terrain already available, the ritual techniques for creating local subjects would be abstract, thus sterile. The long-term reproduction of a neighbourhood that is simultaneously practical, valued and taken-for-granted depends on the seamless interaction of localized spaces and times with local subjects possessed of the knowledge to reproduce locality. Problems that are properly historical arise whenever this seamlessness is threatened. Such problems do not arrive only with modernity, colonialism or ethnography. I stress this point now because I will go on to discuss (in the final section of this paper) the special properties of the 'production of locality' under the conditions of contemporary urban life, which involve national regimes, mass mediation and intense and irregular commoditization.

If a large part of the ethnographic record can be re-read and rewritten as a record of the multifarious modes for the production of locality, it follows that ethnography has been unwittingly complicit in this activity. This is a point about knowledge and representation, rather than about guilt or violence. The ethnographic project is in a peculiar way isomorphic with the very knowledges it seeks to discover and document, since both the ethnographic project and the social projects it seeks to describe have the production of locality as their governing telos.[2] The misrecognition of this fact, in both projects, as involving only more humdrum and discrete actions and settings (house-building, child-naming, boundary rituals, greeting rituals, spatial purifications), is the constitutive misrecognition that guarantees both the special appropriateness of ethnography to certain kinds of description, and its peculiar lack of reflexivity as a project of knowledge and reproduction. Drawn into the very localization they seek to document, most ethnographic descriptions have taken locality as ground not figure, recognizing neither its fragility nor its ethos *as a property of social life*. This produces an unproblematized collaboration with the sense of inertia on which locality, as a 'structure of feeling', centrally relies.

The value of reconceiving ethnography (and re-reading earlier ethnography) from this perspective is three-fold: (1) it shifts the history of ethnography from a history of neighbourhoods to a history of the techniques for the production of locality; (2) it opens up a new way to think about the complex co-production of indigenous categories by organic intellectuals, administrators, linguists, missionaries and ethnologists which undergirds large portions of the monographic history of anthropology; (3) it enables the ethnography of the modern, and of the production of locality under modern conditions, to be part of a more general contribution to the ethnographic record *tout court*. Together, these effects would help guard against the too-easy use of various oppositional tropes ('then and now', 'before and after', 'small and large', 'bounded and unbounded', 'stable and fluid', 'hot and cold'), that implicitly oppose ethnographies of and in the present to ethnographies of and in the past.

THE CONTEXTS OF LOCALITY

I have so far focused on locality as a phenomenological property of social life, a structure of feeling which is produced by particular forms of intentional activity and which yields particular sorts of material effects. Yet this dimensional aspect of locality cannot be separated from the actual settings in and through which social life is reproduced. To make the link between *locality* as a property of social life and *neighbourhoods* as social forms requires a more careful exposition of the problem of context. The production of neighbourhoods is always historically grounded and thus contextual. That is, neighbourhoods are inherently what they are because they are opposed to something else and derive from other, already produced neighbourhoods. In the practical consciousness of many human communities, this something else is often conceptualized ecologically as forest or wasteland, ocean or desert, swamp or river. Such ecological signs often mark boundaries which simul-taneously signal the beginnings of non-human forces and categories, or of recognizably human but barbarian or demonic forces. Frequently these contexts, against which neighbourhoods are produced and figured, are simultaneously seen as ecological, social and cosmological terrains.

It may be useful here to note that the social part of the context of neighbourhoods – the fact, that is, of other neighbourhoods – recalls the idea of 'ethnoscape' (Appadurai 1991), a term I used to get away from the idea that group identities necessarily imply that 'cultures' need to be seen as spatially bounded, historically unselfconscious, or ethnically homogeneous forms. In this earlier usage, I implied that the idea of 'ethnoscape' might be salient especially to the late twentieth century, when human motion, the volatility of images and the conscious identity-producing activities of nation-states lend a fundamentally unstable and perspectival quality to social life.

Yet neighbourhoods are always to some extent ethnoscapes, insofar as they involve the ethnic projects of others as well as consciousness of such projects. That is, particular neighbourhoods sometimes recognize that their own logic is a general logic by which others also construct recognizable, social, human, situated life-worlds. Such knowledge can be encoded in the pragmatics of rituals associated with clearing forests, making gardens, building houses, which always carry an implicit sense of the teleology of locality-building. In more complex societies, typically associated with literacy, priestly classes, and macro-orders for the control and dissemination of powerful ideas, such knowledges are codified, as in the case of the rituals associated with the colonization of new villages by Brahmans in pre-colonial India.

All locality-building has a moment of colonization, a moment both historical and chronotypic, when there is a formal recognition that the production of a neighbourhood requires deliberate, risky, even violent action in respect to the soil, the forests, animals and other human beings. A good deal of the violence associated with foundational ritual (Bloch 1986) is a recognition of the force that is required to wrest a locality from previously uncontrolled peoples and places. Put in other terms (de Certeau 1984), the transformation of spaces into places requires a conscious moment, which may subsequently be remembered as relatively routine.

The production of a neighbourhood is inherently colonizing, in the sense that it involves the assertion of socially (often ritually) organized power over places and settings which are viewed as potentially chaotic or rebellious. The anxiety that attends many rituals of habitation, occupation or settlement is a recognition of the implicit violence of all such acts of colonization. Some of this anxiety remains in the ritual repetition of these moments, long after the foundational event of colonization. In this sense, the production of a neighbourhood is inherently an exercise of power over some sort of hostile or recalcitrant environment, which may take the form of another neighbourhood.

Much of the narrative material unearthed by ethnographers working in small communities, as well as much of their description of rituals of agriculture, house-building and social passage, stresses the sheer material fragility associated with producing and maintaining locality. Nevertheless, however deeply such description is embedded in the particularities of place, soil and ritual technique, it invariably contains or implies a theory of context; a theory, in other words, of what a neighbourhood is produced from, against, in spite of, and in relation to.

The problem of the relationship between neighbourhood and context requires much fuller attention than can be afforded here. Let me sketch the general dimensions of this problem. The central dilemma is that neighbourhoods both *are* contexts and at the same time *require and produce* contexts. Neighbourhoods are contexts in the sense that they provide the frame or setting within which various kinds of human action (productive, reproductive, interpretive, performative) can be initiated and conducted meaningfully. Since meaningful life-worlds require legible and reproducible patterns of action, they are text-like, and thus require one or many contexts. From another point of view, a neighbourhood is a context, or a set of contexts, within which meaningful social action can be both generated and interpreted. In this sense, neighbourhoods are contexts, and contexts are neighbourhoods. A neighbourhood is a multiplex interpretive site.

Insofar as neighbourhoods are imagined, produced and maintained against some sort of ground (social, material, environmental) they also require and produce contexts, against which their own intelligibility takes shape. This context-generative dimension of neighbourhoods is an important matter, because it provides the beginnings of a theoretical angle on the relationship between local and global realities. How so? The way in which neighbourhoods are produced and reproduced requires the continuous construction, both practical and discursive, of an ethnoscape (necessarily non-local) against which local practices and projects are imagined to take place.

In one dimension, at one moment and from one perspective, neighbourhoods as actually existing contexts are prerequisites for the production of local subjects. That is, actually existing places and spaces, within an historically produced spatio-temporal neighbourhood, and with a series of localized rituals, social categories, expert practitioners and informed audiences are required in order for new members (babies, strangers, slaves, prisoners, guests, affines) to be made temporary or permanent local subjects. Here we see locality in its taken-for-granted, commonsensical, *habitus* dimension. In this dimension, a neighbourhood appears to be simply a set of contexts, historically received, materially embedded, socially appropriate, naturally unproblematic: fathers yield sons, gardens yield yams, sorcery yields sickness, hunters yield meat, women yield babies, blood yields semen, shamans yield visions, and so forth. These contexts, in concert, appear to provide the unproblematized setting for the technical production of local subjects in a regular and regulated manner.

But as these local subjects engage in the social activities of production, representation and reproduction (the 'work of culture'), they contribute, generally unwittingly, to the creation of contexts which might exceed the existing material and conceptual boundaries of the neighbourhood. Affinal aspirations extend marriage networks to new villages; fishing expeditions yield refinements of what are understood to be navigable and fish-rich waters; hunting expeditions extend the sense of the forest as a responsive ecological frame; social conflicts force new strategies of exit and re-colonization; trading activities yield new commodity-worlds and thus new partnerships with as yet unencountered regional groupings; warfare yields new diplomatic alliances with previously hostile neighbours. And all of these possibilities contribute to subtle shifts in language, world-view, ritual practice and collective self-understanding. Put summarily: as local subjects carry on the continuing task of re-producing their neighbourhood, the contingencies of history, environment and imagination contain the potential for new contexts (material, social and imaginative) to be produced. In this way, through the vagaries of social action by local subjects, *neighbourhood as context produces the context of neighbourhoods*. Over time, this dialectic changes the conditions of the production of locality as such. Put another way, this is how the subjects of history become historical subjects, so that no human community, however apparently stable, static, bounded or isolated can usefully be regarded as 'cool' or 'outside history'. This observation converges with Sahlins's view of the dynamics of conjunctural change (Sahlins 1985).

Consider the general relationship between various Yanomami groups in the rainforests of Brazil and Venezuela. The relationship between settlements, population shifts, predatory warfare and sexual competition can be viewed as a process in which specific Yanomami villages ('neighbourhoods'), in and through their actions, preoccupations and strategies, actually *produce* a wider set of contexts for themselves and each other. This creates a general territory of Yanomami movement, interaction and colonization in which any given village responds to a material context wider than itself while simultaneously contributing to the creation of that wider context. In a larger-scale perspective, the overall network of space–time in which the Yanomami produce and generate reciprocal contexts for specific acts of localization (village-building), also produces some of the context in which the Yanomami, as a whole, encounter the Brazilian and Venezuelan nation-states. In this sense, Yanomami locality-producing activities are not only context-driven but are also context-generative. This is true of all locality-producing activities.

Thus neighbourhoods seem paradoxical, since they both constitute and require contexts. As ethnoscapes, neighbourhoods inevitably imply a relational consciousness of other neighbourhoods, but they act at the same time as autonomous neighbourhoods of interpretation, value and material practice. Thus, locality as a relational achievement is not the same as a locality as a practical value in the quotidian production of subjects and colonization of space.

Locality-production is inevitably context-generative, *to some extent*. What defines this extent is very substantially a question of the relationships between the contexts that neighbourhoods create and those they encounter. This is a matter of social power, and of the different scales of organization and control within which particular spaces (and places) are embedded.

Though the practices and projects of the Yanomami are context-producing for the Brazilian state, it is even truer that the practices of the Brazilian nation-state involve harsh, even overwhelming forces of military intervention, large-scale environmental exploitation and state-sponsored migration and colonization which the Yanomami confront on hugely unequal terms. In this sense, which I will pursue in the next section on the conditions of locality-production in the era of the nation-state, the Yanomami are being steadily *localized*, in the sense of enclaved, exploited, perhaps even 'cleansed' in the context of the Brazilian polity. Thus, while they are still in a position to generate contexts as they produce and reproduce their own neighbourhoods, they are increasingly prisoners in the context-producing activities of the nation-state, which make their own efforts to produce locality seem feeble, even doomed.

This example has wide general applicability. The capability of neighbourhoods to produce contexts (within which their very localizing activities acquire meaning and historical potential) and to produce *local subjects* is profoundly affected by the locality-producing capabilities of larger-scale social formations (nation-states, kingdoms, missionary empires and trading cartels) to determine the general shape of all the neighbourhoods within the reach of their powers. Thus power is always a key feature of the contextual relations of neighbourhoods, and even 'first contact' always involves different narratives of 'firstness' from the two sides involved in it.

The political economy which links neighbourhoods to contexts is thus both methodologically and historically complex. Our ideas of context derive largely from linguistics. Until recently, context has been opportunistically defined to make sense of specific sentences, rituals, performances and other sorts of 'text'. While the production of 'texts' has been carefully considered from several different points of view (Bauman and Briggs 1990; Hanks 1989), the structure and morphology of 'contexts' has only lately become the focus of any systematic attention (Duranti and Goodwin 1992). Beyond anthropological linguistics, context remains a poorly defined idea, an inert concept indexing an inert environment. When social anthropologists appeal to context, it is generally to a loosely understood sense of the social frame within which specific actions or representations can best be understood. Socio-linguistics, especially as derived from the 'ethnography of speaking' (Hymes 1974) has been the main source for this general approach.

The structure of contexts cannot and should not be derived entirely from the logic and morphology of texts. Text-production and context-production have different logics and meta-pragmatic features. Contexts are produced in the complex imbrication of discursive and non-discursive practices, and so the sense in which contexts imply other contexts, so that each context implies a global network of contexts, is different from the sense in which texts imply other texts, and eventually all texts. Intertextual relations, about which we now know a fair amount, are not likely to work in the same way as *intercontextual* relations. Last, and most daunting, is the prospect that we shall have to find ways to connect theories of intertextuality to theories of intercontextuality. A strong theory of globalization, from a socio-cultural point of view, is likely to require something we certainly do not now have: a theory of intercontextual relations which incorporates our existing sense of intertexts. But that is truly another project.

The relationship between neighbourhood as context and the context of neighbourhoods, mediated by the actions of local historical subjects, acquires new complexities in the sort of world in which we now live. In this new sort of world, the production of neighbourhoods increasingly occurs under conditions where the system of nation-states is the normative hinge for the production of both local and translocal activities. This situation, in which the power-relations that affect the production of locality are fundamentally translocal, is the central concern of the next section.

THE GLOBAL PRODUCTION OF LOCALITY

What has been discussed thus far as a set of structural problems (locality and neighbourhoods; text and context; ethnoscapes and lived worlds) needs now to be explicitly historicized. I have indicated already that the relationship of locality (and neighbourhoods) to contexts is historical and dialectical, and that the context-generative dimension of places (in their capacity as ethnoscapes) is distinct from their context-providing features (in their capacity as neighbourhoods). How do these claims help to understand what happens to the production of locality in the contemporary world?

Contemporary understandings of 'globalization' (Appadurai 1990; Balibar and Wallerstein 1991; Featherstone 1990; King 1991; Robertson 1992; Rosenau 1990) seem to indicate a shift from an emphasis on the global journeys of capitalist modes of thought and organization, to a somewhat different emphasis on the spread of the nation-form, especially as dictated by the concurrent spread of colonialism and print capitalism. If one problem now appears to be the dominant concern of the human sciences, it is that of nationalism and the nation-state (Anderson 1991; Bhabha 1990; Chatterjee 1986, 1993; Gellner 1983; Hobsbawm 1990).

While only time will tell whether our current preoccupations with the nation-state are justified, the beginnings of an anthropological engagement with this issue are evident in the increasing contribution of anthropologists to the problematics of the nation-state (Borneman 1992; Falk-Moore 1993; Handler 1988; Herzfeld 1982; Kapferer 1988; Tambiah 1992; Urban and Sherzer 1991; van der Veer 1994). Some of this work explicitly considers the global context of national cultural formations (Hannerz 1992; Basch *et al.* 1994; Foster 1991; Friedman 1990; Gupta and Ferguson 1992; Rouse 1991; Sahlins 1993). Yet a framework for relating the global, the national and the local has yet to emerge.

In this section, I hope to extend my thoughts about local subjects and localized contexts to sketch the outlines of an argument about the special problems that beset the production of locality in a world that has become deterritorialized (Deleuze and Guattari 1987), diasporic and transnational. This is a world where electronic media are transforming the relationships between information and mediation, and where nation-states are struggling to retain control over their populations in the face of a host of sub-national and transnational movements and organizations. A full consideration of the challenges to the production of locality in such a world would require extended treatment, beyond the scope of this chapter. But some elements of an approach to this problem can be outlined.

Put simply, the task of producing locality (as a structure of feeling, a property of social life and an ideology of situated community) is increasingly a struggle. There are many dimensions to this struggle, and I shall focus here on three: (1) the steady increase in the efforts of the modern nation-state to define all neighbourhoods under the sign of its forms of allegiance and affiliation; (2) the growing disjuncture between territory, subjectivity and collective social movement; (3) the steady erosion of the relationship, principally due to the force and form of electronic mediation, between spatial and virtual neighbourhoods. To make things yet more complex, these three dimensions are themselves interactive.

The nation-state relies for its legitimacy on the intensity of its meaningful presence in a continuous body of bounded territory. It works by policing its borders, producing its 'people' (Balibar 1991), constructing its citizens, defining its capitals, monuments, cities, waters and soils, and by constructing its locales of memory and commemoration, such as graveyards and cenotaphs, mausoleums and museums. The nation-state conducts on its territories the bizarrely contradictory project of creating a flat, contiguous and homogeneous space of nationness and simultaneously a set of places and spaces (prisons, barracks, airports, radio-stations, secretariats, parks, marching grounds, processional routes) calculated to create the internal distinctions and divisions necessary for state ceremony, surveillance, discipline and mobilization. These latter are also the spaces and places that create and perpetuate the distinctions between rulers and ruled, criminals and officials, crowds and leaders, actors and observers.

Through apparatuses as diverse as museums and village dispensaries, post-offices and police-stations, toll-booths and telephone booths, the nation-state creates a vast network of formal and informal techniques for the nationalization of all space considered to be under its sovereign authority. States vary, of course, in their ability to penetrate the nooks and crannies of everyday life. Subversion, evasion and resistance, sometimes scatological (Mbembe 1992), sometimes ironic (Comaroff and Comaroff 1992), sometimes covert (Scott 1990), sometimes spontaneous and sometimes planned, are very widespread. Indeed, the failures of nation-states to contain and define the lives of their citizens are writ large in the growth of shadow economies, private and quasi-private armies and constabularies, secessionary nationalisms, and a variety of non-governmental organizations that provide alternatives to the national control of the means of subsistence and justice.

States vary, as well, in the nature and extent of their interest in local life and in the cultural forms in which they invest their deepest paranoias of sovereignty and control. Spitting on the street is very dangerous in Singapore and Papua New Guinea, public gatherings are a problem in Haiti and Cameroon, disrespect to the Emperor is not good in Japan, and inciting pro-Muslim sentiments is bad news in contemporary India. The list could be multiplied: nation-states have their special sites of sacredness, their special tests of loyalty and treachery, their special measures of compliance and disorder. These are linked to real and perceived problems of lawlessness, reigning ideologies of liberalization or its opposite, relative commitments to international respectability, variably deep revulsions about immediate predecessor regimes and special histories of ethnic antagonism or collaboration. Whatever else is true of the world after 1989, there do not seem to be any very reliable links between state ideologies of welfare, market economics, military power and ethnic purity.

Yet, whether one considers the turbulent post-communist societies of Eastern Europe, the aggressive city-states of the Far East (such as Taiwan, Singapore and Hong Kong), the complex post-military polities of Latin America, the bankrupt state economies of much of sub-Saharan Africa or the turbulent fundamentalist states of much of the Middle East and South Asia, they appear to pose a rather similar set of challenges to the production of neighbourhood by local subjects.

Neighbourhoods exist, from the point of the view of modern nationalism, principally to incubate and reproduce compliant national citizens and not for the production of local subjects. Locality, for the modern nation-state, is either a site of nationally appropriated nostalgias, celebrations and commemorations or a necessary condition of the production of nationals. Neighbourhoods, as social formations, represent anxieties for the nation-state, since they usually contain large or residual spaces where the techniques of nationhood (birth-control, linguistic uniformity, economic discipline, communications efficiency and political loyalty) are likely to be either weak or contested. At the same time, it is neighbourhoods that are the source of political workers and party officials, teachers and soldiers, television technicians and productive farmers. Neighbourhoods are not dispensable, even if they are potentially treacherous. For the project of the nation-state, neighbourhoods represent a perennial source of entropy and slippage. They need to be policed almost as thoroughly as borders.

The work of producing neighbourhoods – life-worlds constituted by relatively stable associations, by relatively known and shared histories, and by collectively traversed and legible spaces and places – is often at odds with the projects of the nation-state.[3] This is partly because the commitments and attachments (sometimes mislabelled 'primordial') that characterize local subjectivities are more pressing, more continuous, and sometimes more distracting than the nation-state can afford. It is also because the memories and attachments that local subjects have to their shop-signs and street-names, to their favourite walkways and streetscapes, to their times and places for congregating and escaping, are often at odds with the needs of the nation-state for regulated public life. Further, it is the nature of local life to develop partly by contrast to other neighbourhoods, by producing its own contexts of alterity (spatial, social and technical), contexts which may not meet the needs for spatial and social standardization prerequisite for the disciplined national citizen.

Neighbourhoods are ideally stages for their own self-reproduction, a process which is fundamentally opposed to the imaginary of the nation-state, where neighbourhoods are designed to be instances and exemplars of a generalizable mode of belonging to a wider territorial imaginary. The modes of localization most congenial to the nation-state have a disciplinary quality about them: in sanitation and street-cleaning, in prisons and in slum-clearance, in refugee camps and in offices of every kind, the nation-state localizes by fiat, by decree and sometimes by the overt use of force. This sort of localization creates severe constraints, even direct obstacles, to the survival of locality as a context-generative, rather than a context-driven, process.

Yet, the isomorphism of people, territory, and legitimate sovereignty that constitutes the normative charter of the modern nation-state is itself under threat from the forms of circulation of people characteristic of the contemporary world. It is now widely conceded that human motion is definitive of social life more often than it is exceptional in our contemporary world. Work, both of the most sophisticated intellectual sort and of the most humble proletarian sort, drives people to migrate, often more than once. The policies of nation-states, particularly towards populations regarded as potentially subversive, create a perpetual motion machine, where refugees from one nation move to another, creating new instabilities there which cause further social unrest, and thus further social exits. Thus the 'people' production needs of one nation-state can mean ethnic and social unrest for its neighbours, creating open-ended cycles of ethnic cleansing, forced migration, xenophobia, state paranoia and further ethnic cleansing. Eastern Europe in general, and Bosnia-Herzegovina in particular, are perhaps the most tragic and complex examples of such state/refugee domino processes. In many such cases, people and whole communities are turned into ghettos, refugee camps, concentration camps or reservations, sometimes without anyone moving at all.

Other forms of human movement are created by the reality or lure of economic opportunity (this is true of much Asian migration to the oil-rich parts of the Middle East). Yet other forms of movement are created by permanently mobile groups of specialized workers (United Nations soldiers, oil technologists, development specialists, agricultural labourers, etc.). Still other forms of movement, particularly in sub-Saharan Africa, involve major droughts and famines, often tied to disastrous alliances between corrupt states and opportunistic international and global agencies. In yet other communities, the logic of movement is provided by the leisure industries, which create tourist sites and locations around the world. The ethnography of these tourist locations is just beginning to be written in detail, but what little we do know suggests that many such locations create complex conditions for the production and reproduction of locality, in which ties of marriage, work, business and leisure weave together various circulating populations with kinds of 'locals' to create neighbourhoods which belong in one sense to particular nation-states, but are, from another point of view, what we might call *translocalities*.

The challenge to producing a neighbourhood in these settings derives from the inherent instability of social relationships, the powerful tendency for local subjectivity itself to be commoditized, and the tendencies for nation-states, which sometimes derive significant revenues from such sites, to erase internal, local dynamics through externally imposed modes of regulation, credentialization and image-production.

A much darker version of the problem of producing a neighbourhood can be seen in the quasi-permanent refugee camps that now characterize many embattled parts of the world, such as the Occupied Territories in Palestine, the camps on the Thailand–Cambodia border, the many United Nations organized camps in Somalia, and the Afghan refugee camps in North-West Pakistan. Combining the worst features of urban slums, concentration camps, prisons and ghettos, these are places where, nonetheless, marriages are contracted and celebrated, lives are begun and ended, social contracts made and honoured, careers launched and broken, money made and spent, goods produced and exchanged. Such refugee camps are the starkest examples of the conditions of uncertainty, poverty, displacement and despair under which locality can be produced. These are the extreme examples of neighbourhoods that are context-produced rather than context-generative. These are neighbourhoods whose life-worlds are produced in the darkest circumstances, with prisons and concentration camps being their most barbaric examples.

Yet even these barbaric examples only push to an extreme the quotidian ethos of many cities. In the conditions of ethnic unrest and urban warfare that characterize cities such as Belfast and Los Angeles, Ahmedabad and Sarajevo, Mogadishu and Johannesburg, urban zones are becoming armed camps, driven wholly by 'implosive' forces (Appadurai 1993) that fold into neighbourhoods the most violent and problematic repercussions of wider regional, national and global processes. There are, of course, many important differences between these cities, their histories, their populations and their cultural politics. Yet, in common, they represent a new phase in the life of cities, where the concentration of ethnic populations, the availability of heavy weaponry and the crowded conditions of civic life create futurist forms of warfare (reminiscent of films like *Road Warrior, Blade Runner*, and many others) where a general desolation of the national and global landscape has folded many bizarre racial, religious and linguistic enmities into scenarios of unrelieved urban terror.

These new urban wars have become, to some extent, divorced from their regional and national ecologies, and turned into self-propelling, *implosive* wars between criminal, para-military and civilian militias, tied in obscure ways to transnational religious, economic and political forces. There are, of course, many causes for these forms of urban breakdown in the First and Third Worlds but, in part, they are due to the steady erosion of the capability of such cities to control the means of their own self-reproduction. It is difficult not to associate a significant part of these problems with the sheer circulation of persons, often as a result of warfare, starvation and ethnic cleansing, that drives people into such cities in the first place. In these urban formations, the production of locality faces the twin problems of displaced and deterritorialized populations, and of state policies that disempower the capabilities both of neighbourhoods to be context-producing and of local subjects to be anything other than national citizens. In the most harsh cases, such neighbourhoods hardly deserve the name anymore, since they are barely more than stages, holding companies, sites and barracks for populations with a dangerously thin commitment to the production of locality.

Lest this seem too dark a vision, it might be noted that the very nature of these less pleasant urban dramas drives individuals and groups to more peaceful locations where they are willing to bring their wit, skills and passion for peace. The best moments of urban life in the United States and Europe are owed to these migrants fleeing places far worse than Chicago, Detroit, Los Angeles and Miami. Yet we know that the production of locality in South-Central Los Angeles, on Chicago's west side and in similar parts of large American cities is a highly embattled process.

The third and final factor to be addressed here is the role of mass media, especially in their electronic forms, in creating new sorts of disjuncture between spatial and virtual neighbourhoods. This disjuncture has both utopian and dystopian potentials, and there is no easy way to tell how these might play themselves out in regard to the future of the production of locality. For one thing, the electronic media themselves now vary internally and constitute a complex family of technological means for producing and disseminating news and entertainment. Film tends to be dominated by major commercial interests in a few world centres (Hollywood, New York, Hong Kong, Bombay) though major secondary sites for commercial cinema are emerging in other parts of Europe, Asia and Africa (such as Mexico City, Bangkok and Madras). Art cinema (partly built on a growing transnational network of film festivals, exhibitions and commercial auctions) is spread both more broadly and more thinly across the world, but 'crossovers' (such as *Reservoir Dogs* and *Crying Game* as well as *Salaam Bombay* and *El Mariachi*) are on the increase.

Television, both in its conventional broadcast forms and through new forms of satellite hook-up, increasingly leapfrogs the public spaces of cinema-viewing and comes into forests of antennae, often in the poorest slums of the world, such as those of Rio de Janeiro and São Paulo. The relationship between film-viewing in theatres and on video-cassettes in domestic settings itself creates very important changes, which have been argued to signal the end of cinema-viewing as a 'classical' form of spectatorship (Hansen 1991). At the same time, the availability of video-production technologies to small communities, sometimes in the Fourth World, has made it possible for these communities to create more effective national and global strategies of self-representation and cultural survival (Ginsburg 1993; Turner 1992). Fax machines, electronic mail and other forms of computer-mediated communication have created new possibilities for transnational forms of communication, often bypassing the intermediate surveillance of the nation-state and of major media conglomerates. Each of these developments, of course, interacts with the others, creating complicated new connections between producers, audiences and 'publics', local and national, stable and diasporic.

It is impossible to sort through this bewildering plethora of changes in the media environments that surround the production of neighbourhoods. But there are numerous new forms of community and communication that currently affect the capability of neighbourhoods to be context-producing rather than largely context-driven. The much-discussed impact of news from CNN and other similar 'global' and instantaneous forms of mediation, as well as the role of fax technologies in the democratic upheavals in China, Eastern Europe and the Soviet Union in 1989 (and since) have made it possible both for leaders and nation-states, as well as their various oppositional forces, to communicate very rapidly across local and even national lines. The speed of such communication is further complicated by the growth of 'electronic billboard' communities, such as those enabled by *Internet*, which allow debate, dialogue and relationship-building among various territorially divided individuals, who nevertheless are forming communities of imagination and interest, which are geared to their diasporic positions and voices.

These new forms of electronically mediated communication are beginning to create *virtual neighbourhoods*, no longer bounded by territory, passports, taxes, elections and other conventional political diacritics, but by access to both the software and the hardware that is required to connect to these large international computer networks. Thus far, access to these virtual (electronic) neighbourhoods tends to be confined to members of the transnational intelligentsia who, through their access to computer technologies at universities, labs and libraries, can base social and political projects on technologies constructed to solve information-flow problems. Information and opinion flow concurrently through these circuits and, while the social morphology of these electronic neighbourhoods is hard to classify and their longevity difficult to predict, clearly they are communities of some sort, that trade information and build links that affect many areas of life, from philanthropy to marriage.

These virtual neighbourhoods seem, on the face of it, to represent just that absence of face-to-face links, spatial contiguity and multiplex social interaction that the idea of a neighbourhood seems centrally to imply. Yet we must not be too quick to oppose highly spatialized neighborhoods to these virtual neighbourhoods of international electronic communication. The relationship between these two forms of neighbourhood is considerably more complex. In the first instance, these virtual neighbourhoods are able to mobilize ideas, opinions, monies and social linkages which often directly flow back into lived neighbourhoods, in the form of currency flows, arms for local nationalisms, and support for various positions in highly localized public spheres. Thus, in the context of the destruction of the Babri Masjid in Ayodhya by Hindu extremists on 6 December 1992, there was an intense mobilization of computer, fax and related electronic networks, which created very rapid loops of debate and information exchange between interested persons in the United States, Canada, England and various parts of India. These electronic loops have been exploited equally by Indians in the United States standing on both sides of the great debate over fundamentalism and communal harmony in contemporary India.

At the same time, continuing with the example of the Indian community overseas, both the progressive, secularist groupings and their counterparts on the Hindu revivalist side (members of the Vishwa Hindu Parishad and sympathizers of the Bharatiya Janata Party and the Bajrang Dal – sometimes referred to as the Sangh *parivar* or family) are mobilizing these virtual neighbourhoods in the interest of political projects which are intensely localizing in India. The riots that shook many Indian cities after 6 December 1992 can no longer be viewed in isolation from the electronic mobilization of the Indian diaspora, whose members can now be involved directly in these developments in India through electronic means. This is not entirely a matter of 'long-distance nationalism', of the sort that Benedict Anderson has recently bemoaned (Anderson 1993). It is part and parcel of the new and often conflicting relations between neighbourhoods, translocal allegiances and the logic of the nation-state.

These 'new patriotisms' (Appadurai 1993) are not just the extensions of nationalist and counter-nationalist debates by other means, though there is certainly a good deal of prosthetic nationalism and politics by nostalgia involved in the dealings of exiles with their erstwhile homelands. They also involve various rather puzzling new forms of linkage between diasporic nationalisms, delocalized political communications and revitalized political commitments at both ends of the diasporic process.

This last factor reflects the ways in which diasporas are changing in light of new forms of electronic mediation. Indians in the United States are involved in direct contact with developments in India, that involve ethnic violence, state legitimacy and party politics, and these very dialogues create new forms of association, conversation and mobilization in their 'minoritarian' politics in the United States. Thus, many of those most aggressively involved through electronic means with Indian politics, are also those most involved in efforts to reorganize various kinds of diasporic politics in the cities and regions of the United States. Thus, the mobilization of Indian women against domestic abuse, and the collaboration of progressive Indian groups with their counterparts involved with Palestine and South Africa, suggest that these virtual electronic neighbourhoods offer new ways for Indians to take part in the production of locality in the cities and suburbs in which they reside as American teachers, cab-drivers, engineers and businessmen.

Indians in the United States are now engaged in a variety of ways in the politics of multiculturalism in the United States (Bhattacharjee 1992). This engagement is deeply inflected and affected by their involvement in the incendiary politics of their homes, cities and relatives in India, and also in other locations where their Indian friends and relatives live and work, in England, in Africa, in Hong Kong and in the Middle East. Thus, the politics of diaspora, at least within the last decade, have been decisively affected by global electronic transformations. Rather than a simple opposition between spatial and virtual neighbourhoods, what has emerged is a significant new element in the production of locality. The global flow of images, news and opinion now provides part of the engaged cultural and political literacy that diasporic persons bring to their spatial neighbourhoods. In some ways, these global flows add to the intense, and implosive, force under which spatial neighbourhoods are produced.

However, unlike the largely negative pressures that the nation-state places on the production of context by local subjects, the electronic mediation of community in the diasporic world creates a more complicated, disjunct, hybrid sense of local subjectivity. Since these electronic communities typically involve the more educated and elite members of diasporic communities, they do not *directly* affect the local preoccupations of less educated and privileged migrants. Less enfranchized migrants are generally pre-occupied with the practicalities of livelihood and residence in their new settings, but they are not isolated from these global flows. A Sikh cab-driver in Chicago may not be able to participate in the politics of the Punjab by using *Internet*, but he might listen to cassettes of fiery devotional songs and sermons delivered at the Golden Temple in the Punjab. His counterparts from Haiti, Pakistan and Iran can use the radio and the cassette tape-recorder to listen to what they choose to pick from the huge global flow of audio-cassettes, especially devoted to popular music and devotional music and speeches.

Different groups of Indians in the United States also hear speeches and sermons from every known variety of itinerant politician, academic, holy man and entrepreneur from the sub-continent, while these make their American tours. They also read *India West*, *India Abroad* and other major newspapers that imbricate news of American and Indian politics in the same pages. They participate, through cable TV, VCRs and other technologies in the steady noise of home-entertainment produced in and for the United States. Thus the 'work of the imagination' (Appadurai 1991) through which local subjectivity is produced and nurtured is a bewildering palimpsest of highly local and highly translocal considerations.

The three factors that most directly affect the production of locality in the world of the present – the nation-state, diasporic flows and electronic/virtual communities – are themselves articulated in variable, puzzling, sometimes contradictory ways which depend on the cultural, class, historical and ecological setting within which they come together. In part, this variability is itself a product of the way that today's ethnoscapes interact irregularly with finance, media and technological imaginaries (Appadurai 1990). How these forces are articulated in Port Moresby is different from their articulation in Peshawar, and this in turn from Berlin or Los Angeles. But these are all places where the battle between the imaginaries of the nation-state, of unsettled communities and of global electronic media is in full progress.

What they add up to, with all their conjunctural variations, is an immense new set of challenges for the production of locality, in all the senses suggested in this essay. The problems of cultural reproduction in a globalized world are only partly describable in terms of problems of race and class, gender and power, although these are surely crucially involved. An even more funda-mental fact is that the production of locality – always, as I have argued, a fragile and difficult achievement – is more than ever shot through with contradictions, destabilized by human motion and displaced by the formation of new kinds of virtual neighbourhood.

Locality is thus fragile in two senses. The first sense, with which I began this paper, follows from the fact that the material reproduction of actual neighbourhoods is invariably up against the corrosion of context, if nothing else in the tendency of the material world to resist the default designs of human agency. The second sense emerges when neighbourhoods are subject to the context-producing drives of more complex hierarchical organizations, especially those of the modern nation-state.

The relationship between these distinct forms of fragility is itself historical, in that it is the long-term interaction of neighbourhoods that creates such complex hierarchical relations, a process we have usually discussed under such rubrics as 'state-formation'. This historical dialectic is a reminder that locality as a dimension of social life, and as an articulated value of particular neighbourhoods, is not a transcendent standard from which particular societies fall or deviate. Rather, it is always emergent from the practices of local subjects in specific neighbourhoods. The possibilities for its realization as a structure of feeling are thus as variable and incomplete as the relations between the neighbourhoods that constitute its practical instances.

The many displaced, deterritorialized and transient populations that constitute today's ethnoscapes are engaged in the construction of locality, as a structure of feeling, often in the face of the erosion, dispersal and implosion of neighbourhoods as coherent social formations. This disjuncture between neighbourhoods as social formations and locality as a property of social life is not without historical precedent, since long-distance trade, forced migrations and political 'exits' are very widespread in the historical record. What is new is the disjuncture between these processes and the mass-mediated discourses and practices (including those of economic liberalization, multiculturalism, human rights and refugee claims) that now surround the nation-state. This disjuncture, like every other one, points to something conjunctural. The task of theorizing the relationship between such disjunctures and the conjunctures which account for them, begun in an earlier essay on the globalized production of difference (Appadurai 1990), now seems both more pressing and more daunting. In such a theory, it is unlikely that there will be anything mere about the local.

ACKNOWLEDGEMENTS

This revised version of the paper originally written for the ASA Decennial Conference was presented subsequently at lectures organized by the East–West Center in Hawaii (February 1994) and by the Centre for the Comparative Study of Religion at the University of Amsterdam (March 1994). The revisions owe much to the thoughtful criticisms (and patience) of Richard Fardon. I have also had helpful queries and suggestions from Peter Pels and Marshall Sahlins.

NOTES

1 There is no ideal way to designate 'localities' as actual social forms. Terms such as 'place', 'site', 'locale' all have their strengths and weaknesses. The term 'neighbourhood' (apart from its use in avoiding the confusion between 'locality' as the singular form of 'localities' and locality as property or dimension of social

life) also has the virtue that it suggests sociality, immediacy and reproducibility without any necessary implications for scale, specific modes of connectivity, internal homogeneity or sharp boundaries. This sense of neighbourhood can also accommodate images such as 'circuit' and 'border zone', which have been argued to be preferable to such images as 'community' and 'centre–periphery', especially where transnational migration is involved (Rouse 1991). Nevertheless, it carries the burden of co-opting a colloquial term for technical use.

2 This critique is entirely consistent with (and partly inspired by) Fabian's critique of the denial of coevalness in ethnography and the resulting creation of a fictive time of and for the other (1983). Yet this essay does not take up the vexed question of the relationship between the co-production of space and time in ethnographic practice, nor the debate (see below) over whether space and time tend to cannibalize each other in modern, capitalist societies. The present argument about locality is in part intended to open up the question of 'time' and 'temporality' in the production of locality. I am grateful to Peter Pels for reminding me that the problem of temporality is equally relevant to how ethnography and locality have historically produced one another.

3 At this point my view of 'localization' converges with the general argument of Henri Lefebvre (1991), though Lefebvre stresses the relationship of capitalism and modernity to this negative sense of 'localization'. Lefebvre's own account of the nation-state is brief and cryptic, though it is clear that he also saw the links between the presuppositions of the modern nation-state and the capitalist process of 'localization'. The question of how my argument might relate more to those of Lefebvre (1991) and of Harvey (1989), though important, exceeds the scope of this chapter .

REFERENCES

Anderson, B. (1991) *Imagined Communities: Reflections on the Origins and Spread of Nationalism*, revised edition, London and New York: Verso.
—— (1993) 'Exodus', *Critical Inquiry* 20(2): 314–327.
Appadurai, A. (1988) 'Putting hierarchy in its place', *Cultural Anthropology* 3(1): 37–50.
—— (1990) 'Disjuncture and difference in the global cultural economy', *Public Culture* 2(2): 1–24.
—— (1991) 'Global ethnoscapes: notes and queries for a transnational anthropology', in R.G. Fox (ed.) *Recapturing Anthropology: Working in the Present*, Santa Fe, New Mexico: School of American Research Press.
—— (1993) 'Patriotism and its futures', *Public Culture* 5(3): 411–429.
—— (1995) 'Playing with modernity: the decolonization of Indian cricket', in C.A. Breckenridge (ed.) *Modern Sites: Situating Public Culture in India*, Minneapolis: University of Minnesota Press.
Balibar, E. (1991) 'The nation form: history and ideology', in E. Balibar and I. Wallerstein (eds) *Race, Nation, Class: Ambiguous Identities*, London and New York: Verso.
Balibar, E. and Wallerstein, I. (1991) *Race, Nation, Class: Ambiguous Identities*, London and New York: Verso.
Basch, L., N. Glick Schiller and C. Szanton Blanc (1994) *Nations Unbound: Transnational Projects, Postcolonial Predicaments, and Deterritorialized Nation-States*, Langhorne, Philadelphia and Reading, UK: Gordon & Breach.
Bauman, R. and Briggs, C.L. (1990) 'Poetics and performance as critical perspectives on language and social life', *Annual Review of Anthropology* 19: 59–88.
Bhabha, H.K. (ed.) (1990) *Nation and Narration*, London and New York: Routledge.

Bhattacharjee, A. (1992) 'The habit of ex-nomination: nation, woman and the Indian immigrant bourgeoisie', *Public Culture* 5(1): 19–44.

Bloch, M. (1986) *From Blessing to Violence: History and Ideology in the Circumcision Ritual of the Merina of Madagascar*, Cambridge: Cambridge University Press.

Borneman, J. (1992) *Belonging in the Two Berlins: Kin, State, Nation*, Cambridge: Cambridge University Press.

de Certeau, M. (1984) *The Practice of Everyday Life*, Berkeley and London: University of California Press.

Chatterjee, P. (1986) *Nationalist Thought and the Colonial World: A Derivative Discourse*, London: Zed Press.

—— (1993) *The Nation and its Fragments: Colonial and Postcolonial Histories*, Princeton: Princeton University Press.

Comaroff, J. and Comaroff, J.L. (1992) 'The madman and the migrant', *Ethnography and the Historical Imagination*, Boulder, Col.: Westview Press.

Deleuze, G. and Guattari, F. (1987) *A Thousand Plateaus*, Minneapolis: University of Minnesota Press.

Duranti, A. and Goodwin, C. (1992) *Language as an Interactive Phenomenon*, Cambridge: Cambridge University Press.

Fabian, J. (1983) *Time and the Other: How Anthropology Makes its Object*, New York: Columbia University Press.

Falk-Moore, S. (1993) *Moralizing States and the Ethnography of the Present*, Arlington, Va.: American Anthropological Association.

Featherstone, M. (ed.) (1990) *Global Culture: Nationalism, Globalization, and Modernity*, London: Sage.

Foster, R.J. (1991) 'Making national cultures in the global ecumene', *Annual Review of Anthropology* 20: 235–260.

Friedman, J. (1990) 'Being in the world: globalization and localization', in M. Featherstone (ed.) *Global Culture: Nationalism, Globalization, and Modernity*, London: Sage.

Geertz, C. (1975) 'Common sense as a cultural system', *Antioch Review* 33: 5–26.

—— (1983) *Local Knowledge*, New York: Basic Books.

Gellner, E. (1983) *Nations and Nationalism*, Ithaca, New York: Cornell University Press.

Ginsberg, F. (1993) 'Aboriginal media and the Australian imaginary', *Public Culture* 5(3): 557–578.

Gupta, A. and Ferguson, J. (1992) 'Beyond "culture": space, identity, and the politics of difference', *Cultural Anthropology* 7(1): 6–23.

Handler, R. (1988) *Nationalism and the Politics of Culture in Quebec*, Madison: University of Wisconsin Press.

Hanks, W.F. (1989) 'Text and texuality', *Annual Review of Anthropology* 18: 95–127.

Hannerz, U. (1992) *Cultural Complexity: Studies in the Social Organization of Meaning*, New York: Columbia University Press.

Hansen, M. (1991) *Babel and Babylon: Spectatorship in American Silent Film*, Cambridge, Mass.: Harvard University Press.

—— (1993) 'Unstable mixtures, dilated spheres: Negt and Kluge's *The Public Sphere and Experience*, twenty years later', *Public Culture* 5(2): 179–212.

Harvey, D. (1989) *The Condition of Postmodernity: An Enquiry into the Origins of Cultural Change*, Cambridge, Mass. and Oxford: Blackwell.

Herzfeld, M. (1982) *Ours Once More: Folklore, Ideology and the Making of Modern Greece*, Austin: University of Texas Press.

Hobsbawm, E.J. (1990) *Nations and Nationalism since 1780: Programme, Myth and Reality*, Cambridge: Cambridge University Press.

Hymes, D.H. (1974) *Foundations in Sociolinguistics: An Ethnographic Perspective*, Philadelphia: University of Pennsylvania Press.

Kapferer, B. (1988) *Legends of People, Myths of State*, Washington: Smithsonian Institute Press.

King, A. (ed.) (1991) *Culture, Globalization and the World-System: Contemporary Conditions for the Representation of Identity*, Basingstoke: Macmillan.

Lefebvre, H. (1991) [1974] *The Production of Space*, trans. D. Nicholson-Smith, Cambridge, Mass. and Oxford: Blackwell.

Lewis, G. (1986) 'The look of magic', *Man* (N.S.) 21(3): 414–437.

Mbembe, A. (1992) 'The banality of power and the aesthetics of vulgarity in the postcolony', *Public Culture* 4(2): 1–30.

Munn, N.D. (1986) *The Fame of Gawa. A Symbolic Study of Value Transformation in a Massim (Papua New Guinea) Society*, Cambridge: Cambridge University Press.

Robertson, R. (1992) *Globalization: Social Theory and Global Culture*, Newbury Park, Cal. and London: Sage.

Rosenau, J. (1990) *Turbulence in World Politics: A Theory of Change and Continuity*, Princeton: Princeton University Press.

Rouse, R. (1991) 'Mexican migration and the social space of postmodernism', *Diaspora* 2(2): 8–23.

Sahlins, M. (1985) *Islands of History*, Chicago: University of Chicago Press.

—— (1993) 'Goodbye to tristes tropes: ethnography in the context of modern world history'. The 1992 Ryerson Lecture (29 April), University of Chicago, *The University of Chicago Record* 4 February.

Schiefflin, E. (1985) 'Performance and the cultural construction of reality: spirit seances among a New Guinea people', *American Ethnologist* 12(4): 707–724.

Scott, J.C. (1990) *Domination and the Arts of Resistance: Hidden Transcripts*, New Haven: Yale University Press.

Tambiah, S.J. (1992) *Buddhism Betrayed? Religion, Politics, and Violence in Sri Lanka*, Chicago: University of Chicago Press.

Turner, T. (1992) 'Defiant images: the Kayapo appropriation of video', *Anthropology Today* 8(6): 5–16.

Urban, G. and Sherzer, J. (eds) (1991) *Nation-States and Indians in Latin America*, Austin: University of Texas Press.

van der Veer, P. (1994) *Religious Nationalism: Hindus and Muslims in India*, Berkeley and London: University of California Press.

Name index

Subject index